The Adventures of
Henry Thoreau

THE ADVENTURES OF
HENRY THOREAU

A Young Man's Unlikely Path
to Walden Pond

By MICHAEL SIMS

BLOOMSBURY
NEW YORK · LONDON · NEW DELHI · SYDNEY

Published by Bloomsbury USA, New York

All papers used by Bloomsbury USA are natural, recyclable products made
from wood grown in well-managed forests. The manufacturing processes
conform to the environmental regulations of the country of origin.

LIBRARY OF CONGRESS CATALOGING-IN-PUBLICATION DATA

Sims, Michael, 1958–
The Adventures of Henry Thoreau : a Young Man's Unlikely
Path to Walden Pond / Michael Sims. —First U.S. Edition.
pages cm
Includes bibliographical references and index.
ISBN 978-1-62040-195-8 (hardback)
1. Thoreau, Henry David, 1817–1862. 2. Authors, American—19th
century—Biography. 3. Naturalists—United States—Biography. I. Title.
PS3053.S58 2014
818′.309—dc23
[B]
2013031528

First U.S. Edition 2014

1 3 5 7 9 10 8 6 4 2

Typeset by Hewer Text (UK) Ltd, Edinburgh
Printed and bound in the U.S.A. by Thomson-Shore Inc., Dexter, Michigan

Every child begins the world again....

HENRY DAVID THOREAU

To my son, Vance,
a gift and marvel,
who raced this book and beat it to the finish line.

I loved to hear him talk, but I did not like his books so well,
though I often read them and took what I liked.
They do not do him justice. I liked to see Thoreau rather in his life.

MARIA BRIDGE PRATT (MRS. MINOT PRATT),
A CONCORD NEIGHBOR

Perhaps he fell, all of us do, into his way of living,
without forecasting it much, but approved & confirmed it with later
wisdom.

RALPH WALDO EMERSON

I am a Schoolmaster—a Private Tutor, a Surveyor—a Gardener, a
Farmer—a Painter, I mean a House Painter, a Carpenter, a Mason,
a Day-Laborer, a Pencil-Maker, a Glass-paper Maker, a Writer, and
sometimes a Poetaster.

HENRY DAVID THOREAU

CONTENTS

PART III: ECHO

Overture

DANCING ON THE ICE

WHEN I FOUND a young Henry Thoreau ice-skating through the correspondence of Sophia Peabody Hawthorne, it was like running into a long-lost friend. In the decades since first encountering *Walden* in my late teens, I had often glimpsed Thoreau as the bearded sage of literature, natural history, or civil liberties. Except in his own writings, however, I had seldom met the awkward young man who loved to sing, who ran a private school and applied his engineering skills to the pencil business, who popped popcorn and performed magic tricks for Ralph Waldo Emerson's children, faced his own illnesses and the deaths of loved ones, and tried to make it as a freelance writer in New York City.

Sophia Hawthorne described a lively afternoon in Concord in December 1842 that captured my imagination: a twenty-five-year-old Thoreau skating on the Concord River with both Emerson and Sophia's own newlywed husband, Nathaniel Hawthorne. Emerson skated earnestly and Hawthorne grandly. Thoreau cavorted in what Sophia soon described to a friend as "dithyrambic dances and Bacchic leaps." In ancient Greece a dithyramb was a wild choral hymn and dance, especially one dedicated to Bacchus. Thoreau didn't drink alcohol, but otherwise Sophia Hawthorne found the perfect term for his response to being outdoors, which was indeed ecstatic and pagan.

Thoreau was not an ivory-tower thinker sitting with chin in hand. Contrary to myth, he was not a hermit. Caught up with his friends and his era, he lived most of his life in a busy village and admitted that he considered "homeopathic doses" of local gossip "as refreshing in its way as the rustle of leaves and the peeping of frogs." He spent relatively little time in the wilderness—a few weeks here and there. His Walden Pond cabin provided a solitary working space away from his family's boardinghouse, not escape from all society.

Over the years, I found that some books about Thoreau sharpened rather than assuaged my hunger for more about the real-life young man. As I began writing my own book about him, I realized that I didn't want to admire the marble bust of an icon. I wanted to gambol with a sarcastic radical who could translate Pindar and Goethe, track a fox to its lair, and host an abolitionist rally beside a tiny cabin he had built himself. I didn't want to applaud Thoreau. I wanted to find Henry.

WE ALL HAVE our own Thoreau. I met mine in high school, where he told me that we are rich in proportion to how much we can do without, that the cost of something is how much of our brief time on earth must be exchanged for it. I had no trouble fitting a mental image of Thoreau's 1840s Massachusetts over my 1970s Tennessee and his famous Concord lake over my modest woodland pond. "Aim above morality," this mentor advised, pulling the rug out from under both my fundamentalist upbringing and years of school indoctrination. What I loved most, however, were his observations about nature. His was a new kind of voice in the mid-nineteenth century: a strong mind classically trained, a poetic sensibility steeped in literature and allusion, but also an outdoorsman's viewpoint informed by a growing passion for how nature actually works. His studies were anchored by personal experience—decades of watching passenger pigeons and woodchucks, carrying botanical specimens in his hat, and observing spawning fish until he could gently lower his hand into the water and lift one out.

Other people have a different Thoreau, just as we have different Malcolm Xs, Oscar Wildes, and Virginia Woolfs. "Today Thoreau's words are quoted with feeling," wrote Thoreau aficionado Ken Kifer, "by liberals, socialists, anarchists, libertarians, and conservatives alike." His worldwide reputation as a philosopher and political activist can be traced to several lectures and essays, especially those following his now-famous night in jail—topics that appear later in this book and in its coda. Both Mohandas K. Gandhi and Martin Luther King credited Thoreau with inspiring their nonviolent campaigns. Edward O. Wilson called Thoreau "the father of environmentalism" and insisted that "he also deserves iconic status in the scientific fields of ecology and biodiversity studies." Fifteen years after Thoreau died in 1862, Emerson told a friend, "Thoreau was a superior genius. . . . A man of large reading, of quick perception, of great practical courage and ability,—who grew greater every day, and, had his short life been prolonged would have found few equals to the power and wealth of his mind."

THE ADVENTURES OF *Henry Thoreau* begins in his childhood and ends in his late twenties. To resurrect this odd young man's everyday life, I turned to his nineteenth-century contemporaries. Thanks largely to the support of fellow Concord villager Ralph Waldo Emerson, Thoreau spent his adulthood surrounded by many of the great writers of the period we now call the American Renaissance. Several neighbors wrote memoirs or biographies of him, such as Emerson, Ellery Channing, and Franklin Sanborn. Others observed

Thoreau closely in journals and correspondence, including all of these plus Nathaniel and Sophia Hawthorne, Lidian Emerson, Bronson Alcott, and Margaret Fuller.

I found many other rich primary sources. Only hours after some incidents took place in the school run by Thoreau and his brother, for example, the students involved described them in diaries or in letters to their parents. After Thoreau became famous for his own writings, some former students penned sketches of him, filled with vivid anecdotes, as did a few of his fellow Harvard undergraduates. Many other Concordians documented everyday life in this tumultuous era. Through them I was able to conjure many surprising details—the prevalence of drunkenness in the town, for example, or the look and feel of a Sunday morning at the Unitarian church.

All dialogue, all thoughts and observations attributed to any character, derive from written records by participants, as you can see from the endnotes. I employ terms that Thoreau used in his own writing, such as Man for humanity, Negro for African American, and Indian for Native American. For many proper nouns I followed nineteenth-century spelling, such as Ktaadn for the mountain now spelled Katahdin.

Every historical or biographical narrative slants toward those topics and characters that most intrigue the author, shaped by which incidents are included and which omitted. I'm more interested in Thoreau's imaginative response to nature, for example, than in his role as social critic and moral gadfly, and consequently much of this book takes place outdoors. It also begins before he put away his rifle. Thoreau started in his boyhood as a hunter and later occasionally shot birds for sport or to study them more closely. His constant reexamination of his own values changed his relationship with both society and nature.

Beginning with a Romantic and Transcendental view of natural processes as symbolic, Thoreau grew increasingly committed to a scientific view of nature. At the cabin, after a morning spent reading Anacreon or Chateaubriand, afternoon might find him undertaking a statistical analysis of temperature changes in regional bodies of water. He studied ecology twenty years before the German evolutionist Ernst Haeckel coined the term *Oekologie*. "This world," Thoreau wrote as he immersed himself ever more in the natural sciences, "is not a place for him who does not discover its laws." Later he was quick to see the validity of Darwin's discoveries about how nature changes slowly over time.

During his brief period living at Walden Pond, such careful attention to nature inspired and nurtured the best writing Thoreau had yet done, the seeds of the best he would ever do. There he wrote his first book, *A Week on the Concord and Merrimack Rivers*, and began what would become his best and most famous, *Walden*. My own book moves toward and culminates in this turning point, as a quirky but talented young man named Henry evolves into an original and insightful writer named Thoreau.

Part 1

REFLECTION

Chapter 1

BEHIND THE STARS

W HEN HENRY WAS a child, a schoolmate accused him of stealing his knife. Henry knew the culprit's identity, but instead of exposing him he said flatly to his accusers, "I did not take it."

A few days later the thief was revealed.

"I knew all the time who it was," said Henry. "The day it was taken I went to Newton with Father."

"Why," demanded his exasperated mother, "did you not say so at the time?"

Staying on his own track, as usual, Henry repeated stubbornly, "I did not take it."

He was a thoughtful boy, considered intelligent and perceptive, even though, after being awarded a school medal for geography, he asked his mother, "Is Boston in Concord?" Once he solemnly asked Phebe Wheeler, mistress of the infant school, "Who owns all the land?" A few years later, Mrs. Wheeler was teaching a private class for older children, mostly girls, and looked up in surprise to find Henry and his older brother John barefoot in the doorway. The public school term had ended and Cynthia Thoreau sent her boys to Mrs. Wheeler's so that they might absorb a few more days of knowledge.

Young Henry was not adept at interpreting facial expressions, and often he failed to look at the face of the person with whom he was speaking. Earnest thinking aloud became his hallmark. At the age of three he was told that, like the pious heroes of the catechism, he must someday die. He took the news calmly. Later, however, as he came indoors from sledding, he announced that he did not want to die and go to heaven, because he could not carry his sled with him. Other boys had told him that because the sled's runners were wood instead of iron, it was "not worth a cent." He was used to owning unimpressive toys and clothes. Mrs. Thoreau made John's shirts and pantaloons out of their father's castoffs, and most of Henry's were further handed down from John. The single time he received new boots he was so excited he wore them to bed.

Constrained as usual by the family's shortage of money, Henry once carried a basket of young chickens to be sold to an innkeeper as food. In front of him, in order to immediately return the basket, the man took out one cheeping, fluffy chick at a time and efficiently wrung each fragile neck. The boy showed no emotion. At an early age his solemnity and frequent lack of expression inspired lawyer Samuel Hoar, Concord's leading citizen and a neighbor of the Thoreaus, to nickname Henry "the Judge." His parents said that as a baby he had suffered baptism by the Reverend Ezra Ripley, minister of Concord's First Parish Unitarian Church, without tears.

Stoic one moment, Henry might be timid the next. Thunder would send him running to his parents' room, where he would announce preemptively from the doorway, "I don't feel well." Other village children knew that Henry never let tree or mudbank slow his investigation of anything that sparked his single-minded curiosity, but they also knew that when racing after a quarry he might not pause to help a friend across a ditch. Henry was woven of contradictions. He loved to sing and dance but hated parades.

As a small boy, Henry shared a trundle bed with John, crowded by his longer limbs. Mrs. Thoreau would pull their flat bed, which rode on casters, out from under the parents' high four-poster. A trundle bed made economical use of a room, especially in rented houses, with two sleeping areas stacked in the space of one and the lower tucked out of sight during the day. Its flat drawerlike structure, however, couldn't accommodate a full straw or feather mattress and wound up padded only with blankets, barely superior to a pallet on the floor.

After a day of exploring outdoors, the boys would tumble into their hard bed and soon John would be fast asleep. Henry, in contrast, often lay awake thinking or daydreaming. Once Mrs. Thoreau came back upstairs long after putting the boys to bed, only to find Henry lying beside his sleeping brother and staring out through the parted curtains at the clear night sky.

"Why, Henry dear," she exclaimed, "why don't you go to sleep?"

"I have been looking through the stars, to see if I couldn't see God behind them."

AS THEY GREW older, skinny John became the handsome brother, with his sisters' wavy brown hair and large dark eyes. His rounder, less pronounced features usually wore an open expression seldom seen on Henry's solemn, big-nosed face. John was more popular, not awkward or difficult as Henry could be. Both were imaginative, trusting children, as were their sisters Helen and Sophia. Helen (born only five months after her parents' wedding in 1812) was five years older than Henry, John two years older, and Sophia two years younger.

Each Christmas Eve, Mrs. Thoreau reminded them to hang their clean stockings on the hearth. During the night, she explained, Santa Claus, a generous and good-natured sprite who flies through the air astride a broomstick, would come down the chimney. On Christmas morning naughty children found a stocking stuffed with a rotten potato, a letter of reprimand from Santa, and possibly even a rod with which they might be whipped. Once John's Christmas dreams were smashed by the discovery of a stinking potato and a letter, which he was too young to read, so he had to suffer through someone else's recital of his faults. The rod, however, was too small for use, so clearly it was intended as a warning. Good children, in contrast—and most of the time John was considered a well-behaved child, perhaps especially after this warning from above—could look forward to a stocking sagging with sweet-scented doughnuts and sugarplums. One year John determined to wait up for this elusive benefactor. He slumped in a low chair by the fireplace, staring up the chimney, and kept his eyes open a full hour after his usual bedtime. The next morning he woke in his own bed to discover that Santa crept in after the sentinel dozed.

On Christmas as well as Thanksgiving, Mrs. Thoreau invited poor neighbors and friends to join her family for a modest holiday repast. Although few people gave significant gifts, Christmas was slowly gaining in importance as a holiday. In December 1823, two days before Henry's sixth Christmas, an anonymous poem called "A Visit from St. Nicholas" appeared in the Troy, New York, *Sentinel*. It was widely reprinted. The author—later identified as Clement Clark Moore—borrowed details from the traditional British notion of Father Christmas and the American idea of Santa Claus, both of which drew upon folklore inspired by the generosity of the historical fourth-century Saint Nikolaos of Myra. Moore also drew from Washington Irving's vivid sketch of St. Nicholas in his 1809 *History of New York*, which Irving had published under one of his pen names, Diedrich Knickerbocker.

Many people, however, were unfamiliar with the idea of Santa Claus. Christmas was not an official holiday. At school on one Christmas Day, the Thoreau children asked a girl what sort of treats

Santa Claus had brought her. She didn't understand the question. Patiently the boys explained the rewards they had received, and even showed her some of the candy. Her father was a shop owner, the skeptical girl replied, and she had watched Mrs. Thoreau purchase that candy only the day before. Outraged, disbelieving, Henry and John raced home after school to interrogate their mother. She confessed all. The children never again hung up their stockings and never again found sugarplums and doughnuts on Christmas morning.

HENRY ENUNCIATED *R*'s with a Gallic burr. His father's family hailed from Jersey off the Normandy coast, source of the French surname whose accent in the New World had migrated from the second to the first syllable, evolving into *thorough*. They fled the French-dominated island after Louis XIV revoked the Edict of Nantes in 1685, making Protestantism again illegal, and in time Henry's grandsire became a privateer along the Atlantic coast of North America. One neighbor who knew the Thoreau ancestry considered Henry's quiet tradesman father not only a gentleman but a French one, from snuff box to shrug. French support during the Revolutionary War lent cachet to their lineage, and nothing enlivened a family tree like the pirate that Henry's grandfather had been.

Christened David Henry, he was named for his father's brother David, who died a few weeks after Henry's birth on the twelfth of July 1817. He was born in an upstairs bedroom that faced the sunrise, in the home of his mother's mother, Mary Jones Dunbar Minot, in quiet farmland between the Concord River and the Lexington Road. A second family occupied the other end of the house. An old building of unpainted gray boards, with a steep roof that almost touched the ground in the rear, it stood alone by the winding

Virginia Road, a mile and a half east of Concord. Cynthia grew up there. Her father died when she was a child and she was raised by her mother and grandmother. Her grandmother told how her second husband, Captain Jonas Minot, would leave a glass of fresh milk on the night-stand beside their bed, for when he woke during the night—until one morning she rose to find the glass still full and Jonas cold beside her.

The house stood on a grassy, unfenced plot amid sprawling meadows and peat bogs, facing a brook that ran into the nearby Shawsheen River, a tributary of the Merrimack. During the day, at home with three children, Cynthia could hear little other than birdsong, grasshopper buzz, the gabble of geese, and the lazy sound of cattle lowing. She felt less lonely when she heard a neighbor cheerfully whistling to his team of oxen. Night was even more still. Sometimes Cynthia got up long after dark and sat on the doorstep, where the loudest sound was in the house behind her—a clock counting the hurrying minutes.

Beginning in 1818, when Henry was little more than a year old, the family lived in Boston and such suburbs as Chelmsford. Mr. Thoreau worked as a sign painter, sold groceries, and—after getting a license that required a character testimonial from Reverend Ripley back in Concord—sold ardent spirits. He also worked in nearby Salem with an inventor and chemist named Joseph Dixon, who had recently begun making pencils.

The family moved back to Concord in the spring of 1822, a few months before Henry turned five. One of his earliest memories was a vision of a beautiful lake that his family took him to visit shortly afterward. Called Walden Pond, it was about half a mile wide and three-quarters of a mile long, surrounded by hills clothed in thick woods, pine sprinkled with oak and maple. After the sometimes frightening bustle and clamor of Boston—Henry was sensitive to noise—he loved the pond's quiet seclusion, where only sunshine and shadow seemed to vary a stilled, enchanted landscape. He began to daydream about this haven as if he had read of it in a fable.

To many residents, the village of Concord lived up to its name—a harmonious setting, if lacking grandeur. The Sudbury and Assabet meandered through meadow and bog, finally uniting to form the Concord River. Its wandering course provided no sandy shores, permitting meadows to grow to the edge. As a boy, Henry loved the fields and woods beside the river and considered the land itself generous. Walnut and chestnut trees rained nuts for easy gathering. Thorny briars of sweet blackberries crowded the roadsides, and the pastures were fringed with huckleberry bushes. Henry could not resist berries and ate his way along many a pathless hillside. This bountiful land and gentle confluence had drawn both Indians and Europeans. In early days, the fur trade thrived on a dense population of beaver, marten, fox, and otter. Moose and bears were plentiful. Descendants of settlers who organized wolf hunts, Concord farmers now thronged to cattle shows.

Often the Thoreaus took their children on picnics to Walden Pond, Fair Haven Pond, Nawshawtuct Hill, and the banks of the Assabet. Shorter jaunts led to the copse between Main Street and the river. On these outings the children—Helen, the oldest, then John and Henry, and finally little Sophia—explored the woods while John Senior and Cynthia built up a temporary stone fireplace and started a fire and cooked supper. It was said around Concord that tall, talkative Cynthia was so determined to imbue her children with a love of the outdoors that one of her offspring came close to being born on Nawshawtuct Hill.

For the first three years back in Concord the Thoreaus lived in a handsome brick house on Main Street owned by Deacon Parkman, next door to Judge Samuel Hoar. Henry's father enjoyed village life. His family had first moved to Concord at the turn of the century, when he was around twelve, and he knew its business as well as anyone—including past business, because he researched the history of the region. He liked to sit with friends at the post office or in a shop and read the newspaper and discuss the world. He recalled family history—how when very young he would eat breakfast with his father, the son eating the bottom half of a biscuit, the father the top; how he apprenticed to a cooper whose business was later destroyed by the Revolutionary War; and how his own father described a cannonball striking so close by that it cast sand into his face.

While Henry's father enjoyed sitting quietly and talking about the past, Henry raced around with boyish energy. He loved the first ball games of early spring, cavorting in the russet fields near Sleepy Hollow as the last snow melted into mud. When not playing snap-the-whip or the knife game mumble-the-peg, Concord boys played chaotic, rule-free ball games, including a version of cricket. They could learn to swim at Thayer's swimming hole, with its gravel beach that gently slanted for twenty or thirty feet down into the water, and afterward sprawl on the bank and exchange insults while the sun dried them. Forced indoors by rain or snow, they could turn to backgammon, hunt-the-slipper, and blind man's buff.

Despite occasional illnesses, Henry's adventurous childhood led him to think of himself as strong and resilient, and he was impatient with those less rugged. As they grew, the Thoreau boys' free-roaming lives invited adventure. They were good friends with two of their schoolmates, the Hosmer brothers from rural Derby's Bridge—Benjamin and Joseph. Ben especially was close to them, stealing whatever time he could from his apprenticeship to a shoemaker. Black-haired, black-eyed Ben was a restless, wiry boy whom Henry and John enviously considered the best whistler, runner, and stone thrower they knew. Ben also wore a reputation for courage. Once, when he and friends were chased across a field by an angry bull, Ben turned on it and, like David facing Goliath, flung a stone that hit it between the eyes so hard it staggered and fell to the ground. Another time, a friend who couldn't swim fell into a pond and panicked. Although he didn't know how to swim either, young Ben grasped a mooring loop on the boat dock, slipped into the water, and awkwardly maneuvered around until his friend could grab Ben's legs and pull himself out of the water.

The Hosmer boys ate many meals at the Thoreau house and sometimes spent the night. Mrs. Thoreau remarked that whenever she heard doors slamming or found them left open, she would soon hear one of her boys call out, "Ben has come, Mother!"

Young people were charmed by Henry's talkative and welcoming mother, who was renowned for her sweet puddings and pies, and quiet John Senior was a tradesman with the gracious manners of a gentleman. During lean times, meat might not be seen on the Thoreau table, but there was always a wide array of vegetables from the garden and the melon patch, as well as aromatic fruit. The scent of Mrs. Thoreau's fresh bread filled the house. When her daughters were young, she removed luxuries such as sugar, tea, and coffee from the weekday menu, and with the savings funded their piano lessons.

Some mornings Henry and John would grab food for a picnic lunch, explain to their mother that they would not be home until dark, and race outdoors with their friends. At nightfall they came trudging back. Usually they were mud-splashed and tired, full of stories about what they had seen at Egg Rock or Fairhaven Hill or even four miles away at Lincoln, or perhaps on the waters of the nearby Sudbury River or Walden Pond.

★   ★   ★

"IT WAS THE wild midnight—" Henry recited grandly. "A storm was in the sky— The lightning gave its light, and the thunder echoed by . . ."

It was August 1830 and he had recently turned thirteen. For two years he had been studying under the preceptor Phineas Allen at the Concord Academy, where John was also a pupil. He was naturally drawn to books and learning and was mocked by other youngsters as "the fine scholar with a big nose." Allen required all students to participate in classroom declamations. Henry was reciting from "The Death of Leonidas," by the Irish writer and divine George Croly. An epic about the legendary Spartan king who led three hundred soldiers against the legions of Xerxes at the Battle of Thermopylae, it was melodramatic enough to please any thirteen-year-old boy:

> *The torrent swept the glen, the ocean lashed the shore,—*
> *Then rose the Spartan men, to make their bed in gore!*

Henry's friend Henry Vose had just recited to the class a passage from Italian historian Carlo Botta's *History of the War of the Independence of the United States of America*, the first major history of the Revolution. After listening closely and watching their performance, Mr. Allen scrawled *decent* in his notebook for Vose's presentation and *good* for Henry's.

Several of the textbooks concerned natural philosophy. One important volume that helped introduce Henry to thinking about nature—rather than merely enjoying its bounty and beauty—was *Institutes of Natural Philosophy: Theoretical and Practical*, by the English Unitarian minister William Enfield. Enfield had fawningly dedicated it to the chemist Joseph Priestley, his countryman famous for discovering "dephlogisticated air"—soon known as oxygen—and for inventing carbonated water. Through such books, Henry imbibed appreciation for nature's complexity and realized that the simplest inquiry could unveil new mysteries. Enfield's volume was divided into Mechanicks, Hydrostaticks, Astronomy, Opticks, and other categories, with sections ranging from an analysis "Of the Equation of Time" to an aside about a recent invention, "Of the Magick Lantern." Book V, "Of Electricity," exemplified Enfield's approach. It began with a definition: "The earth, and all bodies with which we are acquainted, are supposed to contain a certain quantity of an exceedingly elastick fluid, which is called the *electrick fluid.* . . . Proposition I. The ELECTRICK FLUID, being excited, becomes perceptible to the senses." The first experiment was typical:

EXP I. Let a long glass tube be rubbed with the hand, or with a leathern cushion; the electrick fluid, being thus excited, will attract light substances, and give a lucid spark to the finger, or any metallic substance, brought near it.

The glass tube is called the *electrick*, and all those bodies which are capable, by any means, to produce such effects, are called *electricks.* The hand, or any other body that rubs an electrick, is called the *rubber*.

Many of the nature-related textbooks included biblical arguments. Samuel Whelpley's *Universal History*, whose title page continued "a comprend of history, from the earliest times; comprehending a general view of the present state of the world, with respect to civilization, religion, and government: and a brief dissertation on the importance of historical knowledge," opened with a defense of "The Credibility of Mosaic History." Strangled with commas, Whelpley gasped, "That the existence of the human race, has no rational claim to higher antiquity, than is allowed in the Mosaic history, may be argued from two considerations: 1. The total want of evidence of a higher antiquity. 2. Various evidences, that the scripture chronology is correct." Rather than trying to refute evidence against biblical chronology, Whelpley simply dismissed "the pretended antiquity of the Chinese and Indians" and asserted that the Hebrew account of an ark capable of housing representatives of every creature of land, sea, and air was perfectly credible.

After starting classes with Phineas Allen, Henry wrote an essay, "The Four Seasons," about one of his favorite experiences in nature:

> There are four Seasons in a year, Spring, Summer, Autumn, and Winter, I will begin with Spring. Now we see the ice beginning to thaw, and the trees to bud. Now the winter wears away, and ground begins to look green with the new-born grass. The birds which have lately been to more southern countries, return again to cheer us with their morning song.
>
> Next comes Summer. Now we see a beautiful sight. The trees and flowers are in bloom. Now is the pleasantest part of the year. Now the fruit begins to form on the trees, and all things look beautiful.
>
> In Autumn we see the trees loaded with fruit. Now the farmers begin to lay in their Winter's store, and the markets abound with fruit. The trees are partly stripped of their leaves. The birds which visited us in Spring are now retiring to warmer countries, as they know that Winter is coming.
>
> Next comes Winter. Now we see the ground covered with snow, and the trees are bare. The cold is so intense that the rivers and brooks are frozen. There is nothing to be seen. We have no birds to cheer us with their morning song. We hear only the sound of the sleigh bells.

Samuel Whelpley's biblical viewpoint was not enough to satisfy Henry. He didn't merely enjoy nature; he looked closely at it from an early age. Like other boys, he hunted and fished, but he also spent time peering into nests and following tracks. He obsessively watched fish in their alien realm. His essay for Phineas Allen reflected a growing preoccupation: the slowly turning wheel of the seasons, the great natural rhythms of life.

Chapter 2

SEEK YOUR FORTUNE

I N AUGUST 1833, shortly after turning sixteen, Henry applied
to Harvard College, which was about twenty miles northwest of
Concord—three or four jouncing hours on the Cambridge Turnpike in the Harvard & Groton Accommodation Coach, with its
jumble of trunks high in the back caked with dust. Although
Cambridge was larger than Concord, it, too, was a quiet, tree-filled
village, except for the rowdy taverns and hostelries that catered to
teamsters hauling country goods to Boston. Under construction
beside the campus, in the edge of the grassy lawn called Harvard
Square, was the fifth incarnation of the First Parish Church, a
historic institution dating back to the 1630s. The current minister,
the Reverend William Newell, had presided over the church's
evolution into a more progressive Unitarian congregation. The
wooden Gothic Revival building was designed by the famed architect Isaiah Rogers, who a few years earlier had designed the
neoclassical Tremont Hotel in nearby Boston, the first hotel in the
United States to offer indoor plumbing and steam-powered running
water and gas with which to heat it. The church was dedicated
during Henry's first term as a freshman.

He narrowly passed the entrance exams, which ranged across
Cicero's orations, the Greek Testament, and the entirety of Virgil.

Most students were listed as "on probation" in one subject or another, taking classes to raise their competency in various subjects. Henry was required to enroll on probation in all three primary areas of study: Latin, Greek, and mathematics. "You have barely got in," said the college's president, Josiah Quincy. Soon, however, Henry raised his grades and standing. By spring he had earned a very respectable 4,038 points in the byzantine scoring system that both faculty and students complained about, making him eligible for twenty-five dollars of "exhibition money" from the school to offset expenses. Over the course of Henry's college years, points were deducted for tardiness and unexcused absence, but mostly he stayed on course.

Since Unitarians had become dominant at Harvard in the first decade of the century, the university had been leading a gradual secularization of American higher education. The 1820s saw a flowering of Unitarianism under the rhetoric that its commitment to reason, to the notion of a humanity not damned by God but inherently holy, was an almost inevitable next step for a democracy. Harvard's founding as a pious school for Puritan divines was already two centuries in the past, and Increase Mather's replacement of classical volumes with Christian had long since been reduced to a historical anecdote. Now the emphasis was almost entirely on ancient classics, the lingua franca of Western education in the New World as in Europe. At President Quincy's inauguration in 1829, he and Massachusetts governor Levi Lincoln addressed each other entirely in Latin, as usual, although the custom was fading.

In his early sixties, Quincy was tall and martial, with a high forehead and receding hair that formed an intellectual halo around the back of his head. Formerly a legislator and three times mayor of Boston, he was more of an administrator than an educator. He was often at war with the undergraduates. The so-called Great Rebellion in 1834 resulted in destroyed furniture and smashed windows, not to mention a rocket set off in chapel—revealing, after the smoke cleared, the words *A Bone for Old Quin to Pick* written on the wall. Students had been protesting Quincy's dismissal of a student who refused to recite his Greek lesson in order to denounce the unfairness of the hoary score-keeping system.

Quincy did, however, accomplish what his predecessors had not bothered to do. Against great opposition among both students and parents, he reined in the rowdy student body, which was infamous for its disregard of persons and property, celebrating even jail-worthy hazing practices. Not until Quincy's administration were Harvard students even considered subject to Cambridge laws while on campus. Henry did not indulge in the college's time-honored antics of drunkenness and vandalism, although apparently he did collaborate in the occasional prank. He failed to hide his distaste for his more raucous fellow students, and some in turn considered him a prig.

Not all of Henry's classmates knew the five-foot-seven yokel with the unkempt light brown hair. He had a distinctive shape—sloping shoulders led to long arms contrasting with short legs—and some recognized him from a distance by his unusual and purposeful stride, which reminded them of an Indian's. He took a shortcut whenever possible, sometimes walking with his hands behind his back or clenched into fists at his side. During his years in Cambridge, he often kept to himself. Some fellow students noticed his earnest expression as he walked across campus with his eyes on the ground, distracted, as if looking for something he had lost. He tended to dominate a conversation and even turn it into a monologue; otherwise his self-absorption and awkwardness became standoffishness.

But his earnest excitement transcended the plain features and quirky personality and attracted young men who were equally serious about life. A few intimate friends—such as Henry Vose, his chum from Concord Academy who became a Harvard roommate—witnessed Henry's love of natural history, his tendency to notice animals more than people. On many winter days he visited a nearby apple tree, in the hollow of which lived an ermine, an elegant but bloodthirsty short-tailed weasel whose fur turned white in winter. Henry wasn't hunting. He simply liked to know the animals. He kept a close eye on the pigeon woodpeckers, or flickers, who enlivened his walk across campus with their *ki-ki-ki-ki* laugh and undulating flight with its characteristic flap-flap-swoop. One had a nest in the grove on the eastern side of the Yard. Several of Henry's fellow students vied with each other in the common pastime of stealing eggs from birds' nests, or sometimes taking the entire nest. It was a curious aspect of the growing interest in natural history as a hobby. These students plagued the woodpecker—who, Henry noticed, kept laying new eggs like a hen until a reckless student destroyed the entire nest with a hatchet, apparently in his zeal to excavate more eggs. Henry did not find such destructiveness, however common it might be, appealing; he wanted to know the living animal. He found another bird of the same species in an adjacent field, nesting in a hollow it had chipped two feet deep into a stump.

Vose and a handful of others saw the playful, imaginative side of Henry—his ecstatic response to nature and love of kittens, his obsession with Indians and the notion of a more natural savage life, his fondness for rural characters rather than what he saw as staid townsfolk. Friends enjoyed his easygoing affection for his family and his daft punning letters from back home in Concord. They knew his practical side, that at sixteen he had built his own boat, *The Rover*, and that before approving his enrollment in college his parents had considered apprenticing him to a cabinetmaker.

★　　★　　★

EACH DAY AT Harvard began with brief morning prayers in the chapel at six, after which many students went into class. Yawning scholars tended to snuff out the candles that made the Bible visible, and gradually the time of chapel service was moved forward so that it always took place after daylight. They were forced to concentrate despite an empty stomach, because breakfast wasn't served until 7:20. Buttered hot rolls and coffee were considered sufficient to break the fast. Such fare was seldom supplemented by meat unless an enterprising diner had the foresight the night before to stab a piece of roast with a two-pronged fork that would hold it pinned to the underside of a table.

Luncheon at one invariably offered meat, bread, and pudding. Beef dominated—roast on Sunday, corned beef on Monday, steak on Wednesday—with veal, mutton, and fish for other days, in a schedule as inviolate as the Decalogue and apparently as old. Dinner echoed breakfast, with hasty pudding or baked rice as typical side dishes. Tables were anchored to the floor, to prevent the formerly common practice of tossing them out a window. Diners tended to commit to a particular table and form an unofficial eating club. During Henry's senior year, the students at one table took turns purchasing each monthly installment of a rollicking novel, *The Posthumous Papers of the Pickwick Club*, by an up-and-coming writer named Charles Dickens.

Henry spent much of his time in the library, which filled the second story of Harvard Hall. All but a handful of its fifty thousand volumes were available to the young men who labored over their forensics and themes at a great table in the center of the room. Nearby could be found the thirty-nine volumes of that comprehensive resource, *The Cyclopædia; or, Universal Dictionary of Arts, Sciences, and Literature*, edited between 1802 and 1820 by the Welsh Nonconformist minister Abraham Rees—"with the assistance of

Eminent Professional Gentlemen," as the title page of each volume declared. Writing during the Napoleonic Wars and already under suspicion for religious nonconformity, Rees and his contributors took great pains to represent their love of England, even going so far as to anglicize the names of French kings from *Louis* to *Lewis*. Nature-minded students such as Henry must have pored over the six volumes of plates, featuring elegant artwork, including beautiful up-to-date steel engravings of beetles in all their baroque splendor, their articulate legs arching across pages as if about to crawl off. Students could find diversion in bound copies of the *Gentleman's Magazine* dating back to 1731, the first periodical to employ the French word *magazine* ("storehouse") to represent the breadth and richness available in a single publication.

Henry's rooms in red-brick Hollis Hall, near the elm called variously the Liberty Tree or the Rebellion Tree, were spartan in their appointments: desk, table, two or three chairs, wash-stand, rocking chair. Not even the allegedly wealthy Southern students could afford such luxuries as the threadbare carpets leased to students at an extortionist's rate, although the occasional devil-may-care senior indulged in one. Only the feather bed in its pine bedstead seemed even theft-worthy.

No furnishings could keep Boston winters at bay. Snow often buried Harvard Yard for weeks at a time. For decades, a few East Coast companies had imported into North America a small amount of coal. Recently discovered coal deposits near Pittsburgh and elsewhere, along with new mining methods, were helping provide cheaper fuel for a larger market. But coal, like many other advances, had gained little headway at the rather backward college. Every student was supplied with a cannon-ball that could be warmed in his room's fireplace to a red glow and then rolled onto an iron skillet from which it could radiate heat for a few hours. (Unheated cannonballs also guaranteed a satisfying uproar when tumbled downstairs during the night.) One student, who was normally not at all bookish, mysteriously kept borrowing from the Harvard library one of its largest books—an oversized volume of theological maunderings—until he was discovered heating it before his fire to use as a bed warmer before he climbed between the sheets.

Recent years had seen the introduction of the smelly and dangerous lucifer match—a splint of wood dipped in a burgoo of sulfur, gum, potassium chlorate, and a sulfide of antimony. Soon the antimony was replaced with white phosphorus, but even this marginally more stable innovation had not yet made its way to Harvard dormitories. Instead, to light a fire or a lamp, a student would take out his small metal tinderbox and strike a forged carbon-steel striker, usually C-shaped for a better grip, against a chunk of flint or quartz. Sparks had to fall directly onto a blackened linen char-cloth, or onto straw or jute, after which the smoldering tinder could be applied to a piece of punk wood. After many strikes, a student could start a fire in the grate, eventually banking coals for the night.

Not all the smoke in dormitories came from fireplaces. A funk from cigars and pipes hovered constantly, only to be worsened by the fire-starting process. Henry didn't smoke, beyond once in his youth trying to puff dried lily stems. He refused to smoke or drink just to be sociable. He never strove to be popular and seemed not only resigned to not fitting in but to sometimes revel in it. At Harvard a black jacket was required for chapel attendance, but sometimes he wore green. He seldom bothered to black his boots. One fellow student, John Weiss, disdained Henry's homespun look and found his moist, indifferent handshake emblematic of the man. He considered Henry's stiff expression like that of an Egyptian idol lost in a kind of mystical arrogance.

★   ★   ★

As a freshman at Harvard, Henry launched into Xenophon's *Anabasis* and the orations of Demosthenes; as a sophomore, Sophocles and Cicero; later came *The Iliad*. By his senior year, although he was no longer studying Latin and Greek courses, he wrote reviews of such books as Henry Nelson Coleridge's *Introduction to the Study of the Greek Classic Poets*. He also studied four contemporary languages—Italian, French, German, and Spanish, from two to five semesters of each. In his last year there he began exploring Persian literature and other Eastern texts.

Edward Tyrrell Channing, a professor in the Department of Rhetoric and Oratory, assigned most of the essays that Henry wrote during his college years, many of them on ethical and philosophical themes. Channing taught Archbishop Richard Whately's *Logic* and *Elements of Rhetoric* and introduced Henry to the Scottish rhetoricians and aestheticians. He studied philosophy extensively, and found himself repelled by what was called Scottish Common Sense Realism, represented by Dugald Stewart, which was increasingly popular in conservative religious circles for its notion of intuitive "first principles" on which religion and morality could be based. Yet Henry also disliked the hard-headed, sense-based empiricism in John Locke's *Essay Concerning Human Understanding*. Instead he was drawn more and more to Plato's idealism, with its central thesis that the world through which Henry strode was a reflection of an ideal reality.

Henry studied geometry, algebra, trigonometry, and calculus, and was introduced to optics and electricity, mechanics and astronomy. His sole course in any topic that could be described as natural history was a term of lectures on botany. Few institutions offered academic courses about the natural world. In their place were influential tomes such as *Natural Theology; or, Evidences of the Existence and Attributes of the Deity*, by the popular British philosopher William

Paley. Henry discussed the *Evidences* in a recitation class during his junior year, along with Joseph Butler's *Analogy of Religion*. Religious commentators were eager to counterbalance the growing evidence of an ancient world appearing in scientific books. A revolution in thinking had been fomented by books such as James Hutton's 1795 *Theory of the Earth* and Charles Lyell's *Principles of Geology: Being an Attempt to Explain the Former Changes of the Earth's Surface, by Reference to Causes Now in Operation*, which appeared in three volumes between 1830 and 1833. Many religious thinkers felt compelled to fight back against the growing notion that the Earth was more ancient than biblical history indicated. The year that Henry graduated, Harvard's own Andrews Norton, Professor of Sacred History, published a long-winded summary, *The Evidences of the Genuineness of the Gospels*.

Only weeks before graduation, Henry wrote an essay on part of *Natural Theology*, a volume that was like a return to the religion-based natural philosophy texts of his childhood. In this book, published in 1802, William Paley opened with an analogy that in the years since had become popular in discussions of religion and natural philosophy:

> In crossing a heath, suppose I pitched my foot against a stone, and were asked how the stone came to be there; I might possibly answer, that, for any thing I knew to the contrary, it had lain there for ever: nor would it perhaps be very easy to show the absurdity of this answer. But suppose I had found a watch upon the ground, and it should be inquired how the watch happened to be in that place; I should hardly think of the answer which I had before given, that, for any thing I knew, the watch might have always been there. Yet why should not this answer serve for the watch as well as for the stone? why is it not as admissible in the second

case, as in the first? For this reason, and for no other, viz. that, when we come to inspect the watch, we perceive (what we could not discover in the stone) that its several parts are framed and put together for a purpose, e. g. that they are so formed and adjusted as to produce motion, and that motion so regulated as to point out the hour of the day; that, if the different parts had been differently shaped from what they are, of a different size from what they are, or placed after any other manner, or in any other order, than that in which they are placed, either no motion at all would have been carried on in the machine, or none which would have answered the use that is now served by it.

Although Paley was responding in part to philosophers such as the eighteenth-century Scot David Hume, who argued against evidence of design, he reiterated a theme that had appeared in theology and philosophy at least since Plato's notion of the divine Artificer. Cicero, in his first-century-B.C. meditation *The Nature of the Gods*, made a similar point: "It can surely not be right to acknowledge as a work of art a statue or a painted picture, or to be convinced from distant observation of a ship's course that its progress is controlled by reason and human skill, or upon examination of the design of a sundial or a water-clock to appreciate that calculation of the time of day is made by skill and not by chance, yet none the less to consider that the universe is devoid of purpose and reason, though it embraces those very skills, and the craftsmen who wield them, and all else beside."

By graduation, Henry was impatient with revealed religion and opposed to dogma. Yet he thought he saw all around him evidence of the kind of divine attention that Paley nicely expressed: "The hinges in the wings of an earwig, and the joints of its antennae, are as highly wrought, as if the Creator had nothing else to finish. We see no signs of diminution of care by multiplicity of objects, or of distraction of thought by variety."

Asked to write an autobiographical note for his Harvard class book, Henry turned in a few disarming remarks about his own shortcomings. He dismissed the considerable amount of work he had accomplished during these college years and implied that Harvard, where he had learned French and German, Spanish and Italian, Greek and Latin, where he had become a thinker and a writer, had not been worth the effort:

> At the age of sixteen I turned my steps toward these venerable halls, bearing in mind, as I have ever since done, that I had two ears and but one tongue. I came—I saw—I conquered—but at the hardest, another such victory and I had been undone. "One branch more," to use Mr. Quincy's own words, "and you had been turned by entirely. You barely got in." However "A man's a man for a' that," I was in, and did not stop to ask how I got there.

> Suffice it to say, that though bodily I have been a member of Harvard University, heart and soul I have been far away among the scenes of my boyhood. Those hours that should have been devoted to study have been spent in scouring the woods, and exploring the lakes and streams.

A FEW MONTHS before he graduated in 1837, nineteen-year-old Henry asked his mother which profession he ought to pursue.

"You can buckle on your knapsack," she replied playfully, "and roam abroad to seek your fortune."

More than ever, Mrs. Thoreau was known for her spunk and sass, but at the thought of leaving home Henry's eyes began to fill with tears.

He was back home visiting his beloved Concord. Just beyond the Thoreaus' front door, creaking ox-carts, laden with grain for local markets, passed women and men trudging to and from the new mills. Concord boasted a lead pipe factory and a steam-driven smithy, six warehouses, two gristmills, and two sawmills. Forty stage-coaches came through town each week, carrying as many as 150 passengers in a single day. One-horse shays raced about, their drivers resting their elbows on their knees, with behind them a folded-back roof rattling and at night twin gig lamps casting double haloes ahead.

Henry was fond of his doting mother and naturally sought her advice. At fifty, tall and handsome and plucky, Cynthia, like her two Thoreau sisters-in-law in the village, was the efficient hostess of a clamorous boardinghouse. It was a hive of activity—boarders' shoes drumming on the stairs, pans clanging in the big kitchen, the whir of a spinning wheel, a butter churn's gurgle and tap. Strangers bantered over breakfast and there were few peaceful evenings. Henry's sister Sophia complained that the din was "enough to drive a man to Nova Zembla for quiet." Down the street their placid, now somewhat deaf father, also fifty, ran the pencil business. He also dealt in miscellaneous related items such as marbled papers, plumbago (graphite), and stove polish, which required a high percentage of plumbago. Henry worked with his father whenever he was home from Harvard, and during his college years had at least once accompanied him in selling pencils to New York City shops.

Mrs. Thoreau stated her opinion bluntly and did not hesitate to denounce behavior she felt unworthy, as in her vocal opposition to slavery. She had little patience for fools, but she was famously generous. Once, eager to help a struggling servant, she opened a bank account in her name and deposited what little money she could spare to encourage the girl to save a tithe of the pittance they paid her. With her family, Mrs. Thoreau was tolerant and affectionate. She tended to indulge her precocious but difficult younger son—"my David Henry," she was often heard to say warmly. He had always prided himself on his stoicism. She had seldom seen him in tears, yet here he was a grown man, crying at the thought of leaving home.

Although only seventeen-year-old Sophia actually still lived with their parents, Henry's sister Helen was home that day. The eldest at twenty-five, she worked as a teacher in Taunton, more than fifty miles to the south. For the last four years, both she and John, who was twenty-two and also a teacher, had joined their parents in contributing driblets of their modest incomes toward the couple of hundred dollars annually that Henry's attendance at Harvard required. Even their aunts had helped. Known for a quick smile and easygoing sympathy, John was more popular than his brother. He was bright and ambitious, but he lacked Henry's voracious appetite for books, which had led to the younger son's becoming the family's only college student.

Shy, polite Helen had dark eyes so large they made her face look small, especially when she pulled back her hair. Like Henry, she had strong dark brows and a tall receding forehead, but her arching Dunbar nose wasn't as prominent as his. His own beak jutted over a puritanically pursed upper lip that rested uneasily on a sensuous lower lip. His strongest feature was deep-set blue-gray eyes, earnest and wary, prominent under drooping lids. Only his receding chin seemed weak. Even in his mother's parlor he sat stiffly, unable to slouch or relax, his body tensed for the next action as if he dared not waste a moment.

Usually, especially when home from college, Henry dressed in rustic drab—heavy boots, a straw hat, sturdy trousers that resisted thorns and would not rip when their owner clambered up a tree to admire the sanctum of owl or raccoon. The ladies of the Charitable Society once observed Henry's unnecessarily urchin-like clothing and meekly asked their cofounder, his own mother, if he might accept a donation of shirts from them. At the next meeting Cynthia Thoreau reported, "I told my David Henry that you would like to make him some unbleached cotton shirts. He said, 'Unbleached, mother. Unbleached. Yes, that strikes my ear pleasantly; I think they may make me some.'" A hard-working farm wife, probably tired of Henry's notorious eccentricities, muttered to the woman beside her, "Strike his ears pleasantly, indeed. I guess they'll strike his back pleasantly when he gets them on."

On the day of his tearful distress, Helen came to Henry's rescue. She hugged her contrary, shabby, affectionate brother and kissed his cheek. "No, Henry, you shall not go," she reassured him patiently. "You shall stay at home and live with us."

He stopped crying.

Chapter 3

MORE BEAUTIFUL THAN USEFUL

G RADUALLY HENRY OVERCAME lack of discipline, shortage of funds, and illness to raise his Harvard points to 14,397 and his rank to nineteenth out of forty-three graduates in the Class of 1837. He was barely in the top half, but his acknowledged intelligence and writing skill were enough to get him invited to participate in the commencement proceedings. The two dozen or so students chosen to contribute were notified by the president's freshman dogsbody, who instructed them to see Mr. Quincy himself for particulars. At his office each young man was handed a slip of paper with instructions, such as *Jones—a disquisition, four minutes*, or *Brown—an English oration, twelve minutes*. During summer term students worked up their presentation. They were expected to first deliver it before Professor Channing, who would help them vent its inflating rhetoric. Next they rehearsed. Then came a trip to the dusty shop of Ma'am Hyde in Dunster Street near the school, where fifty cents would rent for the day one of many aging black silk gowns that she stocked.

Soon Henry found himself declaring, "The characteristic of our epoch is perfect freedom—freedom of thought and action." He liked to hold forth and on this day he was addressing his favorite theme—personal and intellectual freedom. "The indignant Greek, the oppressed Pole, the jealous American assert it," he continued. "The skeptic no less than the believer, the heretic no less than the faithful child of the Church, have begun to enjoy it."

Years of public discussion had cured him of stage fright. The Concord Academy Debating Society had served him well, and each year at Harvard he had participated in requisite exhibitions. He spoke calmly as he looked down at other members of the notoriously rowdy class, students from other grades, President Quincy, the twenty-seven professors and instructors and proctors who comprised the Harvard faculty, the governor, church officials, and other members of the audience. The host of the commencement was Cambridge's still new First Parish Church. For this occasion it had been equipped with a speaker's platform, from which Henry could look down at the center and side aisles and the box pews along the north and south walls.

Since before dawn, on this sweltering next-to-last day of August 1837—three months after the end of his senior year—covered handcarts and other vehicles, most driven by Negroes, had been rattling down the streets from Boston and surrounding the green fields of Cambridge Common. Few students partook of these foods and games, which were intended to provide sustenance and diversion to the jostling herd of locals who gawked at the proceedings. Harvard's commencement was one of the town's liveliest holidays. Early that morning, Massachusetts governor Edward Everett, escorted by cavalry, had departed the State House in Boston, driven in a fashionable barouche with facing seats behind the elevated driver.

Henry's fellow students were a varied crew. They ranged from John Fenwick Eustis, scion of a Southern-born general and first in the class, to Manlius Stimson Clarke, earnest son of a poverty-haunted liberal clergyman. After an absence of two years serving as a merchant seaman, Cambridge-born Richard Henry Dana had returned and was graduating from Harvard's law school. Following the summer holiday, students had returned for commencement, which was always scheduled for the last Wednesday in August. Class Day had taken place on the eighteenth of July, less than a week after Henry turned twenty. The valedictory mischief had been so besotted and disorderly that Josiah Quincy had already forbidden such carousal in the future.

Now, in contrast to the carnival-like commencement period, Henry and two other sweating graduates were presenting a formal debate—a conference, it was called: "The Commercial Spirit of Modern Times, Considered in its Influence on the Political, Moral, and Literary Character of a Nation." The conference participants were listed as Charles Wyatt Rice of Brookfield, David Henry Thoreau of Concord—although sometimes he reversed the order of his given names—and Henry Vose of Dorchester. Friends for years with Vose, Henry also liked Rice, the son of a blacksmith, who had been a roommate first and then became a close friend. Before their turn arrived, the trio had had to sit through other speakers. It was customary for the best writer of Latin to deliver in the language of classical education an overture in which he flattered the governor, complimented professors, and joked about the girls present. Then came a paper on the religiously charged poetry of William Cowper and Edward Young, and finally an essay on "The Effect upon Literature of a Belief in Immortality." After every few speakers, the college band struck up a yawn-preventing diversion. But the speeches were expected to drag on from nine in the morning until three or four in the afternoon, when Quincy began handing out diplomas, which were rolled and tied with a blue ribbon. Now and then restless audience members strolled outdoors and someone else wandered in to fill the empty seat.

Finally Henry and his partners rose to debate the idea of the new American commercial spirit that had arisen from the many changes during the decades since the war with England and the founding of the United States. "The winds and the waves are not enough for him," Henry asserted of modern man; "he must needs ransack the bowels of the earth, that he may make for himself a highway of iron over its surface." Ever since the successful performance of the pioneer steam locomotive *Tom Thumb* in 1830, when Henry was thirteen, trains had promised ever greater commercial possibilities that would further change society. And at this time dreamers were trying to perfect nothing less miraculous than instantaneous communication. Only a few months earlier, the English inventors Charles Wheatstone and Sir William Fothergill Cooke had patented something called an electric telegraph. Henry, who enjoyed engineering especially, liked to keep up to date about technology.

Some of Henry's friends were former roommates who had spent enough time around him to get past his stoic façade. One, James Richardson, watched admiringly from the audience as Henry summed up their shared intellectual excitement about the prospects ahead for American men of this age. A younger friend was John Shepard Keyes, also from Concord Academy. Keyes was at Harvard that week for his entrance examinations, having ridden up from Concord the previous Sunday evening, lugging a carpetbag bulging with books, food, and an unrealistic certificate of moral character scribbled by the Concord minister Barzillai Frost. Henry had found his young townsman standing, with sagging bag in hand, at the college gates where the five o'clock mail coach dropped him. He took him up to his room in four-story red-brick Stoughton Hall, where Keyes stayed during this commencement weekend visit. Keyes was anxious about his upcoming days and awed by the venerable stone walls of Harvard, until a herd of Henry's raucous classmates exploded into his room. Keyes enjoyed their tomfoolery. Fresh from the summer holiday, the seniors were loud in their casual disrespect for people whom Keyes had heard spoken of reverently over Concord dinner tables. When the fellow students learned that Keyes was also from Concord, Henry himself was chaffed for his provincial pride in his hometown.

Whatever his difficulties with real people, Henry found it easy to speak about humanity in the abstract. In his speech, thinking of telegraph wires and train tracks crossing the continent, Henry continued, "Man thinks faster and freer than ever before. He, moreover, moves faster and freer. He is more restless, because he is more independent than ever." In writing and speaking, as in tramping the Massachusetts countryside, he sought a panoramic view. He liked to climb mountains and reduce civilization to a sandbox observed from Olympus. His side of the graduation debate was his farewell to college, where he had learned to read classical poets and contemporary German newspapers, where he had devoured economics and politics, but where he had seldom felt happy. As he spoke, he drew back from his fellow human beings more than he had in his classroom essays and imagined how human life would look through a telescope viewing Earth from somewhere out among the stars. A celestial observer would see the characteristics of this age, Henry decided, as scurry and bustle: "There would be hammering and chipping in one quarter; baking and brewing, buying and selling, money-changing and speechmaking in another." He made explicit his contrarian view of such chaos: "This curious world which we inhabit is more wonderful than it is convenient; more beautiful than it is useful; it is more to be admired and enjoyed than used."

After characterizing a lust for wealth as "unmanly," Henry admitted grudgingly in his closing remarks, "The spirit we are considering is not altogether and without exception bad. We rejoice in it as one more indication of the entire and universal freedom that characterizes the age in which we live—as an indication that the human race is making one more advance in that infinite series of progressions which awaits it."

After Rice, Vose, and Henry sat down, a young man rose to deliver his speech—a "literary disquisition," the audience read in their catalogs, on "Modern Imitation of the Ancient Greek Tragedy." The moment toward which Henry had been working for months was over. Four years of college were behind him. Like every other graduate in the room, he wondered what lay ahead.

Henry was not bound by the prohibitions that kept his mother and sisters from walking alone in the world. Unlike the more than two million slaves shackled in the South or the tens of thousands of Indians who were being pushed ever farther into the West, Henry had been able to attend college and earn a degree. He could go anywhere he chose in the New World or elsewhere, could see everything, learn anything. But he wasn't going to use his own freedom to traverse the twenty-six states or the violent, exotic territories beyond. Certainly he wasn't about to explore tropical islands or Himalayan plateaus. He was going back home to live with his parents.

NEARBY THAT DAY as Henry spoke during commencement was his Concord schoolmate and recent roommate Charles Stearns Wheeler. Boyish and round-faced, the friendly son of a prosperous farmer, Wheeler was a brilliant scholar who ranked second in the graduating class—far ahead of Henry, who greatly admired him. After rooming together, they had been friends throughout their college years. One day in early October 1833, shortly after they met as freshmen, Henry evaded both morning and evening chapel to walk to Concord with Wheeler. It was almost twenty miles, and the long last two Henry limped in his stocking feet because his shoes had rubbed blisters. It took him three hours just to walk from Lincoln, and necessarily his visit home was brief, but he had great conversations with Wheeler. Although Wheeler was an insatiably curious young devourer of books, he was otherwise an unlikely chum for contentious Henry—always smiling, happy to obey the college rules.

Precocious and industrious, Wheeler had already worked in publishing for a couple of years, editing manuscripts, creating indexes, laboriously writing out fair copies. His early efforts on the *Library of American Biography* series led to editorial work with the writer and philosopher Ralph Waldo Emerson, whose book *Nature* Henry had devoured after its publication in late 1836. The acclaimed Scottish essayist Thomas Carlyle had been unable to arrange a book publisher for his semi-autobiographical novel *Sartor Resartus*, only to find an American champion in Emerson. Carlyle's experimental tale thus first appeared between covers in the United States, with a preface by Emerson. It became available only because Wheeler spent many hours in the mansion on tree-lined Pearl Street that housed the handsome Boston Athenæum, painstakingly—and without pay—transcribing every word of Carlyle's book from the dense two-column pages of London's *Fraser's Magazine*, its only previous publication.

Recently, during the break between the end of classes and commencement, Henry had spent a few weeks living with Wheeler in the rough summer hut he had built the year before under trees near the edge of Flint's Pond, a large shallow lake a couple of miles southeast of Concord, near Lincoln. Wheeler invited various college chums to stay with him and his family, and often they slept in the shanty, although they ate at the family house. Henry enjoyed visiting the pond. He loved the miles of woodland, rich in flourishing plants and animals, between his home on Main Street and the shores of the pond—a solitary ramble in a garden larger than kings could afford. Flint's Pond was shallow and Henry loved wading in it. Although the sand beneath his bare feet was soft, its sculpted ripples felt surprisingly firm. He admired the view of a reedy island cleverly in its midst dubbed Reed Island. He liked to climb the mountain beyond the lake and peer back across the woods that hid his route there. It looked like a painter's landscape, tinted and faded by the air itself, romanticizing the view toward Concord and the mountains beyond, and providing an almost bird's-eye view of his beloved Walden Pond, a mile and a half from Concord.

Even the rustling straw bunks in Wheeler's cabin didn't spoil Henry's first taste of restful solitude, which contrasted greatly with the noise of the Thoreau boardinghouse. His family had moved from one abode to another throughout his life; he had never had a place to call home for long. The image of a lakeside cabin lingered in his mind.

Chapter 4

MEADOW RIVER

SOME OF THE boarders in the Thoreau house were strangers who needed temporary residence, and occasionally Mrs. Thoreau even took in a transient who came to the door with a reference from a mutual acquaintance. Most, however, were relatives or friends who lived there for years. The majority were women. Cynthia Thoreau's maiden sister, Louisa Dunbar, had moved in after the death of their mother in 1830. Two maiden aunts from the Thoreau side, Maria and the almost deaf but still talkative Jane, boarded there at times. Other resident boarders included Mrs. Prudence Ward, widow of a Revolutionary War soldier, and her daughter Prudence, who were friends of Aunt Maria. The younger Prudence was known for her love of plants; she identified wild ones, sowed and raised domesticated ones, and painted accomplished portraits of them.

Aunt Louisa spent much of her time rushing from one meeting to another, to battle what she saw as the unnecessary pain that people inflict on each other. Both of Henry's parents were known as "comeouters" on various issues. Ever since abolitionists had boarded with the Thoreaus in the mid-1830s the entire family had opposed slavery. The past few years had seen an international growth of abolitionist support by strong women such as Louisa and Cynthia,

who organized rallies and kept up an onslaught of petitions to legis-
lators. Mrs. Ward and Prudence had been reading the abolitionist
organ the *Liberator* for two and a half years prior to their arrival in
Concord in 1833.

Henry regularly saw one of the venerable, and considerably less
progressive, spirits of Concord's past strolling down Monument Street
in black stockings and broad-brimmed hat, his ancient black cloak
swirling—the Reverend Ezra Ripley. The balding and bespectacled
minister liked antique fashions in ideas and clothing. He remained
loyal to the Puritan notion of a hands-on deity who received thanks
for every time an overturned carriage did not kill anyone but never
received blame for toppling the carriage. He also remained loyal to
the most recent style in coats he had admired—from the Revolutionary
War when he was in his mid-twenties. In front the lapels couldn't
meet across his considerable belly, so Ripley wore an heirloom waist-
coat that swathed his trunk from neck to thigh.

Ripley was Emerson's step-grandfather. In his mid-eighties in
1837, Ripley had been minister of the First Parish Church almost
sixty years, since 1778, two years after graduating from Harvard,
where he had been nicknamed Holy Ripley. When General
Washington commandeered Harvard's dormitories to house troops
during the Revolution, young Ripley invited his alma mater to
continue classes down the road in the Concord Meeting House.
Two years after returning to town and boarding with Phebe Bliss
Emerson—the widow of his predecessor and Emerson's paternal
grandmother—he had married her. In 1812 he performed the
marriage service for John Thoreau and Cynthia Dunbar, and five
years later he christened Henry. Over the decades he had provided
ready counsel and stern admonition to Concordians, while always
finding time to chat gallantly with the ladies, and he was renowned
for his lively stories around the fire.

His church was one of the town landmarks. Above its fluted white columns, above the dark faces of its faithful clock, above its open bell tower and restless weathervane, a spire towered over the Common. Inside the bare, uncarpeted meetinghouse, Ripley climbed a long flight of stairs to his high pulpit, which looked down on the four deacons' seats and the ranks of square, un-cushioned pews with their old-fashioned high wooden backs. There was little leg room between pews, so when the congregation rose for a prayer they raised the hinged seats as well, and Ripley's "amen" signaled a gunshot volley of seats slamming down as people sat. Like most regions of the country, Concord had its unique pronunciations; some veterans of the Revolution, for example, still called bayonets "bagnets." When the congregation sang Isaac Watts's joyful late-seventeenth-century hymn "Let Every Creature Join," Ripley's antique diction rang out from the sounding boards on three sides of the church: "Let every critter jine . . ."

From his vantage point, Ripley could look down upon the history of Concord, with several Revolutionary veterans gazing back at him. The now wrinkled and bent Amos Barrett, who had been a spry corporal in Captain David Brown's Concord Minute Man Company, described seeing the redcoats' first volley of shot splash into the water to his right as he approached along the river road, with his musket freshly loaded and ready to fire, while in the village black smoke hovered above carriages set afire by the plundering soldiers.

Over time, Ripley came to think of himself as God's regent in Concord. Little acquainted with other literature and resistant to ideas beyond his ken—parishioners knew they could visit him at any time, because he was seldom caught reading—he concentrated on an ancient Hebrew view of the world. He was famous for his prayers to coax rain and repel maladies. When Emerson was a child, Ripley drove him about the parish in a carriage, pointing out the homes of people who had broken off from his church and emphasizing that divine misfortune had dogged each thereafter. Once, during a drought, when a junior colleague offered to lead the congregation in prayer, Ripley said slyly, "This is no time for you young Cambridge men. The affair, sir, is getting serious. I shall pray myself."

Although they passed each other on the streets, Reverend Ripley seldom saw young Henry Thoreau in a pew. He had a provocative habit of walking in the woods on Sunday morning, cheerfully enjoying God's creation instead of hearing His word.

MUSKETAQUID, THE MASSACHUSETT Indians had called the river, for the grassy fields that surrounded it. It meant "meadow river" or "grass-ground river," adapting the Algonquian word for grass, *muskeht*. European settlers optimistically renamed it the Concord, but Henry preferred the original name. Its current was so slow that newcomers had trouble deciphering its direction of flow, and a fisherman piloting a skiff might find it as easy to row against the current as with it. In summer, yellow water lilies stood on their unobtrusive stalks, just above the surface, surrounded by leathery flat leaves on which frogs perched, and blue pickerelweed stood up from leaves shaped like arrowheads.

Founded in 1635, Concord was the first inland English settlement in the New World. Two centuries later, with the population nearing two thousand, mail arrived and departed sixteen times a week. The Mill Dam was the center, crossing over Mill Brook, which ran through the village between Walden Road and the Cambridge Turnpike. The Mill Dam had anchored Concord since the Reverend Peter Bulkeley had built a gristmill on the site in the seventeenth century. The bustling Anderson Market was there, along with an array of businesses essential for a modern society—milliner, tinsmith, barber, currier, tanner. During Henry's life great changes had taken place in this part of Concord, thanks to the formation in 1826 of the Mill Dam Company, which had torn down older buildings, drained the venerable mill pond, divided up land and sold lots, and set itself up as landlord of new buildings. While Henry was at Harvard, the Company headed the building of a temple to the village's mercantile ambitions, the Concord Bank and Middlesex Mutual Fire Insurance Company, whose four Doric columns now lent gravitas to Main Street.

Loafers sprawled around the town pump, from which boys measured local distances; it was half a mile, for example, to Thayer's swimming hole. Able-bodied men between the ages of eighteen and forty-five were required to muster for militia inspection in May each year, and usually they did so on the Common. Dressed in old clothes and with only token training, most made poor soldiers and were chaffed by critical boys. Artillery and infantry kept up a good-natured competition, with rival companies importing bands from Boston. People still talked about legendary bugler Ned Kendall, who led a marching band in a quickstep three-quarter-time version of a polonaise. Even a small muster was accompanied by fife and drum, their volume rising and falling as the militiamen marched behind a barn and out again. Boys played soldier. Those pretending to be marauding Indians wore long white shirts adorned with strips of red flannel and carried makeshift wooden spears with which to gig settlers.

Concord had been the site of the first Provincial Congress and in 1792 served as the capital for some months. Ever since the early 1690s, it had been a shire town, a seat of county government. Its courthouse, which dominated the Common, saw trials from across Middlesex County, whose population in 1837 was approaching one hundred thousand. Within the courthouse lurked relics of Concord's past. In the basement stood an old array of stocks before which offenders had sat, knelt, or stood with head and arms immobilized between wooden bars, exposed to weather and humiliation, with passersby allowed to throw rotten eggs, offal, even manure. The basement housed a gallows used to hang the only man executed in Concord. Out front stood an elm that tradition claimed had been planted on the nineteenth of April 1776, the first anniversary of the Concord battle. From 1790 to 1820, three years after Henry's birth, the tree served as the town's whipping post. An iron staple anchored eight feet above the ground had secured the hands of felons receiving lashes, but in the last seventeen years scaly gray bark had grown over it. The courthouse faced across Monument Square toward the red-brick Masonic Hall. Down the block, the Middlesex Hotel stood across the Common from the tall brick chimneys of Wright's Tavern, where Minutemen had gathered in 1775 after learning that British troops were approaching. Behind the hotel rose the yellow spire of the Unitarian Meeting House.

Main Street in Concord was a buzz of commerce, as manufacturing began to catch up with agriculture in economic importance. Since his move to Concord two decades earlier, the businessman David Loring had manufactured first lead pipes and then wooden pails, evolving into a major employer and an influential citizen. The cotton mill employed dozens of locals. Most were women, but their numbers didn't compare with the more than seven thousand women who worked in the nearby Lowell textile mills, whose thirteen-hour days had been revealed recently in a newspaper exposé.

A parade of flatbed wagons convoyed dry goods from Boston to New Hampshire and Vermont, stopping overnight at Concord's rowdy taverns. So many public and private coaches came through town that tavern barns soon filled with horses. As long lines of coaches stretched down the streets near taverns, their animals spent the night hitched to the back of the conveyance they had pulled into town. Drink was rampant. Temperance leaders made no more headway in Concord than elsewhere in the nation. The prominent Concordian Nathan Brooks admitted that, after he delivered a lecture (requested by the selectmen) on temperance, he and other town leaders strolled to a tavern for a drink. It wasn't unusual to find prominent, highly regarded farmers staggering down a Concord street or even lying drunk beside it.

Each drinking spot drew its own clientele. The three-story Middlesex Hotel, with its portico under which mail and passenger coaches lined up, catered to locals and stage travelers, leaving for rowdy teamsters the coarse fare at Hartwell Bigelow's tavern on Main Street above the burial ground. Patrons gathered around a stove large enough to accommodate massive logs, from whose red coals protruded iron loggerheads to use in heating flip. A decoction of fermented roots, hops, and spruce, flip was mixed in a pewter mug, filled two-thirds full of weak local beer, sweetened with molasses, laced with a gill of rum, and heated by plunging a red-hot loggerhead into it—causing it to seethe like a witch's brew and acquire a scorched bitter taste. At night a walker on the street could hear the clatter of a toddy stick frothing sugar and rum inside the bar.

Periodically the village routine was enlivened by a quack medicine salesman in his long schooner of a wagon that rattled with heavy glass bottles of tinctures and elixirs—nostrums for gout, quinsy, tissick, and dropsy; miraculous water from the Dead Sea and herbs of mythological potency; tonics to banish languor and philters to dissolve romantic qualms. There were some national brands of alleged medicaments, such as Samuel Lee's Bilious Pills, whose patent dated to 1796, but many were concocted in the back of a wagon. Usually the hucksters had moved on to Lincoln before disillusionment arrived in Concord.

Chapter 5

THE NEW SCHOOLMASTER

F OLLOWING HIS RETURN to Concord, Henry had less time
than usual to stroll at Walden Pond. Two weeks after Harvard's
commencement, he began his first job. In mid-April, while Henry
was in his last term at Harvard, the Centre Grammar School had
run an advertisement in the *Yeoman's Gazette* for a teaching position. Henry applied. The Centre was one of seven districts that
comprised sixteen schools, half for girls and half for boys. With
more than three hundred students, it required four teachers: two
women and two men. Most of the male teachers in the region
earned only about one hundred dollars per year, which was still two
and a half times what women earned for the same work. Concord
devoted the largest portion of its civic budget to schools—$2,132.55
during the upcoming academic year. The next largest expense was
assistance to the poor.

Henry got the job. Fresh out of college amid a severe national
recession, he found himself with a well-paid position that required
not a move to Taunton or the Missouri Territory but a stroll through
the village. Most Concord teachers were recent graduates—many,
like Henry, straight from Harvard—and they regarded teaching as a
temporary profession that required few skills and little commitment. Yet education was becoming a Thoreau family tradition, with

John and Helen both teaching, and Cynthia's sister, Aunt Louisa Dunbar, and father, Asa Dunbar, having taught, as had John Senior himself for a time.

Henry was hired for the Centre School by a three-person committee that included Deacon Nehemiah Ball. No more than forty, Ball had a hand in practically every public activity in Concord. A trial justice and the town clerk, he was also a board member of the Mill Dam Company and secretary of the School Committee. Abstemious and judgmental, broad and pompous, he seldom smiled and almost never laughed; Concord wits considered him the antidote to humor. He was never seen to walk quickly or pick up a tool. Once when Ball was serving as justice of the peace, a witness in a dispute about a sale of potatoes remarked that the potatoes had been "deaconed." Ball demanded icily, "What was meant by that remark?" and his anger turned his face ever more red as the man explained that the good-looking potatoes had been piled on top in the barrel, with the worthless runts hidden underneath.

Frequently Ball was lampooned behind his back for quirks of speech, such as overuse of the phrase "I apprehend," especially in his lectures for the Lyceum that, in 1828 and early 1829, replaced the village's Debating Club. The series of lectures and debates were held in various venues around town until settling in the Town Hall. When he demonstrated the first magic lantern to be seen in the Concord area, Ball projected a drawing of a lion onto the bed sheet that had been hung up as a screen, stared at the figure for a moment, and said to the delight of his enemies, "This, I apprehend, is a ferocious beast."

School was in session all year, six days a week, broken up by four one-week vacations. Fast days were holidays, as was Thanksgiving. Most holidays concerned celebration of or maintenance of the young nation. Students were off for the May day on which the militia performed its public training, and they were also free on the varying date when the state militia's Day of Muster occurred in Concord. A favorite holiday for many students was called simply "Cornwallis." It took place on October 19, the anniversary of the British General Charles Cornwallis's surrender to American and French forces at Yorktown in 1781. Each year Cornwallis featured a reenactment of the enemy's humiliation. Men in red British uniforms represented the invaders, while an appropriately ragtag band of volunteers, clad in antique clothes and carrying muskets, portrayed American settlers. Every Cornwallis battle ended satisfyingly with colonists parading their redcoat captives.

The trudge of school days throughout the year was made more oppressive by the close quarters. Most of the cheaply built school buildings had no windows that would open or in some cases no windows at all. During school hours the atmosphere grew increasingly foul, until both students and master nodded from the shortage of fresh air. The school committee found the stench in some schools disgusting and repellent when they visited to inspect, but they were slow to improve the situation.

IN MOST AMERICAN schools at the time, students worked under the threat of physical punishment. Frederick Augustus Porter Barnard alluded casually to this situation in his 1830 *Treatise on Arithmetic*:

> 1. *John made 3 marks on one leaf of his book, and six on another. How many marks did he make? 3 and 6 are how many?*
> 2. *His teacher punished him, for soiling the book, by giving him 4 blows on one hand, and 5 on the other. How many blows did he strike him? 4 and 5 are how many?*

When they weren't fighting among themselves—and violence in the public schools was one reason why the Concord Academy had been founded in 1822, just in time for Henry and John to attend—students were facing violence from their teachers. Mild offenses resulted merely in incarceration in the classroom while the rest of the students cavorted outdoors during a brief recess, or perhaps in extra study after the other students left. But a long menu of rule breaking elicited a violent response. Even in the "infant schools"— the lower grades taught mostly by women, also known as dame schools—thrashing was an ever-present risk for the rambunctious student. A Concord schoolmistress might whip a child with the sole of her shoe or whatever else was handy, but most women walked into the schoolroom every morning armed with a more serious weapon. For centuries the corset had been uncomfortably sculpting women toward an ideal silhouette, and doing so required many stays of whalebone or pliant wood; in front, a narrow pocket in their long, high-necked dress housed a busk, a posture-minding center stay that could be unsheathed to whip students. Thrashing was more common and more harsh in the higher grades. Many teachers kept a cowhide whip in the desk.

A few years before Henry's birth, a towering giant of a teacher named Elijah Paige, who was quite popular and respected among townsfolk despite his brutal methods, would strip off a rebellious boy's coat, tie his hands to a high rope that dangled him with his feet unable to touch the floor, and flog him with willow rods that he had sent other students to cut. Until recent years, another regular form of punishment had been to discipline boys by forcing them to sit painfully doubled beneath the master's desk in a posture of abject humiliation. One legendarily cruel master had tried to inflict this torture on a fourteen-year-old boy recently arrived from Canada, but not even beating could compel obedience, until finally his case had been taken before a school committee that included the allegedly kind-hearted Dr. Ripley. The committee was inclined, as usual, to enforce the viewpoint of the master, even after the student pointed out that his teacher regularly spat and blew his nose on the floor. "I will not sit down," he bravely proclaimed, "in that *spit* and *snot* which is all over the floor under the desk."

Some school board members recalled that proper conduct and high scholarly standards had been maintained in the classroom of gentle Samuel Barrett, but he taught school for only a couple of years in Henry's childhood, and unfortunately other teachers did not adopt his pacific example. In Henry's time feruling and flogging still were common. Many teachers kept a cane or ferule—a flat-ruler-like board—in cautionary view alongside inkwell and paper. A student would stand with hand held out and facing upward, and the teacher would strike the ferule hard across the open palm, causing blistering pain. Sometimes boys were even sent to cut and trim a supple willow rod for their own flogging.

The school's regulations advised teachers to keep corporal punishment down to as little as they considered "practical," but Henry's students were not rowdy and he saw no need to resort to physical discipline. One day, however, only two weeks after Henry began teaching, heavy-featured Deacon Ball, solemn as Job, dropped by the class unannounced and strode in to observe the young man's teaching methods. Soon, finding students behaving with what he considered unseemly animation, he told Henry firmly that he must not spare the rod, that the school would be ruined if he did not thrash the children now and then.

During the next day or so after Ball reprimanded him, Henry— apparently both angry at the interference in his classroom and worried about his job—thrashed several students for various reasons, or perhaps for no reason. Naturally they were outraged. Ten-year-old Daniel Potter thought he was included because he followed the rule among the female teachers he had formerly studied under at the district school: when you finish a lesson, put your book away and sit quietly with arms folded to indicate that your work is done. At the Centre School, in contrast, each student was required to keep a book visible on the desk, and here the arms-crossed posture may have seemed a taunt, a declaration of idleness. For whatever infraction, Henry called young Daniel to the front of the class and quickly whipped him. Furious at this unjust treatment, the boy stomped back to his seat, swearing to himself, "When I'm grown up, I'll whip you for this, old feller!" That others were similarly treated didn't quell his anger.

Henry's outburst remained a mystery to the students and apparently to Henry himself. Parents probably didn't care, because thrashing was the usual form of punishment at home. Those citizens who knew Henry outside the school were surprised, because he was considered a mild and inoffensive man, other than for his occasional sarcastic remarks and aggressive nonconformity.

Immediately afterward, in another move as sudden and irrational as his decision to punish the students, Henry resigned his job. He told his superiors that he wouldn't keep school any longer if he was expected to whip children. Although at the last he had indulged in a paradoxical bout of violence, Henry—always a master of rationalization—managed to tell himself that he had otherwise stood by his principles, renouncing corporal punishment. Perhaps he had also peered into the future and seen a sobering image of himself as a servant of the community, trapped by a regular income, rather than his dream job of gadfly. After only a fortnight employed in a coveted position, he joined the uncountable jobless men who milled about during the national financial panic that had followed the crash in the spring. He walked east down Middle Street to the boardinghouse to tell his parents that next week he would not be leaving home every morning. In his anger at Nehemiah Ball's interference, and his discomfort with working inside a public system, he had quickly thrown away his best chance to stay near his family and his beloved woods and ponds. The next available job might be well beyond sight of Walden.

FOR HENRY, ABANDONING his teaching job meant a necessary return to the pencil business, which had supported the family since 1823. During his brief time living in Chelmsford, while working with the inventor Joseph Dixon, John Thoreau Sr. seems to have learned the essentials of pencil manufacturing, which was a rudimentary profession in the New World. Because of its similarity to lead, graphite was called *plumbago*, "that which acts like lead," and had also at times been named after various words referring to its blackness, such as *black-cowke*, *ochra nigra*, and *crayon noir*. The word "graphite" had been coined in Germany as recently as the late eighteenth century, from the Greek *graphein*, "to write."

Dixon mixed plumbago from Ceylon with clay and water and rolled the resulting paste into strips. He found plumbago readily available because his father was a ship owner whose vessels carried it from Ceylon—where the dense and heavy substance could be found cheaply—as ballast during their voyages homeward to New England. Afterward they dumped it into the bay at Marblehead, Massachusetts. Dixon learned that this waste plumbago could be used to make pencils. After baking the flattened mixture in his mother's kitchen oven, Dixon pressed it into boards of grooved cedar, joining two boards to encase the graphite. He constructed his own hand-cranked machines to cut and groove the slats of cedar and to extrude the plumbago.

But Dixon's American pencils were gritty and could not compete with European brands. Europe had dominated the pencil market since the middle of the sixteenth century, when a mine in Cumberland, England, began producing sticks of graphite encased in tubes of wood or wrapped in string. Gradually this humble beginning blossomed into a profitable industry. Within a century, enterprising inventors in Nuremberg were gluing sticks of graphite between two pieces of wood, and a few decades later they were filling the pencil cores with a mixture of graphite, sulfur, and a binding agent that was less sturdy than England's natural sticks of pure graphite. In 1812 William Munroe in Boston introduced to the United States market wood-cased lead pencils that he manufactured himself, but unfortunately their core of unfired graphite paste left them brittle. When Joseph Dixon tried to peddle his pencils in Boston, he was advised to sell them under a counterfeit European label if he expected to make inroads into the market. He continued to tinker with plumbago in stove polish, lubricants, and other uses, and eventually added his own successful pencil business.

In 1821, not long before John Thoreau brought his family back to Concord, Charles Dunbar, Cynthia's ne'er-do-well brother, discovered a plumbago deposit near Bristol, New Hampshire, and he himself briefly gambled on the pencil business. In 1823 he asked his sister's husband to join him. John Senior had been paying attention in Chelmsford and quickly he mastered the manufacture of pencils. By the next year, Thoreau pencils were receiving special commendation at an exhibition of the Massachusetts Agricultural Society. "The Lead Pencils exhibited by J. Thorough & Co.," reported the *New England Farmer*, "were superior to any specimens exhibited in past years." They could compete with Munroe and other American manufacturers because all pencils then made in the New World were similarly inferior to European pencils. With

British plumbago unavailable, and French processes not yet known in the United States, Americans used impure and poorly ground plumbago and mixed it with poor binding agents such as spermaceti and bayberry wax. Henry's father improved the process enough to compete, and by the time Henry returned to Concord, the family business was well established.

John Thoreau Sr. had the early training with Dixon and years of experience, as well as a fondness for reading about chemistry. Henry—already interested in engineering, usually happy in both manual labor and solving a problem—had an impatient and eager imagination. Together they tackled the challenge of improving pencils. Henry knew that the plumbago they were using was excellent, so he determined that the problem lay in either the filler materials or the process of lead making. Apparently through research in the Harvard library, he got the idea of replacing the additive sulfur with heat-resistant clay. Experimenting with combining plumbago and clay, he immediately produced a darker pencil lead, but it was still coarse and gritty.

Deciding that the plumbago needed to be ground more finely, the Thoreaus extended the chamber that surrounded the millstones into a seven-foot-tall space like a churn, which opened into a broad shelflike box. An upward draft of air carried the finest plumbago dust to this height, after heavier particles had fallen to the bottom to be ground further. This refinement of the pencil lead itself vastly improved the product, and sales of Thoreau pencils steadily climbed upward.

Chapter 6

SAVAGE BROTHERS

T OWARD THE END of a Sunday afternoon in late September 1837, a few weeks after he quit his job teaching, Henry and his brother John went tramping in search of Indian relics. John was enjoying a short break from teaching in Taunton, more than fifty miles to the south. Intoxicated with the unwritten history that had saturated the banks of the Musketaquid River before white settlers confidently renamed it the Concord, the brothers walked to the mouth of Swamp-Bridge Brook and thence toward, as usual, the nearest steep rise, Fair Haven Hill.

Their Concord neighbors were used to seeing the Thoreau boys ranging the hillsides and loafing on the ponds—short, muscular Henry, lean but rather thick-waisted, with his steady unusual stride; John slight and underweight, taller but not stronger. His quick sympathy, his optimism and easy humor—including a lighthearted patience with children, the elderly, the infirm—inspired affection. John was more traditionally religious, not the questioner that Henry had been since childhood. He was considered to have a clean, gentlemanly mind, although he clearly enjoyed the company and attentions of girls. He remonstrated when a friend called the girls around them "flat and insipid." Like Henry, John enjoyed playing the flute that their father had bought two years earlier—a handsome instrument made of warm reddish-brown fruitwood, with shiny metal keys and ivory trim. John had his gloomy days, although he didn't talk much about them. He was known to frequent graveyards in solitary meditation. He insisted, however, that they made him think not of the decaying mortal body but of the immortal spark within that transcended natural laws.

Sometimes they were kept indoors by illness. John frequently suffered digestive problems he called colic, and for several years he had occasionally suffered from nosebleeds so sudden and violent that he passed out. Every family knew what these symptoms might mean. Consumption, or tuberculosis, haunted many New England families. It was more prevalent there than in most parts of the country, and at the time was the leading cause of death in the Boston region. In Europe one death in four was attributed to consumption. It stalked mostly young adults, especially women. People watched anxiously as a cough developed, or a fever, but the disease was not considered contagious, so victims were seldom isolated. Henry and John's grandfather had died of consumption.

The most common prescription was outdoor activity, fresh air, and a wholesome diet, all of which the Thoreau family tried to maintain. As often as possible, the brothers tramped the fields and woods. They followed dainty overlapping mink tracks in the snow and watched dense gray flocks of passenger pigeons fly straight across a clearing. They fished and hunted. Henry bragged that he could carry a rifle all day without finding it heavy, even if he seldom got around to firing it. He had developed a strong, muscular body at an early age and maintained it with ascetic devotion—little meat, no tobacco, no spirits, and a glory in sweaty manual labor and tramping outdoors. Although every year he had less interest in hunting for sport, he felt grateful for his childhood introduction to hunting and fishing—adventures with a fowling piece before his teen years, solitary hours angling on the river—which resulted in early acquaintance with animals and places he might otherwise never have known intimately. Henry had a good sense of direction and seldom got lost—not that he could lose himself around Concord, where he knew all the land from Merrick's Pasture to the Andromeda Ponds, from Bear Garden Hill to Beck Stow's Swamp.

From childhood, Henry had been the more guarded of the two, but he loved John and valued his respect. Henry enjoyed the company of his parents and sisters, and was devoted to them—especially to younger Sophia—but John he idolized. Outdoors with him, away from other human beings, Henry relaxed. His face lost its stiffness, its frequent mask of superiority that hid the uncertainties behind it. Throughout their early years an ardor for the past had grown as well, and by the time Henry was twenty and John twenty-two, they were knowledgeable about the region's history. John was first to develop a passionate interest in Indians, but Henry soon followed, as he often followed his brother in other ways. Recently they had discovered a pestle and other shards to add to their collection, a find that had stoked their zeal.

The hills and valleys that Henry and John explored differed greatly from those that the Indians had silently trod in deerskin moccasins. Early white settlers quickly turned the rich Concord meadows to hay for their livestock, but the sandy and less fruitful uplands to the south, especially around Walden Pond, yielded mainly firewood. This region had been subdivided into lots and each generation inherited one for wood. Henry couldn't walk around the pond during daylight hours without hearing an ax attacking a tree trunk. For many years Concordians had also been cutting down other trees at an ever greater pace, for cordwood and for construction of new homes. During Henry's two decades, the townsfolk had enjoyed their strong share in the national economic boom before the recent crash.

These straight-edged buildings and treeless clearings were visible from the hill that Henry and John climbed that day in the autumn of 1837. The serpentine meander of the Concord River lay to the left, Walden Pond reflecting shore and sky to their right. Ahead, beyond the village, stretched Punkawtasset and Hubbard's and Buttrick's hills, and beyond them the faint outline of larger rises, Mount Monadnock and Mount Wachusett. When down on mundane earth beside them, Henry considered buildings an artificial blot on the natural curves of his beloved landscape, but he had to admit that from this prospect they became a soothing focus for a pensive gaze. Hay-makers were not as visible as earlier in the season, changing the tint of a green-brown field as they scythed across it; cut buckwheat, for example, looked red from a distance. But across the almost treeless village the brothers could see small figures leading lumber-hauling oxen or driving brisk shays. More than a quarter of the land was pasture marked off with straight stone or post-and-rider fences. Along the Mill Brook heading into the Mill Dam, plots were outlined by brooks straightened into angular drainage ditches. Houses and cattle were visible in every direction. Herds had to be driven down the roads, so fences lined each side to keep them from wandering astray. Old pastures were thick with scrub pine and barberry. Houses, barns, sheds, brick schoolhouse, the yellow-painted spire of Reverend Ripley's church— the map of their daily life was visible from up there, as if they had been lifted from two dimensions into three.

THE THOREAU BROTHERS' imaginations were full of primary-colored scenes that seemed more heroic and savage than pastel Concord. Numerous books gathered folklore, legends, and one-sided accounts of Indians. A few authors even made an effort to accurately describe what was known of the lives of North American natives prior to the arrival of Europeans. Most of these, however, were tinted by Romantic melancholy about doomed innocents, tangled with misconceptions about what the French philosopher Jean-Jacques Rousseau had referred to almost a century before, in his *Second Discourse*, as the "noble savage." In their natural world, Rousseau maintained, all human beings exist in a state of amoral virtue, prior to either the corruptions of civilization or the development of higher moral laws that curb human beings' inborn drift toward depravity. Smugly civilized and with moral criticism of Europe in mind, Rousseau found American Indians a useful metaphor.

In 1828, when Henry was nine, the lexicographer Noah Webster defined *savagism* in his *American Dictionary* as "the state of rude uncivilized men; the state of men in their native wildness and rudeness," without suggesting that often it might exist more in the minds of the civilized than in the realities of the uncivilized. With a broad brush, Webster sketched Indians as his example: "The savages of America, when uncorrupted by the vices of civilized men, are remarkable for their hospitality to strangers, and for their truth, fidelity and gratitude to their friends, but implacably cruel and revengeful toward their enemies."

Henry devoured stories about Indians and there were many from which to choose. Benjamin Bussey Thatcher, for example, published *Tales of the Indians* in 1831, followed four years later by *Indian Traits: Being Sketches of the Manners, Customs, and Character of the North American Natives*. Thatcher included information on every topic—hunting and divorce, toys and weapons, tattooing and snowshoe making. From the first page of the later book, he established an Edenic vision of what he regarded as a fated race:

Two centuries ago, the entire surface of this vast American continent was covered with an Indian population. From the

Atlantic Ocean to the Pacific, and from the broad waters of
Canada to the Gulf of Mexico, the Red Man roamed in his
native wilderness, fearless and free as the deer that fled from the
sound of his footstep. The smoke of his wigwam rose peacefully
from every hill-side and every riverbank . . .

Some accounts were less poetic. The 1832 volume *Indian
Biography* was a thick compilation of alphabetical listings, ranging from Acoompanet, "one of the Eleven Christian Indians
accused as concerned in the murder of the people of Lancaster,
22d Aug. 1675," to Yumanum, "the last Sachem of the Pequots."
It was written by Samuel Gardner Drake, who in Boston in 1828
had founded the first antiquarian bookstore in the twenty-four
United States.

From books such as their neighbor Lemuel Shattuck's *History of
the Town of Concord*, which had been published while Henry was at
Harvard, Henry and John learned much local Indian folklore. They
loved the story of the chief, or sachem, Nanepashemet. According
to Shattuck's account, just before the coming of the first Europeans,
little more than two centuries earlier, Nanepashemet ruled the
Pawtucket confederation of Indian tribes. His influence reached
from the Piscataqua in what became New Hampshire, westward to
the Musketaquid, and eastward to the Mattacuset—a river that
Charles I later renamed for himself—around what became Boston.
Shattuck estimated that in 1612 pestilence reduced the natives'
numbers by ninety percent and he reported that some villages
disappeared entirely. "This great mortality," he wrote, "was viewed
by the first Pilgrims, as the accomplishment of one of the purposes
of Divine Providence, by making room for the settlement of civilized man, and by preparing a peaceful asylum for the persecuted
Christians of the old world."

The local sachem had been Tahatawan, although his name was recorded with various spellings. After Nanepashemet died in 1619, his widow—who was called merely Squaw Sachem in most early records—and Tahatawan negotiated the sale of the Concord region to the European settlers. The official Colony Records duly reported:

> 5th. 6mo. 1637. Wibbacowett; Squaw Sachem; Tahattawants; Natanquatic, alias Old Man; Carte, alias Goodmand; did express their consent to the sale of the Weire at Concord over against the town: and all the planting-ground which hath been formerly planted by the Indians, to the inhabitants of Concord; of which there was a writing, with their marks subscribed given into court, expressing the price.

To the Thoreau brothers, the Indians personified a need for wildness, and in their imaginations they still hunted the riverside at dusk.

To the east across the little valley, beyond the Concord Academy and the western end of Main Street, rising just beyond the river, was Nawshawtuct Hill. From its height Henry had surveyed his local cosmos many times. The previous summer, in August 1836, shortly after turning nineteen, he had beached his small homemade boat, the *Red Jacket*, beneath Nawshawtuct following an amateurish ten-minute sail on the river.

This name, too, was a tribute to Indians. Henry christened the boat after a Seneca chief—an act in itself deliberately confrontational and a testament to his passion for native history. The Seneca had sided with Britain during the Revolution. The Wolf clan chief Sagoyewatha took the nickname "Red Jacket" after a handsome embroidered coat he was given by the Crown to honor his services during the war. After England's defeat, he played an important role as a representative of Indian concerns in dealing with the new United States government. Henry admired resistance to dogmatism, of which Red Jacket was an example eloquent enough to stand with Cicero. He was best known for his reply to the Christian missionaries who, at a Buffalo, New York council in 1825, informed the gathered Indians that they had always lived in darkness, unaware of their need to worship the same god as the Europeans, and that they could never be truly happy without adopting the white man's religion. In the twelve years since its delivery, and the seven since Red Jacket's death, his polite appeal to reason and tolerance had become legendary. The Great Spirit made this land for his red children because he loved them, said Sagoyewatha, and they had always worshipped him with thankfulness. Just as the Great Spirit had made for his red and white children different skins and customs, so must he have given each the religion he wanted them to have:

> Brother, you say that there is but one way to worship and serve the Great Spirit. If there is but one religion, why do you white people differ so much about it? Why not all agree, as you can all read the book? ... Brother, we are told that you have been preaching to white people in this place. These people are our neighbors; we are acquainted with them. We will wait a little while and see what effect your preaching has on them. If we find it does them good, makes them honest, and less disposed to cheat Indians, we will then consider again what you have said.

At the end of his speech, Red Jacket added, "As we are going to part, we will come and take you by the hand, and hope the Great Spirit will protect you on your journey, and return you safe to your friends." But the head missionary refused to shake hands with the

Indians. Witnesses reported that he said "that there was no fellow-ship between the religion of God and the works of the devil, and therefore could not join hands with them." The same reporters noted that after the missionary's rejection was translated to them, "they smiled, and retired in a peaceable manner."

To the childhood friend who would later become a partner in his graduation speech, Charles Wyatt Rice, Henry had recounted his *Red Jacket* expedition in mock-heroic terms and parodied his own vessel. "If men have dared the main to tempt in such frail barks, why may not wash-tub round or bread-trough square oblong Suffice to cross the purling wave and gain the destin'd port?" He described the local response to the boat's landing: "Natives, a harmless, unoffensive race, principally devoted to agricultural pursuits—appeared somewhat astonished that a stranger should land so unceremoniously on their coast."

ON THE DAY that Henry and John neared the top of the rise that looked down on the panorama of the Concord River, Henry was contrasting the present bucolic view with the savage woodlands of the past. "There on Nawshawtuct," he said, gesturing dramatically toward the east, "was their lodge, the rendezvous of the tribe."

Henry pointed in a different direction. "And yonder, on Clamshell Hill, their feasting ground. This was, no doubt, a favorite haunt. Here on this brow was an eligible lookout post. How often," he speculated, "have they stood on this very spot, at this very hour, when the sun was sinking behind yonder woods and gilding with his last rays the waters of the Musketaquid, and pondered the day's success and the morrow's prospects—or communed with the spirit of their fathers gone before them to the land of shades."

He always found it easy to imagine himself into the past life of the natives. "Here stood Tahatawan!" he exclaimed to his brother, gesturing wildly. "And there"—he pointed at a spot nearby on the ground—"is Tahatawan's arrowhead!"

Agreeable John went along with this fancy, and they sat on the rough ground where Henry had pointed. To further his little joke, Henry reached down, pretending to pick up Tahatawan's legacy. He grabbed the nearest stone and held it up for his brother to see.

To their astonishment, it was indeed an arrowhead. Its flint was so sharp it seemed to have just been chipped, as if its maker lurked in the forest nearby—a ghost watching from the past.

THE DISCOVERY OF what he thought of as Tahatawan's arrowhead furthered Henry's sense that he was not only surrounded by the past but might in fact be part of it. He continued to devour all he could find to read about Indians, and he and John watched the ground more than ever. Often Henry kept his eyes on a path as he walked, and he was famous for finding more arrowheads than anyone else. Once during their walk a friend remarked, "I do not see where you find your Indian arrowheads."

Henry stooped to pick up something from the ground and held it out. "Here is one."

Soon John returned to the school in Taunton. In mid-November, Henry wrote him a playful letter that was saturated with their current favorite topic. It was in the style of treaties and Indian speeches as they appeared in Shattuck and other writers. The style also resembled that of James Fenimore Cooper, the New Jersey novelist whose sagas about heroic frontiersman Natty Bumppo had appeared during Henry's childhood and achieved international popularity, despite being ridiculed by critics as vulgar and silly.

Musketaquid two hundred and two summers—two moons—eleven suns since the coming of the Pale Faces. Tahatawan—

Sachimausan—to his brother sachem—Hopeful of Hopewell—hoping that he is well.

Brother, it is many suns that I have not seen the print of thy moccasins by our council-fire, the Great Spirit has blown more leaves from the trees and many clouds from the land of snows have visited our lodge—the earth has become hard like a frozen buffalo skin, so that the trampling of many herds is like the Great Spirit's thunder—the grass on the great fields is like the old man of many winters—and the small song sparrow prepares for his flight to the land whence the summer comes.

Brother—I write thee these things because I know that thou lovest the Great Spirit's creatures, and wast wont to sit at thy lodge door—when the maize was green, to hear the bluebird's song . . .

Henry went on to apprise John of the goings-on in Concord, referring to the Boston State House as a "council house" and describing solemn and large-nosed Samuel Hoar as "Eaglebeak." He signed the letter "Tahatawan." Under the signature he wrote *His mark* and drew a bow arcing like two hills above a horizontal bowstring, across them an arrow pointing toward the sky.

Chapter 7

GOD AND NATURE FACE TO FACE

I N EARLY SEPTEMBER 1837, Henry had received a letter from his Harvard chum James Richardson Jr., who had been in the First Church in Cambridge applauding Henry's commencement conference with Henry Vose and Charles Wyatt Rice. "I hear," wrote Richardson, "that you are comfortably located, in your native town, as the guardian of its children, in the immediate vicinity, I suppose, of one of our most distinguished Apostles of the Future— R. W. Emerson."

Although he had quickly abandoned the role of guardian of Concord's children, Henry saw more and more of the distinguished apostle. Before they were fellow villagers, he and Ralph Waldo Emerson had been crossing paths for years. Emerson had not only attended Harvard, beginning in 1818, but had lived in the same building. Emerson had spoken at Harvard more than once during Henry's time there, and he had also given public lectures in Concord. They met as early as February 1835, when Emerson was among those examining Henry and other sophomores to determine how well they retained and understood Richard Whately's 1828 book *Elements of Rhetoric*.

Soon after the publication of Emerson's book-length essay *Nature* in September 1836, Henry went to the library at Harvard and checked out a new black-leather-bound copy. Often falling into the tone of Emerson's Unitarian preaching days, its ninety-two pages comprised a manifesto for radical change in American life that had been provoking impassioned discussion for the last several months. It fed Henry's growing passion for independence and for a personal relationship with the natural world.

Emerson was a calm and lyrical revolutionary. "Our age is retrospective," he began. "The foregoing generations beheld God and nature face to face; we, through their eyes. Why should not we also enjoy an original relation to the universe? Why should not we have a poetry and philosophy of insight and not of tradition, and a religion by revelation to us, and not the history of theirs?" Beginning to be called Transcendentalists, after a reference in Immanuel Kant's 1781 *Critique of Pure Reason*, Emerson and his loose coalition of intellectual colleagues sought to establish the validity of each individual's quest for an original relation to the universe. Emerson had been showered with praise and damnation for his argument on behalf of a spirituality inherent in each human being, an assertion that carried with it an implicit rejection of much of biblical Christianity. He had been preceded, however, by other thinkers such as the Reverend William Ellery Channing, who delivered his sermon "Likeness to God" eight years before Emerson published *Nature*, and by the idealism of the Romantic poets such as Coleridge and Wordsworth. Emerson's beloved Harvard was sometimes denounced for serving as a breeding ground for radical freethinkers who wanted to reform both religion and society.

In 1832, only three years after becoming an assistant pastor of Boston's Second Church, he had written in his journal, "I have sometimes thought that, in order to be a good minister, it was necessary to leave the ministry. The profession is antiquated. In an altered age, we worship in the dead forms of our forefathers."

That year he resigned and had not held a church position since. In *Nature* he divided his study of attitudes about nature into eight sections that explored how human beings think of the world from which they come and upon which they depend: Nature, Commodity, Beauty, Language, Discipline, Idealism, Spirit, and finally a section on possible changes entitled Prospects. Emerson's overall theme was that divinity was to be found throughout nature, and that nature included human beings. The divine was within all, not bottled up in a deity.

Henry eagerly devoured the book, from the vague epigraph by Plotinus ("Nature is but an image or imitation of wisdom, the last thing of the soul; nature being a thing which doth only do, but not know") to the grand summation in the last section:

> Adam called his house, heaven and earth; Caesar called his house, Rome; you perhaps call yours, a cobbler's trade; a hundred acres of ploughed land; or a scholar's garret. Yet line for line and point for point, your dominion is as great as theirs, though without fine names. Build, therefore, your own world. As fast as you conform your life to the pure idea in your mind, that will unfold its great proportions.

Henry especially embraced comments encouraging him in his independent and freethinking ways. Happily steeped in classical literature—he didn't like to admit it, but he had been profoundly influenced by his Harvard years—Henry nonetheless shared the prevailing American doubts about decadent Old World literary values. It was a time of strident nationalism and on this point as on many others Henry joined the already established chorus. His natural bent was always toward scholar as much as naturalist, poet as much as social critic.

Some of Emerson's phrases evolved almost into Henry's mottoes: "To go into solitude, a man needs to retire as much from his chamber as from society. I am not solitary whilst I read and write, though nobody is with me. But if a man would be alone, let him look at the stars."

EARLIER IN 1837, Henry's own writing—and Emerson's clear influence on it—had come to the older man's attention in a roundabout way.

Boarders at the Thoreau house included Lucy Jackson Brown, from Plymouth. She was the sister of Emerson's wife, Lydia Jackson Emerson, whom Emerson called Lidian. In 1834, two years after resigning his position as minister of the Second Unitarian Church in Boston, Emerson had moved up the turnpike to Concord. After her husband spent their money and abandoned her, Mrs. Brown moved to the village with her two children. At first Lidian was glad to have her nearby, because her presence made Concord less boring in comparison with festive Plymouth. But Lucy spent almost six months living with the newlywed Emersons, and the strain was too much for all of them. When Lidian next encouraged her sister to return to Concord, she did not invite Lucy and the children to live with her, so they moved into the Thoreau boardinghouse. There she met Henry.

Mrs. Brown was famously kindhearted and encouraging to young people. She became friends first with Sophia and gradually with her siblings. When, in the spring of 1837, Mrs. Brown and Sophia went to hear the lively and charismatic Emerson speak about manners—repeating a talk he had already presented in Boston—Sophia leaned close to whisper that Emerson's comments reminded her strongly of some paragraphs that Henry had written recently. Back home she dug out the passage and showed it to Mrs.

Brown. Struck by the similarity to her brother-in-law's philosophy—she did not know that Henry had just read *Nature* and was
thinking aloud in imitation of it—Mrs. Brown took the writing to
Lidian. Her sister was known for her reliable generosity and charitable interest in neighbors. About once a week during winter, for
example, a boy would pull a large sled along the snowy, horse-shoe-
patterned Concord streets, stopping at the homes of Lidian's friends
to deliver a still-warm pie.

The Emersons lived in a plain, white two-story house called
Bush, set at an angle to the road, with tall chestnuts in the backyard
and one side shielded by a small grove of fir and pine trees. It was
just past the eastern edge of the village, beyond the Unitarian meetinghouse and across from the primary school, where elm-lined
Main Street diverged into the Lexington Road and the Cambridge
Turnpike—where the British had marched in April of 1775. In the
V of the intersection Emerson owned an apple orchard. They had
bought the house only two years earlier, with money from Emerson's
first wife's estate, and were still planting trees and flowers. Residing
with them was Emerson's colorful and fervently religious mother,
Ruth Haskins Emerson.

Lidian in turn showed Henry's writing to Emerson. Always
interested in young people, and already establishing a habit of
mentoring young men, the thirty-four-year-old Emerson invited
Henry to come meet him the next time he was back in Concord.
Soon Henry did so.

They were a study in contrasts. Emerson was a slim six feet tall
and carried himself with the air of a gentleman, his dark hair parted
high on the left and half covering his ears; Henry shorter by a few
inches, long-armed, with unkempt light brown hair. Even Emerson's
aquiline nose seemed more refined, quite unlike Henry's beak.
Only his narrow sloping shoulders resembled Emerson's. Emerson

was naturally graceful, Henry awkwardness personified. Yet they were immediately drawn to each other and soon began a habit of regular conversations and walks.

DISCOMFITED AROUND GIRLS his own age, Henry was often drawn to older women who treated him kindly and whose intelligence and quirky wit could match his own. He seems to have been attracted, possibly romantically, to the smart and pretty thirty-nine-year-old Mrs. Brown, with her dark hair and slightly pointed chin. One day in May, during a walk through the warm spring woods and fields of Concord, he gathered a wild bouquet for her—several fresh purple blossoms of violets, as well as sheep sorrel. To farmers, sorrel was a weed. Its young leaves, clustered at the base below an almost leafless stem of tiny red flowers, were egg-shaped, but as the plant grew the leaves became more pointed like an arrowhead. Henry admired the way by mid-June its tiny blossoms could paint a field red.

He wrapped the bouquet in a piece of paper on which he had written a romantically melancholy poem. Then he tied the bundle with a wisp of straw and tossed it through the open window of Mrs. Brown's room in the boardinghouse. The verses distilled out of the bouquet and its wrapping every ounce of symbolism a bookish, nature-loving nineteen-year-old could find, as if the bouquet itself were the poem:

SIC VITA

I am a parcel of vain strivings tied
By a chance bond together,
Dangling this way and that, their links
Were made so loose and wide,
Methinks,
For milder weather.

A bunch of violets without their roots,
And sorrel intermixed,
Encircled by a wisp of straw
Once coiled about their shoots,
The law
By which I'm fixed . . .

TWO YEARS EARLIER, in 1835, the year he settled in Concord and purchased Bush, Emerson had been asked to write a lecture celebrating Concord's two centuries. Later, after trying several other speakers who turned out to be unavailable, the North Bridge Battle Monument Committee approached him about writing a poetic tribute to accompany the unveiling of the Concord Monument, a marble obelisk to commemorate the battle at the North Bridge, which launched the Revolutionary War. Reverend Ripley had donated land for it beside his venerable Manse (as some parsonages were called). Emerson planned his poem to be sung to the familiar strains of the "Old Hundred," a hymn by Louis Bourgeois that dated back to the sixteenth-century Genevan Psalter. It acquired its nickname through association with the 100th Psalm ("Make a joyful noise unto the Lord, all ye lands"), but its best known incarnation was in Thomas Ken's beloved Anglican hymn "Praise God, from Whom All Blessings Flow." It was in long meter, four lines of eight syllables each. Like most poets writing about military triumphs, Emerson promoted the battle to a symbolic level, celebrating victory over oppression and the founding of a new kind of government.

By the rude bridge that arched the flood,
Their flag to April's breeze unfurled;
Here once the embattled farmers stood;
And fired the shot heard round the world . . .

Delays had pushed the celebration into 1837, enabling Henry's and Emerson's paths to cross in new ways. In June, just before the end of Henry's senior year at Harvard, Emerson wrote a letter to the college's president in praise of Henry's scholarly and personal virtues. Josiah Quincy had found Henry a bit insubordinate and lax in his studies and Emerson defended him. He didn't yet know him well, but he was generous in his support of talented young men.

Then on Independence Day Henry sang in the choir that performed the song Emerson called the "Concord Hymn." Henry loved to sing. He sang alone and in groups, at home and in informal gatherings. Sometimes, like his father and brother, he accompanied others on a flute. On the fourth Samuel Hoar gave a speech, but Emerson himself was in Plymouth at the time. In his absence, his poem was first read aloud and then sung by Henry and the rest of the choir.

Emerson was becoming known as a writer and lecturer, but he had yet to build a reputation as a poet, so the response to his "Concord Hymn" was heartening. He had written about the bridge that he himself could see from the Manse, where he had lived briefly in 1834. From its second-floor window, Emerson's grandmother had held up her daughter Mary, Emerson's aunt, to see the redcoats approaching in 1775.

"Do you keep a journal?" Emerson asked Henry in late October 1837, a couple of months after his return to Concord.

Emerson believed passionately in the value of maintaining a diary, both for recording and analyzing experience and for working out thoughts prior to writing them up in more public form. He had maintained one off and on since entering Harvard in 1817, at the age of fourteen, and more and more frequently since his early twenties. One way Emerson mentored his various young charges was by encouraging them to be more like him. Like many of his Transcendentalist colleagues, Emerson esteemed friendship highly. The notion of ideal friendship, in fact, haunted his relationships with actual acquaintances. Only the day before discussing journals with Henry, Emerson had written vaguely in his own, "friendship is good which begins on sentiment & proceeds into all mutual convenience and alternation of great benefits."

Henry did not regularly keep a journal, despite a passionate urge to write. For years, however, he had written occasional autobiographical notes and stabs at personal essays. In late 1834, as a sophomore at Harvard, he wrote for Professor Edward Tyrrell Channing an essay entitled "Shall We Keep Journals?" Henry began with a swipe at the frustrations of writing on demand for class: "As those pieces which the painter sketches for his own amusement in his leisure hours are often superior to his most elaborate productions, so it is that ideas often suggest themselves to us spontaneously, as it were, far surpassing in beauty those which arise in the mind upon applying ourselves to any particular subject." Then he went on to quote Francis Bacon, the patron saint of short essays, and to enthuse about the possibility that a journal might serve as a vehicle of self-discovery and a way to maintain a kind of personal authenticity. If each person, he argued,

> would occupy a certain portion of each day in looking back upon the time which has passed, and in writing down his thoughts and feelings, in reckoning up his daily gains, that he may be able to detect whatever false coins have crept into his coffers, and as it were, in settling accounts with his mind, not only would his daily experience be greatly increased, since his feelings and ideas would thus be more clearly defined, but he

would be ready to turn over a new leaf, having carefully perused the preceding one, and would not continue to glance carelessly over the same page without being able to distinguish it from a new one.

Henry had written these words at the age of seventeen and had not yet taken them to heart in a systematic way. Three years later, primed by Harvard with the resources and desire to communicate, he felt both a thirst for experience and ambition as a writer, so a nudge from an admired elder was precisely what he needed. The day that Emerson encouraged him, Henry acquired a large red folio, opened it to the first page, dipped a pen in a bottle of strong dark ink—probably some of the stock that his family made at home— and began to settle accounts with his mind. In his still rather adolescent scrawl, he wrote *Oct. 22* and quoted his friend's prompt to keep a journal. Then he centered in capital letters the word *solitude* and wrote under it, "To be alone I find it necessary to escape the present, to avoid myself. How could I be alone in the Roman emperor's chamber of mirrors? I seek a garret."

Over the next few weeks, the journal became Henry's repository for the joy that spilled over from his ecstatic response to nature. "We have always," he scrawled, "a resource in the skies." He meditated upon the delights of paddling a gentle stream. Happily he wrote up his September experience on Fair Haven Hill with John and the finding of Tahatawan's arrowhead. "Crossed the river today on the ice," began one entry. He mentioned that a friend had discovered "a new note in nature, which he calls the Ice-Harp." Pebbles tossed upon the surface of the pond had produced a musical melody because of the chambers of air underneath the ice, inspiring Henry to add, "Herein resides a tenth muse, and as he was the man to discover it probably the extra melody is in him." Awakening to his own facility for language, and to the thrill of practicing a craft, Henry gloried in description itself. "The snow gives the landscape a washing-day appearance," he noted one day. The Concord River was "the jugular vein of Musketaquid." Describing dawn and sunrise, he noted that it began with "the gray twilight of the poets."

He described in detail watching elegant and colorful wood ducks—sometimes called summer ducks—swimming under water some distance before resurfacing. But he couldn't resist investing the scene with imagination: "Just before immersion they seemed to give each other a significant nod, and then, as if by a common understanding, 't was heels up and head down in the shaking of a duck's wing. When they reappeared, it was amusing to observe with what a self-satisfied, darn-it-how-he-nicks-'em air they paddled off to repeat the experiment." Although he could be eloquent, often a phenomenon quickly inspired an immature symbolic interpretation. When dense fog limited his view to hazy mountaintops, Henry responded with a scrawled, "So when thick vapors cloud the soul, it strives in vain to escape from its humble working-day valley . . ."

Naturally thoughts about his ever-expanding reading poured into the journal as well. He casually included phrases from ancient Latin and Greek sources as well as contemporary German texts. He hiked through science and history, poetry and drama, religion and philosophy—at twenty, finding most of it still new and untrodden territory. "How cheering it is," he observed, "after toiling through the darker pages of history,—the heartless and fluctuating crust of human rest and unrest,—to alight on the solid earth where the sun shines, or rest in the checkered shade." Henry copied long passages from Goethe's 1790 play about the sixteenth-century Italian poet Torquato Tasso, including the lines, "Often he ennobles what appeared to us as common, / And the prized is as nothing to him." He was inching toward making such a philosophy his own, but often he simply responded to nature with delight. One November morning Henry rose at dawn, as usual, and peeked out above the frost on the window to find every eastward-facing window in nearby houses bouncing the sunrise light into his eyes. He wrote in his journal, "I am at home in the world."

Now and then he added cryptic remarks suggesting his life was as troubled as that of most twenty-year-olds. On the evening of November 13, he stared out the window at the bright moon, which was a day past full, and wrote, "This shall be the test of innocence— if I hear a taunt, and look out on this friendly moon, pacing the heavens in queen-like majesty, with the accustomed yearning." He was watching himself closely, advising himself on how to behave. The evening before, he had written, "I yet lack discernment to distinguish the whole lesson of to-day; but it is not lost,—it will come to me."

Storing up investment in himself as entries in this journal fueled his literary ambitions. On the twenty-fifth of November 1837, he had the pleasure of seeing the Concord *Yeoman's Gazette* print his first published words—an obituary for Miss Anna Jones, a survivor of the Revolutionary War who died at the age of eighty-six: "She was as it were, a connecting link between the past and the present— a precious relic of days which the man and patriot would not willingly forget. . . . Poverty was her lot," Henry added, "but she possessed those virtues without which the rich are poor."

BACK HOME IN the Thoreau boardinghouse in late 1837, Henry was free of his college routine for the first time in years. On Concord winter nights, he could light a tallow candle at the parlor fireplace and carry it upstairs in its tin candlestick to start his own fire, or heat a warming pan over the coals and slide it back and forth between sheets to make his cold bachelor bed more inviting. There was little more he could do. Henry recognized that his own century was a revolutionary time, especially in the technologies of everyday life and communication, but the changes were slow to affect the lives of most human beings. For millennia there had been no portable nighttime illumination beyond candles or a smoking rag wick in a bowl of animal oil or fat. Only half a century had passed since Frenchman Aimé Argand had introduced an efficient oil lamp that featured nestled brass cylinders—outside to feed oxygen to the wick, inside to feed it oil—and a glass chimney and metal wick holder. By the 1830s improvements in glass were providing lamps made mostly of blown glass. Whale oil had become the most popular fuel.

Still, every cold morning, after a night buried under many layers of cover, Henry would find the windows adorned with fernlike patterns of frost crystals. Frigid air seeped in around the bubble-warped glass panes. Usually any water left in the house would be frozen by morning, despite being left in a kettle hanging by the cold fireplace, near its pile of banked ashes. Fresh water would require an early-morning jaunt to the well, if it was sunk low enough in the ground to escape freezing.

Some domestic technologies had evolved, but while reading Virgil on these shivery nights, Henry found it satisfying to be reminded that the ancient Roman had lived a life much like his own. Across the eighteen and a half centuries since the death of Publius Virgilius Maro, the natural world had continued its predictable, nourishing rhythms. *"Jam laeto turgent in palmite gemmae,"* Corydon observes to Thyris in the *Eclogues*, and later *"Strata jacent passim sua quâeque sub arbore poma."* Peering at the page of Latin in his school text, Henry dipped his pen in an inkwell and scribbled the lines down in his journal. "Now the buds swell on the joyful stem," he later translated. "The apples lie scattered everywhere, each under its tree." Two centuries before the birth of Christ, Cato described farming techniques in *De re rura*, and every day around Concord Henry could see the same rituals enacted. Then as now, farmers spread manure-rich compost over the ground and broke up the dry chunks with a mallet.

Sitting upstairs in his room, trying to marshal vagrant thoughts into a parade, he heard his sister Sophia or boarders banging out a tune on the piano in the parlor a couple of floors below. He hated the discord of scales and other practice, but he liked a coherent tune. He could even tolerate "The Battle of Prague," the sonata by Bohemian composer František Kočvara that, since its publication in 1757, had become painfully familiar to every piano student of even moderate skill. From upstairs, Henry could hear the slow, hymnlike opening march, the labored attempt to evoke the general's commands, the bugler's and trumpeter's optimistic clarion, dandified trills of the Prussian attack, even cannons and galloping cavalry.

A neighbor's overheard burst of music could remind him of the Hindu Vedas' archives of timelessness. All kinds of sound distracted Henry—crickets, whose chorus seemed anxious and made him wonder about the future; frogs, who sounded in contrast complacent, unworried in their ancient truce with time. He heard music in the clang of tools. He enjoyed working outdoors in part because random overheard sounds piqued his imagination. Trimming a branch by the pond, he might hear the splash of an oar and pause, his head tilted like a robin's as he waited for another. Like a child he yelled simply to hear his own echo reply from the woods. As he walked, if his cane sparked noise from a stone he would strike it again to duplicate the sound. Naturally he talked about music in the kind of broad symbolic terms he applied to everything else. "A flitting maiden," he called it, "who now lives just through the trees yonder, and now at an oriental distance."

Around the house Henry could hear family members and the servant girl and boarders clomping on the stairs, opening and closing doors, rattling pots and pans and dishes in the kitchen, bantering over meals. When he thought about living in a cabin in the woods—a cabin such as the one he had stayed in with his Harvard chum Charles Stearns Wheeler—he didn't have to contemplate the abandonment of civilized luxuries. Village life offered few conveniences that he would have to renounce, but the woods offered a luxury Henry had almost never experienced at home. It was summed up in the first word he wrote in his new journal: *solitude*.

Part 2

SHADOW

Chapter 8

HOW COMIC IS SIMPLICITY

B Y LATE OCTOBER 1837, Emerson was recording Henry's amusing quirks. During a philosophical conversation among Emerson and friends, a local farmer named Edmund Hosmer argued that he didn't wish to claim a distinction between the mind of Jesus and that of a normal human. Then suddenly he changed his tone and remarked that Jesus created the world and was the eternal God.

"Mr. Hosmer has kicked the pail over," observed Henry.

That night Emerson wrote in his journal, "I delight much in my young friend, who seems to have as free & erect a mind as any I have ever met."

In December, Emerson informed Henry that he would be launching the lecture season at the Masonic Temple in Boston. Knowing the state of his unemployed friend's finances, Emerson gave him a free-admission pass to the lecture. When he stopped by the Thoreau boarding-house on the day of the talk, apparently to offer a ride, Emerson found that Henry had departed hours earlier. Unable to afford even the carriage fare, Henry had set out to walk the nineteen miles to the lecture hall.

Flattered and impressed by Henry's eager interest in his words, Emerson invited him to attend a weekly gathering at Bush, granting Henry associate membership in the family. The only other person at the gatherings besides Emerson, Lidian, Lidian's mother, the Emersons' one-year-old son Waldo, and Henry was a friend from Henry's childhood—Elizabeth Hoar, sister of Henry's childhood friend Edward, daughter of judge Samuel Hoar. Elizabeth had been engaged to Emerson's brother Charles, who died before they could marry. Through his new mentor, Henry was being brought into contact with other intelligent, perceptive women besides those he could find at home in the boarding-house. Emerson's influence was showing up in unpredictable ways.

Although Henry had published almost nothing, Emerson saw the young man's potential in his challenging conversation and broad reading. He went out of his way to welcome Henry into Concord's growing literary circle and wrote at length about him in his journal and in letters to friends. Emerson also offered Henry the run of his considerable library—a lure guaranteed to entice a young man who greatly missed the Harvard library. Emerson's was a handsome but not elegant room to the right of the front door, the first of the two large square rooms on the right side of the hall that divided the house down the center. Its books were arrayed on plain and functional rather than decorative shelves that reached from ceiling to low wooden cabinets on only one side of the room, opposite a large fireplace with a low grate.

The winter of 1837–38 brought the two together often. Emerson's city friends hesitated to brave the snow and ice for a journey to Concord. He was receiving considerable criticism for, and misrepresentation of, his recent essays and lectures, and outraged responses to *Nature* were still trickling in; so Emerson was in the mood to hide out in his bucolic oasis, avoiding disputation and turmoil. "My good Henry Thoreau made this else solitary afternoon sunny with his simplicity & clear perception," Emerson remarked to his journal in February. "How comic is simplicity in this doubledealing quacking world. Every thing that boy says makes merry with society though nothing can be graver than his meaning."

HENRY'S GRAVE APPROACH to serious issues derived in part from his mother and sisters. All three were involved in a national movement. Across America, support for the abolition of slavery was growing daily, and women were one of the main reasons. In 1837, in Middlesex County alone, eight anti-slavery groups formed, three of them emphasizing female membership. Seventy percent of the signatures on a petition to abolish slavery in the District of Columbia were from Massachusetts women. "The destiny of the slaves is in the hands of the American women," the abolitionist William Lloyd Garrison had proclaimed in 1833, "and complete emancipation can never take place without their co-operation." British women had organized on behalf of abolition in the 1820s and United States women were trying to catch up.

Massachusetts had banned slavery in 1783 and thousands of citizens in the state had since joined the growing movement to outlaw it across the nation. Locally, women organizing for public works dated back at least to 1814, with the founding of the Concord Female Charitable Society. The Concord Female Anti-Slavery Society held its first formal meeting on the eighteenth of October 1837. The sixty-one women who attended included Cynthia Thoreau with both Sophia and Helen; their boarders Mrs. Joseph Ward and her daughter Prudence; and Lidian Emerson. In early September, the Reverend John Wilder's Trinitarian church had hosted a visit from a pair of famous—or notorious—abolitionists and advocates of women's rights, sisters Sarah and Angelina Grimké. Crowds flocked to hear them in Concord, as they did all over New England. The sisters lodged at the Thoreau boardinghouse, and

Henry and his family found them inspiring. Emotional speeches were followed by liberal financial donations. "I think I shall not turn away my attention from the abolition cause," wrote Lidian Emerson, "till I have found whether there is not something for me personally to do and bear to forward it."

The Grimké sisters knew whereof they spoke. At the age of five Sarah had witnessed the brutal whipping of a slave. She told audiences that in response she tried to run away from home aboard a ship, hoping to voyage to a land without slavery. The sisters' father, John Faucheraud Grimké, who had died in 1819, had been chief judge of the South Carolina Supreme Court and a wealthy landowner, an upper-class Charlestonian who owned hundreds of slaves. As an aristocratic Southerner, he had never publicly opposed slavery. After Sarah nursed him through a mysterious fatal illness, however, she joined her younger sister in devoting their lives to eradicating the practice they saw as the scourge of civilization. And she had inspired the Thoreau family to join the fight.

In Hingham, Massachusetts, the Reverend Albert Folsom warned his parishioners that such political involvement would "poison the soul" of white women. He claimed that Woman was naturally amiable and modest, and that she should not interfere in politics, lest she become "bigoted, rash, and morose. Nor is this all. Self-sufficiency, arrogance, and masculine boldness follow naturally in the train."

Only a few weeks later, in Illinois, a young man named Elijah Parish Lovejoy was murdered. A Presbyterian minister, journalist, and editor, he had just founded an antislavery newspaper called the *Alton Observer*. He was receiving, as quietly as possible to avoid attention, a fourth printing press, this one sent by the Ohio Anti-Slavery Society, because his first three had been destroyed by pro-slavery mobs. On the seventh of November 1837, a mob stormed Lovejoy's office with guns and stones. He was shot and killed. The Lovejoy murder helped ignite nationwide awareness of the urgent need for abolition, and as Henry and his family devoured the sad news stories they began to think of themselves as committed abolitionists.

LIDIAN EMERSON, KIND-HEARTED and intelligent, liked Henry and enjoyed his company. Her admiration for her brilliant and popular husband had originally carried over into his friendships with others; she wanted to like the people he liked. Already, however, she was becoming jealous of Emerson's time and attention in some cases. Their ambitious dream of an intellectually balanced marriage was fading, as Emerson wrote and traveled while Lidian managed the household servants and tended to Waldo. The boy restored the family's enjoyment of life following the death of Emerson's brother a few months before Waldo's birth. He liked to be pulled in a wagon around the barn, barking at dogs and mooing at cows and, when glimpsing a sheep, uttering his favorite exclamation: "Baaaaaaa . . ." Henry enjoyed the company of children more than that of most adults, and Lidian liked his easy familiarity with Waldo, his patience and calm.

Henry was often at the Emerson house. He and his new mentor had more in common than was apparent to others at first sight. Each found his greatest delight in the natural world, although each also applied considerable symbolism to the act of responding to nature. Emerson's comment in his journal—one of many instances of an observation metamorphosing into a symbol during the act of recording it—could have been written by Henry in his own: "In nature all the growth is contemporary. Man's labor in the garden is successive but the weeds and plants swell root & ripen all over the farm in the same instant of time." Henry instinctively cared more about the actual animal or plant before him and tried to respond with open spirit to its presence and uniqueness, while Emerson had difficulty seeing a creature or process without framing it in symbolic terms. He would firmly remind himself, "We must use the language of facts & not be superstitiously abstract," and then ask himself, "Is not the Vast an element in man? Yet what teaching or book of today appeals to the Vast?" Yet his eureka revelation about the interconnectedness of all nature had occurred in the Jardin des Plantes, the great botanical garden of the Muséum national d'Histoire naturelle in Paris, where he discovered the plant taxonomy system of the pioneer French botanist Antoine Laurent de Jussieu.

Both Henry and Emerson responded with dismay to society's parade of demeaning and frivolous diversions. "Then retire & hide," Emerson instructed himself that summer; "& from the valley behold the mountain. Have solitary prayer & praise. Love the garden, the barn, the pasture, & the rock. There digest & correct the past experience, blend it with the new & divine life, & grow with God." At about the same time, Henry was writing in his own journal, "Men are constantly dinging in my ears their fair theories and plausible solutions of the universe, but ever there is no help, and I return again to my shoreless, islandless ocean, and fathom unceasingly for a bottom that will hold an anchor, that it may not drag." Society drove both back to what they thought of as the real world. "Nature is the beautiful asylum," Emerson wrote, "to which we look in all the years of striving & conflict as the assured resource when we shall be driven out of society by ennui or chagrin or persecution or defect of character."

But Henry was restless. Having thrown away an excellent job, he was looking for new employment elsewhere. In the spring of 1838, he solicited testimonials from three prominent individuals whose endorsement might help him find work. Emerson expressed confidence in Henry's intelligence, character, energy, kindness, and scholastic promise, adding, "I shall esteem the town fortunate that secures his Services." Reverend Ripley scrawled, "The undersigned very cheerfully hereby introduces to public notice the bearer, Mr David Henry Thoreau, as a teacher in the higher branches of useful literature . . ." President Quincy at Harvard, having changed his opinion of Henry's commitment and enterprise during his latter years in college, wrote a glowing letter, certifying Henry's graduation and explaining that "his rank was high as a scholar in all the branches, and his morals and general conduct unexceptionable and exemplary. He is recommended as well qualified as an instructor, for employment in any public or private school or private family."

Yet still Henry could not find another job teaching, although the family needed his income. A fierce skin inflammation had forced Helen to abandon her own teaching position in Taunton, and she had moved home for a while. Henry's quixotic abandonment of his first job after Harvard had resulted in more difficulty than he had imagined at the time.

As EMERSON'S OPINION of his protégé rose ever higher, his comments about him surprised those who had known Henry in college. Henry's fellow Harvard '37 graduate David Greene Haskins had had no expectations of Henry and no sense that he exhibited unusual potential. Henry had not been notable as either scholar or writer; he was not a member of literary societies. Unlike Haskins, he did not contribute to *Harvardiana*, the undergraduate literary journal that had been under the university's auspices during his last couple of years there and had folded a year after his graduation. Furthermore, Haskins, along with many of Henry's other classmates, had considered the homespun Concord boy aloof and unsociable. Early in 1838, Haskins corresponded with Henry about a possible teaching position, to which Henry had replied thankfully but with the cool greeting "Dear Classmate." Apparently they had had no other contact since graduation.

Then one day during the summer of that year, while Haskins was studying at the Andover Theological Seminary, he was at his father's office in Boston when he ran into his cousin Ralph Waldo Emerson. Haskins's father, Ralph Haskins, was the brother of Emerson's mother, Ruth Haskins Emerson, who had named young Ralph Waldo after him. In 1826, Haskins had become a student of Emerson's after he took over his brother Edward's school on the second floor of the octagonal Norfolk Bank Building. Haskins had enjoyed Emerson's classes and was fond of him ever afterward. As a child riding on horseback to school in Roxbury, Haskins had often glimpsed Emerson's daily trudge down Roxbury Street to the cemetery across from the Latin School. Emerson was visiting the shaded, quiet grave of his first wife, Ellen Louisa Tucker, after her death at the age of twenty in 1831, less than two years after their marriage. The cemetery visit was a ritual that he observed in all weather until his departure for Europe in 1833 for an educational tour and first encounter with his heroes—John Stuart Mill, Samuel Taylor Coleridge, William Wordsworth, and Thomas Carlyle.

In his father's office that day, Haskins asked Emerson, Do you see much of my classmate, Henry Thoreau?

"Of Thoreau?" Emerson's face lit up as he smiled. "Oh, yes. We could not do without him. When Mr. Carlyle comes to America, I expect to introduce Thoreau to him as *the* man of Concord."

Haskins was dumbfounded. He thought his cousin's estimate greatly exaggerated Henry's talent and potential.

Soon after encountering Emerson in Boston, Haskins visited him at the big white house in Concord. He had been there several times before, bringing his sister with him from Roxbury, on which occasions he had been surprised by Emerson's brief grace before meals: "We acknowledge the Giver." This time Haskins saw Henry again as well and was shocked by changes that had taken place during the past year. Henry seemed to have altered everything about his behavior in conversation. He looked the same physically—the same awkward figure and unimpressive clothes, the same homely features. But he had adopted Emerson's inflections and timbre, manners and figures of speech, even his pauses and hesitations in marshaling thoughts for a sentence he was in the process of forming aloud.

From college Haskins recalled Henry's distinctive voice so well that he thought he could recognize it in the dark. Here the voices sounded so much alike that he decided to test this idea. Sitting in Emerson's study by the wall of books, and listening to Henry and Emerson converse, Haskins closed his eyes in order to compare the voices. He found to his astonishment that most of the time he could not tell them apart. Haskins opened his eyes—and saw that Henry's posture mimicked Emerson's.

Haskins himself found his cousin's personality and style magnetic, and after being in his presence could imitate his manner. He came to think of Henry's curious metamorphosis as a kind of chemical reaction that had taken place within him in response to a powerful catalyst. Many other people noticed Henry's imitation of Emerson. Some observed that his handwriting even came to resemble his mentor's. A student who graduated in 1838, a year behind Henry, felt the same way as David Haskins—Cambridge-born James Russell Lowell, who saw Henry during the same summer and wrote to a friend, "I saw Thoreau last night, and it is exquisitely amusing to see how he imitates Emerson's tone and manner. With my eyes shut I shouldn't know them apart."

Chapter 9

WE CAN TEACH YOU

IN JUNE 1838, having failed to find a job teaching for someone else, Henry opened a small school of his own in the Thoreau home. "I have four scholars, and one more engaged," he wrote to John the next month. He placed advertisements in the *Yeoman's Gazette*, declaring that he had opened a school "for the reception of a limited number of pupils, of both sexes. . . . Instruction will be given in the usual English branches, and the studies preparatory to a college course. Terms—Six dollars per quarter."

The number of pupils turned out to be even more limited than he had imagined. At first he had little success, but then John, with his extensive teaching experience, agreed to come aboard. After a shaky beginning the new school's reputation spread quickly and each quarter brought new students. In February 1839 Henry and John moved their classes to the Academy School. Phineas Allen, who had taught Henry in his early youth—and whose essay assignments had resulted in his early hymn to the seasons—had departed Concord for a school in Northfield, near the Vermont border. Thus Henry was now teaching in the same school at which he had attended classes as a child.

Every new student of the Thoreau brothers was first interviewed by John. "You say you would like to enter our school," he would say. "Why do you wish that?"

The child would list the courses that his parents wanted John and Henry to help him master, from solid geometry and algebra to classical languages and even such practical topics as surveying.

"If you really wish to study those things," John would say pleasantly, "we can teach you, if you obey our rules and promise to give your mind to your studies. But," he added firmly, "if you come to idle and play, or to see other boys study, we shall not want you for a pupil."

His earnest, quiet tone impressed each youngster with the seriousness of the contract between student and teacher. "Do you promise, then, to do what we require?" asked John. "If so, we will do our best to teach you what we know ourselves."

Naturally each child promised. And naturally each broke the promise at some point, only to face John's and Henry's disappointment, which was somehow as powerful an inhibitor as the ferule. Some students reported home that they couldn't understand how a school that rejected corporal punishment still ran so efficiently. Remembering the trauma of his fortnight teaching after graduating from Harvard, Henry refused to whip children, as did gentle John. Each student understood assigned duties and generally executed them without much policing. The secret to a harmonious classroom seemed to be a small number of students and a relationship built upon mutual respect.

School was in session from half past eight in the morning until half past twelve. Following a lunch break, classes resumed from two until four in the afternoon, with a brief recess in both halves of the day. Just before a break ended, Henry would stride into the classroom in his quick purposeful way, ready for work. The moment the children came indoors he would launch into their Greek or Latin lesson, with little patience for students who demonstrated that they had not prepared for their work. John taught English topics downstairs and Henry Greek and Latin above, as well as mathematics.

For his rigorous ways, some of the students called Henry "Trainer Thoreau." With the familiar site of volunteer militia drilling on public grounds, "trainer" had become a synonym for "militiaman," especially during the periodic muster times. Some of the young scholars preferred John to Henry, finding Henry more rigid and less companionable. Other students were particularly fond of Henry. Sometimes, as he started home after the school day, one of the younger students would come up to him and take his hand and walk beside him to continue the day's conversation. John maintained discipline in the classroom, but at recess he was out on the lawn with the students—wrestling with the older boys, turning somersaults. Solemn Henry could look out the window and see John walking across the grass on his hands, with a big grin on his upside-down face.

SOLID GEOMETRY BEGAN the day upstairs. After Henry walked around proposing the problem from his textbook, students drew figures and wrote their demonstration of them on their slates. Then they brought their slate up to Henry's desk for him to check their work. Geography followed morning recess. Henry used Roswell C. Smith's 1835 *Geography on the Productive System; for Schools, Academies, and Families.* Unlike Jedediah Morse, whose popular first American geography text came out in 1784, Smith's text included many maps and illustrations, some associated with his ranking of world cultures on a scale that progressed from "barbarous" to "enlightened." Every week each student had to draw one map, and a half day in class was devoted to the task. One assignment required drawing maps of the states—almost rectangular Pennsylvania, tiny Rhode Island, their own Massachusetts flexing its arm out into the

Atlantic. Cartographers often had to revise U.S. maps, such as adding the Arkansas Territory in 1836 and taking the Michigan Territory out of the Northwest Territory the next year.

Saturday morning was spent writing a new composition. The students worked in unlined writing books with marbled covers, another product created by the elder John Thoreau in his versatile shop. Henry read aloud some of the compositions, which resulted in laughter and chaffing between the students. Half wrote one day and half the next. Those students who boarded with the Thoreaus and had families out of town were permitted to alternate compositions with letters home.

Often, after morning prayers, either Henry or John spoke briefly on a subject about to be studied or on the larger pleasures of learning. Henry yearned to instill in the students a delight in knowledge as much as he wanted to drill them in a particular subject. Vividly he explained one of his favorite themes, the seasons—their source in the tilt and rotation of the Earth and its revolution around the sun, their relationship to the changing lives of animals and people throughout the year, their parade of strikingly different forms of beauty. Such talks made learning seem central to the enjoyment of life rather than some kind of adornment—and, Henry hoped, it set a tone for the school day.

Henry liked to talk about such topics as the glorious design of the universe, which he felt was visible in every detail of nature. He spoke of his own belief in a wise and kind power watching over human lives. Explicitly invoking William Paley's watchmaker analogy from his Harvard days, he asked the students to envision walking into a shop and finding spread out on a bench the pinions, springs, and wheels of a pocket watch. He wondered aloud if they could imagine such an intricate mechanism assembled by chance. This old argument was new to the children in a village school.

As more students enrolled and the school earned an erratic profit, Henry and John purchased a large slate blackboard. Since the turn of the century, American schools had been adopting this innovation, especially after the availability of trains that could safely transport such large items. Writing or drawing on a blackboard provided the first means of demonstration to an entire group of students and was considered a great technological advance in education. Teachers no longer had to repeat an assignment for every student, chalking words or equations on each slate. After they acquired the blackboard, Henry taught a class in natural philosophy, which students such as George Keyes particularly liked. Henry had his students diagram animals and plants on the board, and, apportioning his time and advice to their enthusiasm, he was quick to encourage any interest they demonstrated by careful attention to such matters as correlation and labeling.

Some of the school's other popular innovations concerned fresh air, both indoors and out. Recess was a half hour, not the usual ten minutes. Windows were left open when weather permitted. While they had autonomy, Henry and John weren't about to subject themselves or their students to the stifling, foul atmosphere still common in most schools.

Henry's quirks contributed to the unpredictability of school hours. He disliked profanity, for example, and devised memorable ways to quell its use among the older students. "Boys," he would say in his half-serious, half-satirical tone, "if you went to talk business with a man, and he persisted in thrusting words having no connection with the subject into all parts of every sentence—" he considered an example and interrupted himself to exclaim, "Bootjack, for instance!" and then resumed, "—wouldn't you think he was taking a liberty with you, and trifling with your time, and wasting his own?" Over the next few minutes, to the delight of the students, he emphasized his point by speaking on some innocent topic but suddenly interjecting a random "Boot-jack!" into his sentences.

WHEN NOT TEACHING school, Henry continued to walk in the woods with Emerson, discussing art and nature and society, taking the world apart and trying to imagine putting it back together a different way. One afternoon in November 1838, they strolled to Walden Pond together. Along the way, Henry complained that although the world belonged to him as much as to anyone, land-owners crowded him out of most of God's earth, compelling him to walk in a narrow strip of road. Although he had not participated in building their fences, he must not cross their fields. Suppose, he said to Emerson, that prior to their birth some hugely powerful man had bought the entire globe and thus fenced everyone else completely out of nature.

"Not having been privy to any of these arrangements," Emerson wrote in his journal that evening,

> he does not feel called on to consent to them, and so cuts fish-poles in the woods without asking who has a better title to the wood than he. I defended, of course, the good institution as a scheme, not good, but the best that could be hit on for making the woods and waters and fields available to wit and worth, and for restraining the bold, bad man. At all events, I begged him, having this maggot of Freedom and Humanity in his brain, to write it out into good poetry and so clear himself of it. He replied, that he feared that that was not the best way, that in doing justice to the thought, the man did not always do justice to himself, the poem ought to sing itself: if the man took too much pains with the expression, he was not any longer the Idea himself.

DURING THE SPRING of 1839, John and Henry invested a week in building a wooden boat. From tapered bow to three-and-a-half-foot beam to stern, it was fifteen feet long. Like a fisherman's dory, it had a flat keel and a shallow draft—a strong vessel but heavy, not very maneuverable, reflecting its quick and unskilled creation. They painted it symbolic colors, wedding sky and water to earth through a blue border and gunwale above a green hull. Then they erected two masts in it, one of which could double as a camp tent-pole. Two pairs of oars completed their preparations for later in the year, when they would be ready to launch.

Henry looked over the ungainly vessel and had to admit to himself that he and John had paid little attention to the design advice of nature itself. He thought of the grace of fish, the way their tails guide humans in how to sculpt and place a rudder, how their fins tell where to lock oars. The same analogy applied to birds: the tapered beak and head demonstrating a prow native to the element it negotiates, the wings showing how sails can seduce wind. Henry felt that a well-made boat ought to be an elegant amphibious creature, fish below and bird above—a mythological hybrid.

Theirs, in contrast, was just a boat. But it would serve for the freedom and adventure that awaited them downriver. They installed wheels on one end of the hull so they could roll the boat around waterfalls or other obstructions. Then they christened it, naturally, with an Indian name: the *Musketaquid*. Wherever they traveled, the prow would praise their own Meadow River.

Soon after John and Henry finished the boat, their students were enjoying sailing or rowing on the river or across Walden Pond. Often the Thoreau brothers' natural history studies were continued under the sky, and at least once a week Henry or John took students on an excursion. Their walks led them around one of the ponds such as Walden or Bateman's or off through the woods and meadows.

On one nature ramble with students, Henry was walking with his eyes on the ground, as he often did, when suddenly he stopped and knelt. He plucked a tiny plant and held it up to the nearest student, Henry Warren, and asked him if he could see it.

"Yes," the boy replied. "What about it?"

Henry took a magnifying glass out of his pocket and showed him how the Lilliputian plant looked through it, that it was a perfect flower at the height of its blooming season—one that happened to be too small for most people to notice. Henry explained that because of his attention to the large and small plants in this region, year after year, he now understood their blooming schedule so well that by seeing the flowers around him he would be able to tell, without calendar or almanac, the month of the year. He made it clear that this seemingly arcane knowledge was available to anyone who was curious and patient.

He used these outings in part to teach about the land's inhabitants before the arrival of white settlers. The students' own little village might be two centuries old, but he didn't want their sense of its history to cease only that far back. Naturally some of the students began to share Henry and John's interests. Young Thomas Hosmer, for example, grew fascinated by Indian lore and accompanied the brothers on expeditions in search of the past. Once he found a chunk of white-speckled dark gray stone that must have weighed fifty pounds. Henry and John examined it and pronounced it the same imported flint of which most local spearheads and arrows were made. They explained to Thomas that the closest site where such rock could be found naturally was around Norwich, Connecticut, more than a hundred miles to the southwest, almost to Long Island Sound. Some industrious Indians had brought with them the material for many arrows.

Another time, Thomas was exploring the bluff above the Great Meadows and found what appeared to be a man-made hollow like an amphitheater. He brought Henry there and showed him. "This is artificial," Henry said with excitement, "made by the Indians. And," he added as he looked around, "we ought to find evidences of their fires here." As they dug, they unearthed not only charcoal but prized relics such as a mortar and pestle.

Henry began to watch the riverbanks and hills for any hint of Indian legacy. Once when he took students downstream to the Great Meadows, past Ball's Hill and the Carlisle Bridge, he pointed out a flat, open area on the riverbank and said that it seemed a likely spot to have once held an Indian fishing village. He could imagine, he said, where they would have built their campfires. "We cannot find one today," he remarked to the students, "because we have no spade. But the next time we come, I will see if that was the place of habitation."

A week later, when he brought a boatload of students this way, he remembered to bring along a spade. After they pulled the boat out of reach of the lapping current, the troop walked a short distance along the bank to the area Henry had pointed out the week before. "Do you see anything here," he asked, "that would be likely to attract Indians to this place?"

As the students dutifully looked around for clues, one boy began with the obvious: "Why, here is the river for their fishing!"

Another mentioned that the nearby forest would have provided ample game.

"Well . . ." Both were good points, but Henry nudged further. "Is there anything else?" He pointed out a rivulet that he said must surely trickle from a nearby spring. Such a source would provide cooler water in summer than could be found in the rivers or ponds.

They moved farther inland. Henry scanned the ground carefully before finally stabbing it with the shovel. The blade sank easily into the soil without encountering an obstruction. Henry tried again, moved, again placed his shoe on the butt of the spade and dug. Some of the boys were skeptical about their teacher's ability to predict the location of Indian camps—until they heard the blade suddenly strike a rock or some other buried object. Triumphantly, Henry moved forward a foot or two and tried again. More success. He kept moving, establishing the perimeter of a circle, and dug deeper. Soon he unearthed a cluster of worn red stones and pointed out that in places they had been blackened by a fire. Before he and the students returned to the boat, he respectfully covered up the forgotten campfire, returning it to the earth's archive, the lost history of these people who haunted his imagination.

IN JUNE OF 1839, the widow Mrs. Joseph Ward and her daughter Miss Prudence Ward, the Thoreau boarders who had co-founded the Concord Female Anti-Slavery Society, had visitors. Another of Mrs. Ward's daughters, Mrs. Caroline Sewall, journeyed from Scituate to visit her mother and sister, bringing along her son Edmund. Late in the afternoon of Monday, the seventeenth of June, their coach arrived in time for them to share supper at the Thoreau table.

For Caroline, it was a homecoming of sorts. When Mrs. Ward had first moved to Concord, both Caroline and Prudence lived with her. Caroline, however, soon met the handsome and romantic young Edmund Quincy Sewall, who was studying divinity with Reverend Ripley in the Manse. They married and moved to Scituate. Reverend Ripley had preached Sewall's ordination sermon back in 1819. Their famously beautiful daughter Ellen (named after Ellen Douglas, the heroine of Walter Scott's hugely popular 1810 narrative poem "The Lady of the Lake") was sixteen, and their handsome and lively son Edmund eleven.

Many literate young people kept diaries. By the time of his arrival in Concord at the age of nine, Edmund was writing in one often, as well as scribbling many letters to relatives and friends. One early entry documented his attendance at an antislavery lecture by the renowned abolitionist William Lloyd Garrison. Afterward, he noted, he contributed ninepence to a fund-raising offering, and he recalled his favorite witticisms by the speaker.

Intelligent and spirited, Edmund came from a bookish family and was unusually familiar with literature. At an early age he had enjoyed Charles Dickens's novel *Oliver Twist*. In the spring of 1838 he had begun reading each of the nineteen monthly install-ments of Dickens's new novel *The Life and Adventures of Nicholas Nickleby*, whose young hero is cast into hazard and farce by the death of his father. *Nickleby* was still running when Edmund visited Concord. A fan of epic poetry, he also reveled in the beauty and perils of Walter Scott's 1808 poem *Marmion*, about the sixteenth-century battle between the kingdoms of Scotland and England at Flodden Field in Northumberland, as well as Scott's poem that had inspired Ellen's name. Edmund's father was in the habit of reading aloud to the family in the evenings. By the age of eight Edmund had heard William H. Prescott's three-volume *History of the Reign of Ferdinand and Isabella the Catholic* and even Carlyle's epic of the French Revolution, with its horrific visions of Sophoclean reversals of fortune.

Mrs. Ward and Prudence had often written to Caroline about the goings-on at their boardinghouse, and thus she and Edmund were quite familiar with the Thoreau family. The boy was immedi-ately popular. Henry and John took the Wards and Sewalls on a Concord River expedition in the boat they had built. It was too small for the party, so while Edmund's mother and aunt sat in the boat with him, Henry and John and a boy who was boarding at the house walked along opposite shores. Edmund was disappointed that the wind was so weak the boat's sail was useless. Then Henry led

Prudence and Caroline back home along the riverside paths, while John and the boarder and Edmund rowed on to the north branch of the river. Along the shore they came across a moored boat that John recognized as belonging to a Mr. Haynes, and a moment later they heard the report of a rifle from the woods. John moored his own boat and led the boys to meet Haynes, who was a famous marksman in the region. Accompanied by two hunting dogs, Haynes was firing his rifle at a dollar-sized target about fifty yards away—and never failing to hit it.

Later Henry took Edmund and other boys to the rocky promontory nicknamed the Dover Cliffs. Dense plant growth surrounded an exposed stone peak. Edmund and another boy climbed up as far as they could along a rocky fissure, and Edmund rolled down a stone and had the satisfaction of watching the frightened boys below leap out of the way. While the others walked back to the village, Henry took Edmund to Walden Pond. As they rowed across the water, Henry showed how it was so clear the bottom was visible even at depths of eight or ten feet. He warned Edmund that in most places four steps into the water would bring it over his head.

Henry found Edmund's wide-eyed curiosity and eager intelligence captivating. The boy and his mother left Concord on Saturday, the twenty-second of June, and on that day Henry scribbled in his journal about what Edmund symbolized to him, without actually saying much about the real boy:

I have within the last few days come into contact with a pure, uncompromising spirit, that is somewhere wandering in the atmosphere, but settles not positively anywhere. Some persons carry about them the air and conviction of virtue, though they themselves are unconscious of it, and are even backward to appreciate it in others. Such it is impossible not to love; still is their loveliness, as it were, independent of them, so that you may seem not to lose it when they are absent, for when they are near it is like an invisible presence which attends you.

Two days later, Henry wrote a poem into his journal under the title "Sympathy." The conventional thirteen stanzas were self-conscious imitation of the classical elegiac mode, flavored with Virgil and Milton and other authors Henry had studied at Harvard and read on his own, but anchored in his momentary infatuation with Edmund Sewall:

> *Lately alas I knew a gentle boy,*
> *Whose features all were cast in Virtue's mould,*
> *As one she had designed for Beauty's toy,*
> *But after manned him for her own strong-hold . . .*

> *So was I taken unawares by this,*
> *I quite forgot my homage to confess;*
> *Yet now am forced to know, though hard it is,*
> *I might have loved him, had I loved him less . . .*

Emerson liked elegy and had great patience for vague poetic philosophizing, and he was always eager to praise the potential of young writers, even to the point of raising unrealistic expectations. "Last night," he wrote in his journal on the first of August, "came to me a beautiful poem from Henry Thoreau, 'Sympathy.' The purest strain, and the loftiest, I think, that has yet pealed from this unpoetic American forest."

Chapter 10

NO REMEDY FOR LOVE

O N T H E T W E N T I E T H of July 1839, a month after her brother and mother arrived in Concord, Ellen Sewall joined them, in response to an invitation from Cynthia Thoreau. It wasn't the seventeen-year-old's first trip to the village. She was friends with Sophia Thoreau especially, who was only three years older, but also with Helen. Her mother had often brought her to visit Grand-mother Ward and Aunt Prudence, and later Ellen had been able to make the journey by herself. Seven years earlier, at the age of ten, she had written in her diary about visiting Concord with her parents during Fourth of July festivities—in the morning watching companies of soldiers muster, later sipping mead with her family at the apothecary on the Common, at night listening to a band in the square while watching fireworks rain colors across the sky.

Once when they were small children, Sophia had visited Ellen at her grandmother Sewall's home in Boston. The girls played by the Frog Pond in the northern part of the busy Common until they grew bored. Then Ellen offered to show Sophia the old State House. Although she was too young to understand much about it, the building was the center of United States history. The balcony on the east side looked down on State Street—named King Street until the Revolution—where in 1770 British soldiers fired into a crowd of unarmed men, killing five. After the Declaration of Independence was read there on the eighteenth of July 1776, all symbols of royal power were stripped off, including the Lion and the Unicorn from the roof, and tossed on a purging bonfire whose smoke clouded Dock Square until it drifted away on the wind. Ellen gave Sophia an extended tour of the inside and outside of the building. Eventually they found themselves up inside the dome, climbing around and under beams until they reached the top. It was a dangerous adventure, and later Sophia asked Ellen if it had really happened or if she had dreamed it.

This time, however, Ellen was visiting Concord although Sophia and Helen were both away. Her father suffered alarming respiratory troubles and had begun to experience epileptic fits, even during some of his own sermons. Having been absent from the pulpit many times, including while doctors cupped his scalp to draw blood, he was weighing the possibility of leaving the church because of his health. Ellen may have enjoyed an escape from illness and worry at home.

Apparently she hadn't seen Henry and John in a while, and in the meantime she had grown into a beautiful and charming young woman, with wavy dark hair and striking light-colored eyes. She had a quick sense of humor and an easy empathy with others. Like her younger brother, Ellen kept a diary and copied favorite poems into it. She wrote detailed letters to friends and family. She painted landscapes and pressed flowers that she brought home from walks. And, perhaps most important to Henry, she was notably intelligent. Edmund Quincy Sewall Sr. had taught his daughter as carefully as he had his son Edmund Junior. By the age of six Ellen studied Greek every day under his tutelage. At eleven she began studying logic. By scrimping, her parents later sent her to a good school, although financial woes had often threatened to end her education.

Henry was smitten with the bright, lively, beautiful, almost-adult Ellen during the first day of her visit. That evening he wrote in his journal a poem titled "The Breeze's Invitation," whose six verses concluded,

One green leaf shall be our screen,
Till the sun doth go to bed,
I the king and you the queen,
Of that peaceful little green,
Without any subject's aid.

To our music Time will linger,
And earth open wide her ear,
Nor shall any need to tarry
To immortal verse to marry
Such sweet music as he'll hear.

Over the next two weeks, they walked along the Concord River and trekked woodland paths and climbed hills for a better view. Henry chauffeured Ellen and the Wards in a carriage. He took Ellen and Aunt Prudence on the river in the *Musketaquid*. He even shared his favorite pastime, berry picking, along the north branch of the Concord. Henry was unusually agreeable in Ellen's presence, although he made a couple of stands on principle. Once he declined her invitation to say grace over a meal. Another time, she and others were going to church, and when Henry flatly refused to accompany them, Ellen reproached his heathen ways.

"All outdoors," he replied, "is a church."

On one memorable occasion, Henry escorted Ellen and her aunt to see the exotic animals in a traveling tent show. They admired an elegant little gazelle and had their first chance to observe a camelopard, or giraffe. This remarkable creature towered above them, its long ochre body patterned in brown shapes like cracked mud. Its surprisingly small camel-like head, with furry antler-like protuberances between the ears, made the animal look foreshortened, as if it were even taller than its sixteen feet or more. Ellen wrote to her father about how much she enjoyed seeing "this famous animal" and added, "Oh, I can not tell you half I have enjoyed here, till I get home. I have had so many delightful walks with Aunt ... and the Messrs. Thoreau that a full account of them all would fill half a dozen letters."

One day a party of young people, including Henry and Ellen, tried to decipher each other's fated character by feeling for diagnostic bumps on the skull. The Austrian physiologist Franz Joseph Gall had developed his notions of cranioscopy, also called phrenology, less than half a century earlier. Religious leaders, Franz Joseph II, even Napoleon opposed the idea that the divine mind required a physical home. Gall argued, however, that the brain was the seat of consciousness, that various mental functions were localized within its mysterious precincts, and that they were reflected in the shape of the skull that housed the organ. Phrenology was losing favor already as a scientific concept in much of Europe. Yet it was gaining popularity in the United States, in part because it seemed to lend authority to notions of superior and inferior races destined to remain such because of brain structure.

When Emerson had been at Harvard, his classmate Robert Barnwell from South Carolina, the leading scholar in their classes, had felt the back of Emerson's head, found what phrenologists called the bump of ambition, and informed his patient that it was tiny. In 1839 phrenology was a favorite parlor game. Surrounded by laughing friends, Henry ran his fingers through Ellen's rich dark hair, gently felt for bumps on her skull, and informed everyone that he could find none. More laughter erupted. A complete lack of bumps, someone argued, demonstrated that Ellen must be either an absolute genius or some kind of idiot.

Henry wrote another poem on the twenty-fourth (ending with "Our rays united make one sun / With fairest summer weather"), but the next day words must have failed him. "There is no remedy for love," he wrote in his journal, "but to love more."

HENRY WAS NOT alone in his fascination with Ellen. Her magic worked just as well, if not better, on John. During her time in Concord, both spent as much time with Ellen as possible, usually with Aunt Prudence as faithful chaperone. All three walked to Walden Pond and Fair Haven Bay. They attended parties. Conversation bounced laughingly from one topic to another, but Henry held forth at times, with others asking questions.

The active interest of John and Henry did not keep other young men away. John Keyes, Henry's friend who had arrived at Harvard during Henry's commencement weekend, was a rival during the latter part of Ellen's stay. He was visiting a neighbor in Concord when Prudence Ward came by to show her niece the neighbor's gardens. Keyes had an eye for the opposite sex and he found Ellen dazzling. After a tour of the gardens, he wasted no time in walking her home to the Thoreau house. He went back later, pretending he wanted to borrow the brothers' boat for a sail on the river, but to his annoyance learned that Ellen wasn't there.

Keyes went to a party that night at the Richards house—and there was the beautiful Ellen. Keyes confessed to his diary later that he "pounced upon her." He monopolized her attention for so long that others launched into singing to derail Keyes's occupation strategy. At supper he sat with Ellen and they discussed the virtues of the Boston Athenæum. Afterward, Keyes, not Henry or

John, walked Ellen home to the Thoreau boarding-house. The next day, he made sure to be present at Mrs. Brooks's tea party, where the Thoreau family provided the music and Ellen could be pursued. On the third of August, however, Keyes's tired ploy of asking to borrow the Thoreaus' boat fell flat, because she had left town that morning.

Ellen made clear in her letters home that she preferred the company of Henry and John. She had so much fun with them that she was surprised to find herself sorry when Sophia and Helen returned. Soon she waited while her luggage was arranged on the back of the coach, climbed up into its chatty, crowded interior, and quietly cried all the way to Lexington. As soon as she arrived home, she wrote Prudence a letter that included "affectionate remembrances" to the Thoreau brothers. Her Concord visit was, Ellen said, one of the happiest times of her life.

Unlike Henry, John was not shy with girls. Realizing that Ellen had left behind in Concord some Indian relics that had been given her, John shipped them to Scituate. The package also included a preserved insect that he had mounted in a silly position. The letter John enclosed mentioned that he and Henry were taking a brief holiday from their school. Smitten with the same woman or not, the brothers were finally taking their homemade boat on the river adventure that they had been planning for months.

Dr. Josiah Bartlett asked Henry and John if they would take one of his sons on their river journey—Gorham was thirteen and a student of the brothers at the Academy—so that he might learn something in the real world. They refused. Even though both enjoyed the company of children and teenagers and often spent after-school hours with them, they were unwilling to share this adventure.

★   ★   ★

APPARENTLY THE RIVALRY for Ellen's affections between Keyes and the Thoreau brothers was friendly. On Thursday, the twenty-ninth of August, Keyes came at Henry's invitation to see his arrangements for the long-planned river trip. Henry and John were going to row and sail the Concord River and probably also the Merrimack. Henry excitedly showed Keyes his intricate pack-ing and invited him back that evening for a farewell melon party he was hosting for a few gentlemen. The party was for men, but Elizabeth Hoar came over to see the decorations. She considered a party hosted by Henry Thoreau, of all people, to be the most surprising Concord event in a boring week. Mrs. Thoreau even felt the need to apologize to her for Henry's hosting it, because she had frequently repeated to others his alleged contempt for parties and other social antics.

Keyes and the other men arrived about nine in the warm summer evening. Groaning tables showcased Henry's skill as a gardener, including four dozen melons of fifteen kinds. He raised green-and-blue-striped citrons that framed white flesh, green watermelons with seed-speckled red flesh, and many other varieties. There was an array of apples as well. This private harvest festival was framed with golden blossoms—sunflowers and squash—mixed with green-ish-yellow corn stalks and purple-veined beet leaves. When he left hours later, Keyes was so stuffed with food and wine (the latter possibly brought along with him) that he felt he could barely walk across the street to his father's house. Henry and John's voyage had been properly launched.

THEY DEPARTED ON the last day of August 1839, a Saturday. The morning dawned wet and misty. Warm rain drizzled the hours away, making them worry that they would have to delay their trip. But by afternoon the rain had stopped and the sky began to clear. The boat was already loaded with melons and potatoes and utensils, and they added a few articles of clothing and their rifles and ammunition. They wheeled the boat down to the riverbank and eased it into the sluggish current among the bulrushes and wild flags. With a vigorous shove against the bank, they were off to explore the world beyond Concord.

Downstream, a few friends who had gathered on the riverbank stood waving as Henry and John rowed past. The brothers remained mock-heroically solemn until they were out of sight. Then they fired their rifles into the air and listened to echoes produce a many-gun salute that startled long-legged egrets into flapping up from the reeds. They rowed under Flint's Bridge, passed where the Mill Brook flowed into the river, and then, resting their muscles, drifted past the abutments of what had once been the North Bridge, where the Concord militia had amassed on that historic day. The brothers passed the Manse, facing the river—the rough-hewn stone gate-posts without a gate, and beyond them a single dormer window projecting out of the long roof, with below it the second-floor window from which Emerson's grandmother had held up her daughter to see the red coats of King George's soldiers.

It was a peaceful voyage, traveling on the river—uneventful, but great fun and a welcome diversion from teaching. This was the most extensive trip Henry and John had ever taken together, their longest time away from the rest of the family. In his journal Henry did not mention any discussion of Ellen Sewall. They fished and hunted, dined on bream and passenger pigeon. They slept in buffalo skins that they rolled up in the dawn while their fire's embers still smoked, so eager were they to see around the bend. From their silent watery vantage point, Henry watched sulky-looking bitterns stalk the shore and wondered what viewpoint they developed, deciphering the motions of fish while patiently standing on one leg under sun and moon.

John and Henry rowed in unison, exulting in their youth and strength. Together they sang one of Henry's favorite songs, an adapted Canadian boat song by the British musician Thomas Moore:

Row, brothers, row, the stream runs fast,
The rapids are near, and the daylight's past . . .

Only a couple of days out, they found themselves in Bedford, New Hampshire, talking with a party of hard-working masons. That night the brothers camped in what they thought was a secluded area. Next morning, however, as they were rolling up their tent, they found that the path by their campsite was traveled every morning by the masons. Curious about John and Henry's voyage, they stopped to chat, to examine the boat, and to look over the brothers' rifles, which they had leaned against a tree trunk. Once a young boy who had been reading *Robinson Crusoe* heard the brothers' account of their trip and begged his father's permission to join them.

Such random encounters with locals and fellow travelers kept the journey unpredictable, but the landscape itself also offered variety. Sometimes they raced between high banks and sometimes floated gently in shallow broad water. Solitude would inspire thoughts of the early days of American exploration, and of the natives who had already been on these banks when white people arrived. Then Henry and John would round a bend and encounter a big canal boat approaching with its square sail glaring white in the sun.

At night the brothers hunched around a campfire. Henry enjoyed newspapers but had mixed feelings about how the journalistic trumpery of national and international affairs distracted him from his daily attention to nature and literature. Back home, he devoured the narrow-columned pages of Horace Greeley's influential Whig weekly, the New York *Tribune*, and then felt cheapened by association with its alarums and excursions, as if he had been eating food that was neither satisfying nor nutritious. Still he could not stop. On the river trip, he would hunch near the campfire and read scraps of newspapers he picked up in towns along the way—unfold them, smooth out wrinkles, and try to ignore food stains from someone else's supper. He considered the editorials flimsier than the paper that bore them, but he enjoyed the advertisements; popular items that year included Samuel Lee's Bilious Pills and iridescent taffeta bonnets from Paris. He thought the categories of commodities evocative enough for a poem: Hides and Guano, Logwood and Lumber, Sugar and Cotton. They seemed at least related to nature, like tide tables and weather forecasts. The editorial opinions, in contrast, read like school essays of which everyone involved soon would be embarrassed or even ashamed.

Although various encounters provoked such critical observations from Henry—he liked to express his disappointment with humanity—he and John enjoyed the trip so much they couldn't resist daydreaming about making a living on boats. The boatmen they passed looked contented with their lot and seemed to lead relatively easy lives. Their steady progress past varying shores would make for less monotonous lives than those led by mariners gazing at a flat horizon day after day. Many of the boatmen on the river were friendly and questioned them about their lives. Some of the boats, Henry was impressed to learn, were so solid and reliable that they didn't even rock when he and John stepped aboard.

After passing through the locks near Amoskeag, New Hampshire, the brothers poled their boat a half mile to deeper, more navigable water and there found many canal boats bound for Hooksett. The other boats were empty, and the mild wind barely curved their sails. One boatman offered to tow the Thoreaus' boat. They assented, but when they pulled up alongside the canal boat, the man explained that he had intended to take their little boat on board—so that it wouldn't be in the way of the larger craft—but it was too heavy. While the boatmen rested and ate their midday meal, Henry and John raced ahead of the cluster of boats. Eventually they anchored under some riverside alders and ate their own lunch, during which time the canal boats passed them, with the same boatman genially taunting. After they were through eating, Henry and John raced ahead to shoot past the other boats, yelling out their own offer of towing, and rowed speedily onward, laughing.

Occasionally they split up. One remained in the boat, rowing and guiding and glimpsing the passing fields and woods and infrequent houses from the water; the other went ashore and saw the landed view. They rejoined downstream, one with stories of friendly farmwives and cold milk, the other with tales of otters and egrets. One rainy day they beached the boat and walked in to Plymouth, New Hampshire, to visit the abolitionist Nathaniel Peabody Rogers, with whom they were acquainted. The year before, Rogers had turned from almost two decades of legal practice to edit the then three-year-old abolitionist newspaper *Herald of Freedom*.

Past Manchester, New Hampshire, near Hooksett, they stowed their boat for a week and traveled in stagecoaches, lodged in taverns, ascended mountain trails. In the White Mountains on the seventh of September, they visited Cannon Mountain at Franconia Notch and paid their respects to a local attraction that, since its discovery by white people in 1805, had been called the Great Stone Face—a huge granite profile, with jagged jaw and overhanging brow, projecting from the top of a cliff.

On the last day of their trip, September 13, with the sail raised and both men rowing as well, they traveled the remaining fifty miles to find themselves back home again. Henry thought the bulrushes and flags still looked flattened from the boat's launch a fortnight earlier.

The next day, Emerson thought about them and their generation in his journal:

> We are shut up in schools & college recitation rooms for ten or fifteen years & come out at last with a bellyful of words & do not know a thing. We cannot use our hands or our legs or our eyes or our arms. We do not know an edible root in the woods. . . . Now here are my wise young neighbors who instead of getting like the wordmen into a railroad-car where they have not even the activity of holding the reins, have got into a boat which they have built with their own hands with sails which they have contrived to serve as a tent by night, & gone up the river Merrimack to live by their wits on the fish of the stream & the berries of the wood.

Chapter 11

GIVE HER A KISS FOR ME

A FTER THEIR RETURN from the river voyage in September 1839, John did not remain long in Concord. When he informed others that he was planning to visit Ellen Sewall in Scituate, her Aunt Prudence made it clear she thought such a plan inappropriate, because Ellen's parents were away on a journey to Niagara Falls.

Nonetheless, John arrived in Scituate to a fond welcome from Ellen, whose only companions were her younger brothers, Edmund and George, who had been left in the care of the responsible seventeen-year-old. Edmund was there during the school break that the brothers had filled with their voyage. On the coast halfway between Boston and Plymouth, Scituate was rich in history. The Plymouth Pilgrims had visited the area before 1628 and within a few years were laying out property lines along the cliffs that John and the Sewall siblings visited, such as Colman's Hill, which towered above the rocky coastline.

The Sewall children enjoyed John's tales of his river exploits, although George kept accidentally referring to John as Henry. Soon a friend of the family dropped by the Sewall home, perhaps alerted by Aunt Prudence, and hinted that she would like to remain for a visit. Ellen managed to postpone the woman's stay until after John's departure. Soon she wrote to Aunt Prudence, "I have enjoyed Mr. John's visit exceedingly though sorry father and Mother were not at home."

At Christmastime, Henry and John accompanied Prudence Ward on a visit to Scituate. Their interest in Ellen was visible to everyone. After their departure, Ellen wrote to Prudence:

> The house seems deserted since you left us; I never was so lonely in my life as the day you went away, and I have not quite recovered my spirits yet. . . . I have wished you and John and Henry here a thousand times this week. . . . Does Dr. Thoreau continue to give advice gratis? I do not clean my brasses half as quick without the accompaniment of his flute.

Following their return to Concord, the brothers took turns sending reminders of their affection to the Sewall home in Scituate. Henry mailed a book of poems by Jones Very, another of Emerson's young protégés. While a student at Harvard Divinity School in 1838, Very had proclaimed that he was Christ resurrected. He notoriously cried to students one day, "Flee to the mountains, for the end of all things is at hand." Divinity School administrators were not convinced and dismissed him. Emerson had responded to Very's recent release from a mental institution by helping him publish his first collection, *Essays and Poems*. His book was a curious choice for Henry to send to the Sewalls, but soon Ellen was reporting that the family enjoyed it.

Knowing Ellen's passion for natural history, as demonstrated by a cabinet of curiosities she kept, John sent her some opals that had originated in South America. To his intellectually inclined student, Edmund, John sent books. Little George couldn't read much, if at all, so John slyly sent him a long letter to be read aloud by Ellen. "If sister has read it through to you very carefully," John

added at the end, "you may give her a kiss for me and wish her a
Happy New Year!"

Henry then sent Ellen some of his own poems. They included
"The Assabet," which he had written in his journal the previous
July, during Ellen's visit that had led to all his distracting thoughts
about her:

> *Up this pleasant stream let's row*
> *For the livelong summer's day,*
> *Sprinkling foam where'er we go*
> *In wreaths as white as driven snow.*
> *Ply the oars! away! away!*
>
> *Now we glide along the shore,*
> *Chucking lilies as we go,*
> *While the yellow-sanded floor*
> *Doggedly resists the oar,*
> *Like some turtle dull and slow . . .*

Apparently Ellen's family insisted that, for the sake of propriety,
she communicate with the Thoreau brothers through her aunt. Even
when Ellen forgot for some time to thank Henry for his poems, she
apologized through Prudence. On the twentieth of March, the first
day of spring, Henry scrawled in his journal, "Love never degrades
its votaries, but lifts them up to higher walks of being."

The next day found him confiding to the journal a boundless
ambition and optimism, as well as his recurring yearning to escape
the bonds of society:

By another spring I may be a mail-carrier in Peru, or a South
African planter, or a Siberian exile, or a Greenland whaler, or a

settler on the Columbia River, or a Canton merchant, or a soldier in Florida, or a mackerel-fisher off Cape Sable, or a Robinson Crusoe in the Pacific, or a silent navigator of any sea. . . . I can move away from public opinion, from government, from religion, from education, from society.

IN JUNE 1840 Ellen visited Concord again. "The other day," Henry wrote in his journal on the nineteenth, "I rowed in my boat a free, even lovely young lady, and, as I plied the oars, she sat in the stern, and there was nothing but she between me and the sky. So might all our lives be picturesque if they were free enough, but mean relations and prejudices intervene to shut out the sky, and we never see a man as simple and distinct as the man-weathercock on a steeple." Then the sounds of the night reminded him of his and John's time on the Merrimack the year before—especially of a distant drummer beating his slow ancient rhythm across miles and centuries. For days or even weeks, the effect of this time with Ellen cast a glow over Henry's life. Romantic and susceptible deep within his shell, he walked the fields under moonlight, thinking that even the lowing of cattle sounded friendlier than usual.

Too soon Ellen was gone. And when she left, John did, too, following her to Scituate. In July he went again—still without Henry, this time accompanying the Wards to the beautiful region. In 1837 the painter Thomas Doughty had immortalized Scituate's dramatic coastline, featuring one of the balanced boulders that stood on end as if tossed by giants. Like his older colleagues Asher B. Durand and Thomas Cole, Doughty celebrated the fresh American landscape.

During the War of 1812, locals claimed, the Scituate lighthouse keeper was away when his two daughters spied a British warship anchored nearby and two skiffs of redcoats rowing toward shore.

The older daughter grabbed a fife and launched into the kind of martial airs that would accompany a mustering militia. Fearing that colonists were massing to attack, the redcoats retreated—and Scituate still bragged about its "Army of Two." By the time John and Ellen strolled on the beach, the lighthouse was in poor repair, its brass tarnished and its glass smoked black. Ellen's aunt accompanied them as chaperone, but obligingly leaned against a rock and waited so they could speak privately. During their stroll, John asked Ellen to marry him. She was surprised. Possibly merely caught up in the excitement of the visit and the romance of the moment, the eighteen-year-old said yes.

Almost immediately she had doubts, but she didn't have to face them long. When she returned home, her mother pointedly asked if John had said anything interesting. Yes, Ellen said, he proposed. Her mother was not pleased. Although the Reverend and Mrs. Sewall had trusted Henry and John as teachers for Edmund and Ellen, they were not going to accept one of them as a son-in-law. The Thoreau family was known to be alarmingly progressive in political and religious matters. Sewall was an old-fashioned Unitarian minister, firmly ensconced in the church that Emerson had fled years earlier; he was no Transcendentalist. Her father would not approve of this match, Ellen's mother insisted. She wielded the threat of his ill health, which had a powerful effect on his affectionate daughter. Ellen reversed her decision.

John returned to Concord on the nineteenth. That evening Henry wrote in the privacy of his room, "These two days that I have not written in my Journal, set down in the calendar as the 17th and 18th of July, have been really an aeon in which a Syrian empire might rise and fall." John's report of Ellen's refusal may have improved Henry's mood, because he added, "Night is spangled with fresh stars."

John's modest income may have been a factor in Ellen's parents' decision; possibly they wanted their daughter to avoid the financial woes that had plagued their own marriage. Three nights after his return to Concord, following an overture about poverty's virtues surpassing the alleged convenience of riches, John confided his disappointment to his own journal, with an apparently sarcastic aside about not being "crossed in love."

> Tonight I feel doleful, somewhat lachrymose, and desponding "Bluey." not absolutely suicidal, but viewing the world at a discount disposed to part with my lease of life for a very small "bonus." Can say with truth I think this is the vilest world I have ever been in. I'm getting to be ferocious; rather hope that no small children will come in my way just now; wouldn't be responsible. "bereaved Father," "distressed Mother" have very little weight with me at this instant— Don't feel very wicked neither, am not in debt, not crossed in love or anything of that sort, but still don't feel quite right.

Then, suffering from indigestion ("things in my chemical laboratory don't assimilate kindly"), he distracted himself by complaining at length in his journal about a pudding concocted by the cooks in what he called the Kitchen Cabinet, after the mocking nickname for President Andrew Jackson's new cabinet of cronies following a Washington scandal in the early 1830s.

Soon, however, in his gentlemanly way, John sent Ellen a crystal for her collection.

AFTER SHE WAS forced to renounce her acceptance of John, Ellen Sewall was sent to or chose to visit her uncle Henry's home in Watertown, on the Black River near Lake Ontario in northern

New York. Uncle Henry's daughter, Ellen's first cousin Mary, had attended boarding school with her. Back in Concord, however, Aunt Prudence kept Ellen updated with information about the Thoreaus. Thus Henry learned her address in Watertown.

On the first of November he wrote in his journal as if speaking directly to Ellen or drafting a letter to her:

> I thought that the sun of our love should have risen as noiselessly as the sun out of the sea, and we sailors have found ourselves steering between the tropics as if the broad day had lasted forever. You know how the sun comes up from the sea when you stand on the cliff, and doesn't startle you, but everything, and you too are helping it.

A few days later, while Ellen was staying in Watertown, she received a romantic letter from Henry, who asked her to marry him. He had learned about Indians, played the flute, and taught school as his brother did, and now he proposed to the woman who had refused John's offer of marriage.

This time Ellen consulted her father immediately and his response was predictable. He insisted that she reply at once to Henry and explain—with no possibility of misunderstanding—that she absolutely would not marry him. Ellen agreed with and understood the need for such a plan. That evening, although heartsick, she sat down and wrote a firm no to Henry. She had greatly enjoyed the company of both Thoreau brothers, and she realized that these proposals and her replies might end the easy communication between them.

Soon she was writing to Aunt Prudence in Concord, advising her to not allude to the proposal in letters. Perhaps, she suggested, Prudence could send a letter or two via Mother or Edmund until the family scandal cooled off. Then she added,

I do feel so sorry H. wrote to me. It was such a pity. Though I would rather have it so than to have him say the same things on a beach or anywhere else. If I had only been at home so that Father could have read the letter himself and have seen my answer, I should have liked it better. But it is all over now.

Two months later, Henry was writing in his journal, "When we are amiable, then is love in the gale, and in sun and shade, and day and night; and to sigh under the cold, cold moon for a love unrequited is to put a slight upon nature; the natural remedy would be to fall in love with the moon and the night, and find our love requited."

In her letters Ellen often asked Prudence about Henry. The next summer, eight months after his proposal, she read aloud some of his poems to friends of hers. They liked best "The Assabet," which began with the happy line, "Up this pleasant stream let's row." Later that day she wrote in her diary,

That is the first piece Henry gave me in "days long passed," "in years not worth remembering." I wonder if his thoughts ever wander back to those times when the hours sped so pleasantly and we were so happy. I think they do. I little thought then that he cared so much as subsequent events have proved.—But to quit this painful theme.

Chapter 12

MY FRIEND'S LITTLE BROTHER

B Y THEN A tall and personable twelve-year-old, Edmund
Sewall returned to Concord for the spring 1840 quarter with
the Thoreau brothers. When he arrived on a snowy evening in
March, nine months had passed since he first visited Concord and
inspired Henry's poem "Sympathy." This time he boarded with the
Thoreaus and slept with John in the same room in which the boy
and his mother had stayed the year before.

Although his courses were rigorous, Edmund enjoyed them. "A
very pleasant schoolmaster," he called Henry, in a letter home. He
liked that in this handsome schoolhouse every student had an individual seat. He dived into geography, Latin, geometry, and
composition, and he kept a journal in the writing book his aunt
gave him. When Henry advised him to write about a topic with
which he was unfamiliar, Edmund chose eagles and ostriches. "I
cunningly took half a sheet of paper to write on," he bragged to his
journal, "so on the whole I managed to fill out my pages."

Although homesick—he dreamed about his family and even
about the pail that he used at home to fetch milk—Edmund enjoyed
living with the Thoreaus. He tagged along when John went to the
post office and to Shattuck's store, where slight twenty-five-year-
old John climbed on the scale and was found to weigh only a

hundred and seventeen pounds. John ordered clams from Boston and cooked them for Edmund in a little vessel called a monkey. They visited the dour stone jail with its tall spiked wall, behind the Middlesex Hotel in the center of town.

One snowy day, Henry took Edmund and another student walking through a small, deep valley that Henry called Laurel Glen because of the luxuriant plants growing there. On their way home, Henry saw a slate-colored sparrow. It was one of his favorite birds, chubby and dark gray with a lighter bill, sometimes called a snowbird because often it returned with winter. He admired its cheerful jingling song, which he could hear from indoors. Henry wanted to examine the bird more closely, so he shot it with his shotgun, and he and the boys took the silent corpse with them. He may have wanted to demonstrate his marksmanship as well. At the pond he set a snowball on a post and blasted it, too, with the shotgun.

On another outing, John and Edmund and some other boys were caught in heavy rain. They huddled beneath hemlock branches, but still had to hide under their umbrellas. During a lull in the rain, John went out and returned with a large wood tortoise. He had also shot a towhee to show the boys. It was a dramatically patterned robin-sized songbird with a black hood, white waist-coat, and rich russet sides—a bird whose cheerful call of *drink-your-teeeaaaaa* was far more melodious than the sharp two-syllable exclamation *towhee*, or the sound that had provided its other name, *chewink*. After they examined it, John threw the bird into the river.

Henry took Edmund into the office of the Whig newspaper *Yeoman's Gazette*, where they watched a compositor set type. A descendant of Concord's first regular paper, the *Middlesex Gazette*, it had been founded on the Mill Dam in 1816. Then they went to the shop of Mr. Bratt, the gunsmith, who took time out of regulating a rifle's sights to show them around. Edmund admired a rifle that he hinted about in a letter home to his parents: "one nice little one just big enough for a boy of my size."

Henry and John believed in hands-on education, and probably they also enjoyed free assistance. As Henry plowed the potato garden, Edmund helped sow it. Students were even brought along after school to watch as Henry and John tarred the bottom of their boat with a mixture of half a pound of tallow to four pounds of resin. Later, when the boat developed a leak, Edmund and two other boys were assigned the task of patching it. After they dumped out the water and dried the boat, they heated an iron at Farrar's Blacksmith Shop, which was across the road behind the school, and used it to melt tar to patch the leak.

Frequently Edmund, like the adults who guided him, went to hear a lecturer at the Concord Lyceum. Once a phrenologist was scheduled to explain the predictive abilities of the shape of the head, but he arrived late. While impatiently waiting, Edmund stared in fascination at the phrenologist's equipment, especially the upper half of the skull of a British soldier that had been unearthed at Lincoln. A Minuteman's bullet had drilled a sharp hole in the cranium.

In early April, Emerson delivered a lecture on literature at the Lyceum. Henry invited Edmund and two other students. Afterward, twenty-two-year-old Henry considered how he might apply Emerson's thoughts to his own yearning life. "How shall I help myself?" he scrawled in his journal. He knew almost instinctively that the answer lay within himself. "By withdrawing into the garret," he replied, "and associating with spiders and mice, determining to meet myself face to face sooner or later. Completely silent and attentive I will be this hour, and the next, and forever."

Edmund Sewall, however, was only half Henry's age. "I was not at all interested," he wrote of Emerson's lecture. "He is a tall man with piercing blue eyes."

IN CONTRAST TO the well-educated Edmund Sewall was another good student, a bright but impoverished ten-year-old farm boy named Horace Hosmer. He was the younger brother of Benjamin and Joseph Hosmer from rural Derby's Bridge, Henry and John's childhood friends. It was Ben who had felled the angry ox with a single stone from his sling roughly a decade earlier. Horace came to school eager for knowledge. At a young age he had learned the alphabet from his mother's Testament, after which his sister tutored him. Most storybooks for children were dreary, but Horace was given an illustrated edition of John Bunyan's seventeenth-century allegory *The Pilgrim's Progress*, one of the few diversions that pious families permitted their children on a Sunday. Afterward Horace looked at the hills of Monadnock and Wachusett and saw the Delectable Mountains, imagined battling the giant Despair before scaling Doubting Castle, and felt at home in the Valley of Humiliation.

When his father walked the shy bumpkin to the Thoreau brothers' school in 1840, Horace was a stranger even to the village except for glimpses of it while walking to church. They entered through the door on the eastern side to find John's desk facing them from across the room. Boys were seated mostly to John's left and girls to his right.

John greeted Horace warmly and took him under his wing. "I want you to be a good boy and study," he said pleasantly, "because you are my friend's little brother."

Students came from diverse backgrounds. The quiet, pale fifteen-year-old who sat directly behind him turned out to be George Hoar, a son of Samuel Hoar. Two Cuban-born boys, Andrew and Alexander

Beath, sat in the row against the south wall, to Hoar's right. Several brothers and sisters came together—Sherman and Almira Tuttle, Gorham and Martha Bartlett. Hosmer cousins were scattered around. Horace often ate with the Thoreaus after school, as did other students who boarded with them. He was charmed by Henry's talkative and welcoming mother, and he considered Mr. Thoreau more refined, good-hearted, and well-spoken than the coarse and vulgar men he saw in other Concord families.

Surprised by his respect for his teachers, Horace didn't whisper with his neighbors during the entire first term, and he didn't notice other students whispering. Few sassed the Thoreaus, although neither teacher whipped, threatened, or even publicly reprimanded them. In fact Horace noticed that when John disciplined a child, he did it so quietly that other students seldom noticed.

Soon after Horace's arrival, John called upon him twice in class but the boy didn't reply. Worried that he was sulking, John quietly summoned Horace to his desk and asked him why he was ignoring his teacher.

Horace insisted that he had not heard his name spoken.

John peered closely at the boy and decided that he was telling the truth. As if in apology for questioning him in front of his classmates, John pulled out a couple of books to lend him—the Englishman Thomas Day's 1780s catchall *The History of Sandford and Merton*, cobbled from his own stories and those of others, and *Lazy Lawrence*, a popular excerpt from *The Parent's Assistant*, a 1796 collection of children's stories by the progressive Anglo-Irish writer and educator Maria Edgeworth. Although she was often didactic herself, Edgeworth aimed for more realistic and entertaining stories than the solemn tracts that had harangued her own youth. Horace, who considered any text superior to reading the New Testament aloud to squirrels, went back to his seat and happily dived into *Lazy Lawrence*.

John liked to provide treats. Sometimes students would find in their desks a slice of tangy citron melon, with its mottled blue-and-green skin framing white flesh speckled with light brown seeds. The first time this happened, Horace worried that a fellow student had maliciously stashed food in his desk, but as he ate the juicy melon his opinion of John rose even higher.

The syllabus also included recent works such as John Wilson's 1822 collection *Lights and Shadows of Scottish Life*. John thrilled Horace with his reading of Wilson's stories. He rousingly brought to life Gilbert Ainslee, a character in the story "Moss-Side" who struck a chord in Horace's imagination, perhaps because he reminded him of his father: "Labour, hard and unremitting, had been his lot in life."

Early in the day came literature study, called "defining," which Horace loved. Students had to recite and elaborate upon prose and poetical texts. One day they disastrously mangled William Cowper's long poem "Needless Alarm." After one hundred and thirty dull lines, Cowper's moral appeared: "Beware of desperate steps. The darkest day / Live till to-morrow, will have passed away." The students' painfully labored attempt to decipher this poem ended when young Edward Wood offered his own cautious summary: "Look before you leap!"

At which point a tired and bored John jumped out of his chair, exclaiming, "*Very good* indeed!" and finally the village literary critics and their teacher were free to move on to another topic.

Chapter 13

LOG CABINS AND CIDER

F OR HENRY AND John and their neighbors, the 1840 presidential campaign was a contentious topic in Concord, as it
was in the rest of the country. For the previous three years, since
Henry graduated from college, the financial depression had influenced voting in both state and national elections. For this and
other reasons, the campaign turned out to be the most feverish
and contested the young nation had yet seen. President Martin
Van Buren, a Democrat, was blamed for much of the crash, in part
because he had refused to intervene with failing banks. Many
preachers, however, argued that the financial crisis was God's
punishment for impiety and intemperance, favorite charges lobbed
toward Democrats. Irate Protestants also denounced the Catholi-
cism tainting the Democratic Party, as well as former president
Andrew Jackson's barbaric treatment of Indians—and Van Buren
had been Jackson's vice president.

Shortly after he began taking classes with the Thoreaus, young
Horace Hosmer discovered that he was not only the youngest and
smallest pupil, but also the only boy in the school who had not been
brought up to consider himself a Whig. Like most children, he
parroted the political bias of his parents. Horace suffered much chaffing, not all of it good-natured, and had to weather the occasional

playground fight. He found the battle so tiring he was glad to have Saturdays away from the other students, even though it meant missing John Thoreau's weekend excursions to Egg Rock and Sleepy Hollow, to Walden Pond and the boiling springs, during which he taught students about geology and botany.

John was vocal about his Whig politics and loudly embraced the motto "Tippecanoe and Tyler Too!" as his own. The campaign's rallying cry had been inflated from a minor military victory back in 1811. The Whig candidate William Henry Harrison, then a general and the governor of Ohio although a native Virginian, had led a thousand soldiers against a rising Indian confederation headquartered at Prophetsown, which the mystic and revivalist Tenskwatawa had built upon the ashes of the venerable village Keth-tip-pe-can-nunk (called Tippecanoe by most whites) after U.S. soldiers razed it to reduce Indian power in the region. In the battle, Harrison's troops triumphed against a much smaller force of poorly armed Indians. John Tyler, who was brought in as Harrison's vice presidential candidate, had grown up in the same area of Virginia as Harrison, but unlike him was still associated with it. As a steadfast supporter of states' rights—which usually meant a supporter of slave-owners' rights—he could court the Southern vote.

Harrison's presidential campaign—his second—was rife with exaggeration and myth. Formerly perceived as aloof and superior, Whigs this time imitated the populist methods of Democrats and magically transmuted the sixty-seven-year-old, wealthy, and aristocratic Harrison into a vital, homespun man of the people. They placed this fiction in opposition to their version of the insider machinations of Van Buren and sent Harrison out to woo the populace. Never before had a presidential campaigner made so many stump speeches or shaken so many hands. Such shenanigans kept Henry skeptical about politics.

Democrats mocked Harrison's age and dubbed him "Granny," suggesting that he was fit only for retirement: "Give him a barrel of hard cider and . . . he will sit the remainder of his days in his log cabin . . ." Their disdain backfired. The Whigs embraced both log cabin and cider as populist emblems. A number of Henry and John's students dutifully wore rattan Log Cabin hats and shirt pins; many boys carried the requisite cane with a hard-cider barrel as its head. One Ciderite badge was a silk lapel ribbon showing a Harrison portrait draped in flags and topped by an eagle, with below him a rustic frontier cabin. Above the eagle floated a banner inscribed THE PEOPLE'S CHOICE and below the cabin POOR MAN'S FRIEND. Newspaper cartoons contrasted two visions of the next four years—under Harrison, prosperity and families merrily picnicking; under Van Buren, royal coaches and families going a-begging.

"He leaves the plow to save the country," declared some Log Cabin artifacts. This clever allusion invoked Lucius Quinctius Cincinnatus, a hero of ancient Rome—a patrician who fell on hard times and worked a humble farm until called upon to serve as dictator, after which brief period he returned to private life. The educated class of Henry's and his parents' generation esteemed Cincinnatus as an ideal of civic virtue. His name also brought to mind George Washington, who was considered equally noble and civic-minded for returning to private life after having been granted so much power as president. How much to serve or resist the state, how imperialistic the new nation should try to be, where allegiance should lie, how to define freedom and citizenship—these topics were discussed in newspapers and around Concord pickle barrels, and as Henry grew older he found such themes more and more relevant to his own daily life.

★   ★   ★

ON THE FOURTH of July 1840 Henry rose before sunrise, as usual, and went outdoors to crickets and a dawn breeze. Nearby he found the Light Infantry from Townsend—a small town on the northern edge of Middlesex County, along the New Hampshire border—encamped in a neighbor's field, their linen tents drenched in dew. Henry watched admiringly as soldiers stirred. Uncertain about his own role in the world, often lecturing himself about how he ought to behave, Henry envied soldiers' structured and committed lives. They seemed innately heroic, as if every day they woke with lofty passions, fated for valor.

Outside a tent, a handful of infantrymen gathered with bugle, fife, and drum. They launched quietly into an old Scottish air. No one, Henry thought, could be a coward after waking to the strains of this hymnlike tune, which drifted across the sleeping fields as if it had distilled from dreams that floated in the night from one sleeping man to the next. Then the morning gun sounded and more men emerged from tents. The holiday was under way.

The Fourth was always a big day in Concord, but this year regional Whigs turned it into a Harrison political rally. With cheap cider as a campaign tool, the Concord taverns did a rousing business. It was another hot, sunny day in Middlesex County; since late June, a drought had been baking eastern Massachusetts. The three roads that led into Concord were clogged with noisy travelers, including twelve hundred from Lowell alone. Members of many regional Harrison clubs flooded into town. Carriages and wagons filled the streets; canal boats clogged the river; herds of walkers marched in from every direction. One of the campaign's giant wheeled log cabins was hauled into town by twenty-three straining, lathered horses whose hooves drummed the dry earth, with a hundred and fifty Harrison supporters on board, many of them drunk. These cabins had been featured in many such gatherings, especially back in early May, when the national Whig convention in Baltimore ratified the nomination of Harrison and Tyler, as merchants closed their stores and crowded onto balconies and rooftops alongside their customers.

The Great Ball also arrived on the Fourth, having been rolled at the front of a parade from West Cambridge by many strong-armed men pulling its ropes, and was parked in the Main Street yard of factory owner David Loring. It was twelve feet high and covered in buckskin stretched over a wooden framework—naturally painted red, white, and blue. Little Horace Hosmer walked over and read on its huge and dirty surface inscriptions from campaign songs and slogans:

O'er every ridge we'll roll this ball,
From Concord Bridge to Faneuil Hall

Farewell poor Van,
You're not the man
To guide our ship.
We'll try Old Tip.

Watching from among the jostling roadside crowd, Emerson admired the ball's unlikely grace as it climbed hills and rolled down slopes. "The simplest things are always better than curiosities," he wrote in his journal later. Henry agreed. Although he claimed to dislike hubbub, instead of escaping to the woods on this always drunken and sometimes violent holiday he strolled amid the noisy crowd to watch the ball arrive. A few days earlier he had written in his journal, out of his usual preoccupation with the idea of innate grace, "A man's life should be a stately march to a sweet but unheard music, and when to his fellows it shall seem irregular and inharmonious, he will only be stepping to a livelier measure, or his nicer ear hurry him into a thousand symphonies and concordant variations." The political Great Ball struck him as symbolic in this body-metaphor vein. Often uncomfortable inside his own body, and seldom an admirer of another person's form, he contrasted the Ball's graceful roll with what he saw as the ungainly tread of human beings. "The line of beauty is a curve," he wrote that night. "What shame that our lives, which should be the source of planetary motion and sanction the order of the spheres, are full of abruptness and angularity, so as not to roll, nor move majestically!"

The campaign ball, like the rolling log cabin, was joined by another new development in this campaign, and one likelier to appeal to Henry—songs. Previously, satirical periodicals had often included verses fiercely lambasting candidates, but now this libelous doggerel was set to tunes that became an integral part of rallies. All day on the Fourth, Concord's streets rang with raucous, drunken songs. "We could meet the Whigs on the field of argument and beat them without effort," the poet and jour-nalist William Cullen Bryant had complained in the *New York Evening Post* not six weeks before Independence Day. "But when they lay down the weapons of argument and attack us with musical notes, what can we do?" Often, to make them easier to remember, campaign songs were set to the tune of established classics or catchy popular songs. "Old Tippecanoe" was sung to the tune of "Rosin the Bow," and "The Last Whig Song" to "Old King Cole." The folk song "When This Old Hat Was New" simply acquired new lyrics under the same title and tune, in a Democratic ditty that represented the Whigs as disguised Federalists, which wasn't far from the truth: "When this old hat was new, the Feds despised the poor, / And blushed if ever they were caught within a cabin door."

The folk tune to which Robert Burns had written "Auld Lang Syne" in 1788 also found itself with new lyrics, as a Democratic rebuttal of the Harrison myth:

Oh, no, he never lost a fight—he's even bullet-proof
For why? Whene'er the battle raged, he always kept aloof . . .

'T was very lucky for him too—It was, it was indeed
The more he didn't get a wound, the more he didn't bleed.

The tone of political discourse was changing quickly. Only a few months earlier, in December 1839, Daniel Webster, the legendary Massachusetts senator and conservative orator, had returned from a diplomatic visit to England. He had danced at balls and met Her Majesty, the twenty-year-old Queen Victoria, while wearing court dress of white satin waistcoat and smallclothes— the old-fashioned tight knee breeches that had been replaced by trousers in most situations—and silk stockings with diamond shoe and knee buckles. To campaign for Harrison among homespun Americans, in contrast, Webster wore a practical wide-brimmed hat and a coat of humble linsey-woolsey. Webster also had to tame his public speaking style. In keeping with the revolution in political oratory, he altered the delivery of his notoriously long speeches, which ranged from one hour to three or more, from grand and classically allusive to earnest, colloquial, and at least seemingly extempore.

Webster was still best known in the Thoreau family, however, for an incident that occurred around 1805, long before Cynthia's sister Louisa Dunbar became Henry's Aunt Louisa. Although he was never her beau, back then Webster occasionally drove the innocent young Louisa in his shay and talked so earnestly about religion that she always credited him with her own conversion.

ALSO IN THE crowd that Henry prowled on that hot busy day was John Keyes, whom John and Henry had recently bested in romance again. Mary Russell, a twenty-year-old friend of Lidian from Plymouth, was spending the summer of 1840 with the Emersons as Waldo's tutor. Keyes was smitten with her, but, like Ellen Sewall the summer before, she preferred the company of the Thoreau brothers. Undaunted, Keyes accompanied the trio to visit a Penobscot Indian camp on the river, where he tried to get Mary to help him gather cardinal flowers, a task that would take them away from Henry and John. She quickly mustered two excuses—she had forgotten to bring a shawl and clouds were building up for rain—but Keyes was not deceived. "The Thoreaus," he muttered to his diary, "were the real excuse."

Like Henry, Keyes didn't admire much about Harvard except a few of his brighter fellow students; he hated the points-counting regimen and felt that instructors behaved like enemies of the students. Not quite nineteen years old, he was so excited about Concord's role in the campaign that he returned from school a few days ahead of the big day. Surrounded by pretty girls he had invited for the occasion, he admired the festivities from a commanding vantage point sixty feet in the air, inside the octagonal cupola atop the newly remodeled courthouse facing Monument Square.

Keyes and his entourage watched a slow, dense parade—which he estimated to include between four and five thousand revelers—pass from the battleground north of town to the square below and on to the grassy lot between central Concord and Sleepy Hollow, at the edge of which the New Burying Ground had been established in

1823, on the site of an Indian cemetery. On the lot a huge booth and speakers' stand had been erected during days of hammering and sawing. Then Keyes squired his companions over to the rowdy crowd at the booth, where they were given free crackers and hard cider, which they nibbled and sipped while listening to rousing speeches about the virtues of Harrison and the vices of Van Buren. Keyes enjoyed seeing in person some of the great regional names of the Whig Party. Several speakers were staying at the Keyes home, on Main Street across from the Thoreau boardinghouse. The night before, one had frightened Keyes with a death-rattle wheeze during an asthma attack.

Toward the end of the day, the tipsy, sunburned crowd filed into the largest tent ever seen in Concord, measuring 175 by 200 feet, for more barbecue and hard cider. After the events were over and the drunken crowd had trickled away from the trash-filled field, Keyes went to a wedding reception at the Thoreau home. A couple of days later, the weekly *Yeoman's Gazette*—which was distinctly more pro-Whig than its former incarnations, the *Middlesex Observer*, *Middlesex Gazette*, and *Concord Gazette and Middlesex Yeoman*—called the Independence Day event "The Great Harrison Barbecue."

A FAMILY OF newcomers strolled Concord on that Fourth of July—Bronson and Abigail May Alcott and their three daughters. They had moved to Concord in early April. Nine-year-old Anna was enrolled in the Concord Academy. The bookish Louisa May, who was seven and a half, and Lizzie, who had just turned five, were taught by Mary Russell, the Emersons' tutor. Abigail was eight months pregnant with a fourth child. They were destitute—with some meals consisting of bread and water—yet Abigail sang to herself as she did tasks around the cottage that they occupied for a modest annual rent of fifty-two dollars, while Bronson worked lackadaisically at whatever manual labor he could muster. They were glad to have a roof over their heads.

At the encouragement of Emerson, his longtime supporter, Alcott had brought his family to Concord following a principled but exhausting scandal in Boston. In late 1834, Alcott had launched, in the new four-story Masonic Temple on Tremont Street, a progressive academy called simply the Temple School. Influenced by revolutionary German ideas about early childhood development, Alcott was adamantly opposed to corporal punishment—going so far as to make his point by having a couple of boys strike him instead of his striking them. He was just as passionately in favor of a questioning dialogue and of encouragement rather than reproof. Meanwhile at home he was writing his own "Observations on the Spiritual Nurture of My Children." There was considerable interest in such an educational endeavor. One idealized magazine illustration showed Alcott standing behind a podium opposite a floor-to-ceiling arched window speaking with a semicircle of young pupils while parents lolled on a divan.

Unfortunately, despite his admirable goals and unquestioned ability with children, Alcott's pride went before his fall. Smug in a near-messianic sense of his own spiritual superiority and educational genius, he was a man who could tolerate almost no disagreement. He criticized the mothering skills of his devoted and affectionate wife, and gradually he alienated other close supporters, including his assistant teacher Elizabeth Palmer Peabody. A young Boston woman barely five feet tall, invariably disheveled and distracted, Peabody was full of drive and intelligence and personality. Devoted to Alcott's ideals and goals, she had published an admiring account of his efforts, *Record of a School*, in 1835.

But scandal emerged in response to Alcott's teaching methods. He encouraged open conversation among students about the Bible rather than delivering pronouncements from on high. December 1836 saw publication of his book *Conversations with Children on the Gospels*, which one Boston newspaper denounced as dangerously flippant; one journalist described Alcott as "either insane or half-witted." The uproar led many parents to withdraw their children, but Alcott worked on alone, having alienated his various assistants. His final sin, in the eyes of Boston, was admitting a Negro child to his classes. Soon the Temple School closed.

Emerson had never lost faith in Alcott. His invitation and assistance had drawn the family to Concord, where Alcott immediately met Emerson's young protege and thought highly of Henry's intelligence and independence.

IN JULY 1840, shortly after the campaign ruckus, the first issue of Transcendentalism's own journal, *The Dial* ("A Magazine for Literature, Philosophy, and Religion"), was published, swaddled in a wrapper bearing its manifesto:

> The purpose of this work is to furnish a medium for the freest expression of thought on the questions which interest earnest minds in every community.
>
> It aims at the discussion of principles, rather than the promotion of measures; and while it will not fail to examine the ideas which impel the leading movements of the present day, it will maintain an independent position with regard to them ...
>
> The DIAL, as its title indicates, will endeavor to occupy a station on which the light may fall; which is open to the rising sun; and from which it may correctly report the progress of the hour and the day.

Bronson Alcott had suggested the journal's title, and in his editorial preface to the first issue Emerson unpacked its implications: "And so with diligent hands and good intent we set down our Dial on the earth. We wish it may resemble that instrument in its celebrated happiness, that of measuring no hours but those of sunshine. Let it be one cheerful rational voice amidst the din of mourners and polemics." After claiming that there had been considerable private demand for this kind of journal, and complaining that no one else had come forth to create it, Emerson expressed his ambitious dreams for *The Dial*:

> We do not wish to say pretty or curious things, or to reiterate a few propositions in varied forms, but, if we can, to give expression to that spirit which lifts men to a higher platform, restores to them the religious sentiment, brings them worthy aims and pure pleasures, purges the inward eye, makes life less desultory, and, through raising man to the level of nature, takes away its melancholy from the landscape, and reconciles the practical with the speculative powers.

Most contributions to the inaugural issue were signed with a single initial, such as Channing's poem "To the Aurora Borealis," or Henry's poem "Sympathy," inspired by his response to Edmund Sewall the year before. The issue also included Henry's first published essay, "Aulus Persius Flaccus," in which, while ostensibly critiquing the Etruscan-born Roman poet Persius at Emerson's request, Henry worked in numerous vague observations from his journal. Margaret Fuller had not been enthusiastic about Henry's essay on Persius, but Emerson had lobbied for its inclusion in what he called "our bold bible for The Young America." Reluctantly accepting Emerson's nudges, Henry had revised it to their satisfaction.

Alcott's fragmentary "Orphic Sayings" were the only signed contributions in the first issue, so he alone bore the ridicule later heaped upon them. He hadn't been in Concord long when he presented the manuscript to Emerson, in the hope that he would include the "Sayings" in the planned journal. They comprised a rambling hodgepodge of brief pronouncements, mostly vague and derivative, on a variety of topics. Hidden within was a celebratory Transcendentalist worldview, but Alcott's turgid attempts at profundity obscured it. One observation headed "Faith" was typical: "Sense beholds life never,—death always. For nature is but the fair corpse of spirit, and sense her tomb . . ."

Even Emerson found little to admire in the "Sayings," but he recommended to Margaret Fuller that they publish a few excerpts. Soon after Fuller came on board as editor of *The Dial*, she discovered that Transcendentalists were not a unified or even a well-defined group. "I believe we all feel much alike in regard to this Journal," Emerson admitted to her. "We all wish it to be, but do not wish to be in any way personally responsible for it." Knowing that the enterprise could not succeed financially and might not intellectually, Fuller cautiously accepted the thankless task of editing *The Dial*. Educated in the classics by her father, Fuller was, at thirty, establishing herself as a promising intellectual and writer. Following her first visit—three weeks at Bush in 1836—Emerson wrote in his journal that Fuller was "a very accomplished and very intelligent person." After she taught herself to read German, 1839 saw the acclaimed publication of her translation of Johann Peter Eckermann's weighty *Conversations with Goethe*. She omitted so many passages that it was later called an abridgment, but the preface alone built her an immediate reputation for critical insight and lucid prose.

Fuller had worked with Alcott at the Temple School in Boston. "One grave thing I have to say," Emerson warned her, "this, namely, that you will not like Alcott's papers; that I do not like them." They suffered, he thought, from Alcott's usual flaw as a writer—"cold vague generalities." Nonetheless, thirteen pages of them appeared in the first issue. The untitled opening one built upon the notion of a sundial, and how Alcott's "heart, a soul-flower" turned always toward the sun. The fifth, "Vocation," was a Transcendentalist theme that Henry had long since adopted: "Engage in nothing that cripples or degrades you. Your first duty is self-culture, self-exaltation: you may not violate this high trust."

"A train of fifteen railroad cars with one passenger," the *Boston Post* called the "Sayings." They irreparably damaged Alcott's reputation, which already had attracted mockery. The critic James Russell Lowell soon wrote of him, "When he talks he is great but goes out like a taper / If you shut him up closely with pen, ink, and paper."

Alcott pasted even the most mocking reviews into a scrapbook.

Chapter 14

MELODIES AND INVENTIONS

I N JUNE 1840, Henry had filled the last of 546 pages in his red journal, the book he had opened in October of 1837 with the heading *solitude* and the quoted words, *"Do you keep a journal?"* The diary was becoming ever more important to him. On the thirty-first of January 1841, only six months later, he filled the last of 396 pages in another volume, closed it, and opened a third.

He needed the journal for talking with himself. He kept reminding himself to pay attention, to look more closely at fleeting life. "The present seems never to get its due," he wrote in early February; "it is the least obvious,—neither before, nor behind, but within us." But he also examined his own often awkward behavior: "Any exhibition of affection—as an inadvertent word, or act, or look—seems premature, as if the time were not ripe for it; like the buds which the warm days near the end of winter cause to push out and unfold before the frosts are yet gone." Looking critically at the craft of expression, he was aware of his tendency to speak in metaphor and simile. On the same day, he wrote, "The unpretending truth of a simile implies sometimes such distinctness in the conception as only experience could have supplied."

Early 1841 saw Henry taking stock of his life amid major changes. After rashly exploring the February snowfields "without great coat or drawers," as he noted in his journal, Henry spent a restless time indoors with another exhausting bout of bronchitis. He hunched in a cozy corner by the wide fireplace, sometimes so close to the crackling flames that he could glimpse a rectangle of blue sky at the top of the chimney. Before this seclusion, however, he had approached another local man about renting property, a farmer who replied that he had four acres with soil as good "as any out doors," so Henry consoled himself with dreams of privacy. Nothing came of this inquiry.

In early March, he was invited to join Brook Farm, a new utopian community about to be launched in West Roxbury, near Boston. Founded by the Unitarian minister and reformer George Ripley and his wife, Sophia, Brook Farm joined several dozen other idealistic communities active around the United States at the time. It was unique, however, in its secular approach—explicitly not a religious community but a social cooperative in which each contributor would commit to a share in the manual labor and ultimately receive a share of the farm's profits.

"If wisely executed, it will be a light over this country and this age," Ripley had written in late 1840 to Emerson, a fellow founding member of an informal group nicknamed the Transcendental Club. "If not the sunrise, it will be the morning star." He went on to explain his dream:

> Our objects, as you know, are to insure a more natural union between intellectual and manual labor than now exists; to combine the thinker and the worker, as far as possible, in the same individual; to guarantee the highest mental freedom, by providing all with labor, adapted to their tastes and talents, and securing to them the fruits of their industry; to do away with the necessity of menial services, by opening the benefits of education

and the profits of labor to all; and thus to prepare a society of liberal, intelligent, and cultivated persons, whose relations with each other would permit a more simple and wholesome life, than can be led amidst the pressure of our competitive institutions.

The Ripleys, Alcott, and Margaret Fuller visited Bush in mid-October 1840 to discuss Brook Farm. "I wished to be convinced," Emerson sighed to his journal afterward, "to be thawed, to be made nobly mad by the kindlings before my eye of a new dawn of human piety." But he did not thaw. "What a brave thing Mr. Ripley has done!" he wrote to Margaret Fuller, but then added, "At the name of a society all my repulsions play, all my quills rise and sharpen." He declined the invitation.

Henry, although passionately interested in combining the thinker and the worker in himself, and in encouraging others to do the same, also refused. He doubted that utopian goals could be achieved on other than an individual basis. "As for these communities," he wrote in his journal, "I think I had rather keep bachelor's hall in hell than to board in heaven."

Henry was touched at this time by a gift from Emerson—a day before the book's official publication date, a copy of his new collection *Essays*. Several struck a chord with Henry, such as "Self-Reliance." Emerson inscribed the book to "Henry D. Thoreau, from his friend, R. W. E.," but in his journal reverted to Henry's real order of names, "D. H. Thoreau." Aware of just how much Emerson had helped and inspired him, Henry confided to his journal, "To be associated with others by a friend's generosity when he bestows a gift is an additional favor to be grateful for."

Because it looked as if John's uncertain health might oblige them to close their little school, and perhaps because the situation with John was strained after their mutual interest in Ellen Sewall, Henry was looking around for work outside Concord. In early March, he read an advertisement for the position of assistant teacher at the Perkins School for the Blind in Watertown. It would have been fascinating work. The school had opened in 1832 as the New England Asylum for the Blind. The wealthy merchant Thomas Handasyd Perkins—a Boston Brahmin heir who had also been an opium smuggler in Turkey and a slave trader in Haiti—had donated his Boston mansion, and the school had been renamed in his honor. Henry applied but did not get the job.

He liked to maintain both his spiritual and financial accounts. Besides working with his father in the pencil business and helping maintain the Thoreau boardinghouse, Henry was careful to pay his family for ongoing room and board. The day after the vernal equinox, he did some accounting on the back of a poem:

Dec. 8, 1840—Owe Father	*$41.73*
Paid, Dec. 17	*5.00*
Jan. 1, 1841	*15.00*
Borrowed, Feb. 2nd	*1.35*
Paid, Feb. 8th	*10.00*
Settled up to March 22nd, 1841	

A week later, Henry's finances took a turn for the worse. He and John closed their school. The enterprise had never prospered much beyond its own maintenance, and John's health was suffering. He could no longer summon the energy to rise every day and teach a flock of children. The family realized that his tuberculosis was growing more severe. He was frail. Immediately John took a trip to New Hampshire, where the air was thought to be more nourishing. Adrift, Henry began asking friends again if they might know of teaching positions or other jobs.

One day in April, he was in his attic room when he heard someone downstairs in the kitchen tap the tea kettle with a metal object,
perhaps tongs or a coal shovel. It rang like the cowbells of his childhood. Instantly Henry recalled rambling across the Great Fields,
picking flowers and berries, drifting down the lazy river of a summer
afternoon. He decided that the brass bell dangling around a cow's
neck meant more to him than the tons of cast metal clanging in
belfries. He believed more in the message of the former, even if it
was only an echo chiming across the years.

MONEY WAS SHORT. On the twentieth Henry worked hard
shoveling manure out of a pen, earning seventy-five cents for the
day. Then his mentor rescued him again. Emerson invited Henry to
live with him and Lidian at Bush in a typically generous arrange-
ment. "He is to have his board &c for what labor he chooses to do,"
Emerson wrote to his brother William, "and he is thus far a great
benefactor & physician to me for he is an indefatigable & a very
skilful laborer & I work with him as I should not without him." In
this letter as in many others, he professed faith in Henry's potential:
"Thoreau is a scholar & a poet & as full of buds of promise as a
young apple tree." To Carlyle, at about the same time, he reported
that he and Henry worked together in the garden, and described
Henry as "a noble manly youth full of melodies and inventions."

During Emerson's frequent lecturing travels, Henry would
attend to household needs and serve as occasional companion and
adviser to the children and Lidian. His departure from the Thoreau
boardinghouse might free up an extra room to rent, and living rent-
free at the Emerson house he could still contribute to the family's
income. He settled into a cozy little room at the top of the stairs. In
contrast with the Thoreau home, quiet, shaded Bush housed no
boarders—only a trickle of high-minded guests whose company

Henry came to enjoy—and a handful of servants, Lidian, their young son Waldo, and the man Henry most admired in the world. Soon he wrote to a friend, "I am living with Mr. Emerson in very dangerous prosperity."

Henry was not the only new inhabitant at Bush. Margaret Fuller had arrived for a fortnight's stay. As tutor the Emersons had hired Mary Russell, with whom Henry had enjoyed outings the summer before. A year later, living around her every day, with his feelings for Ellen fading, Henry fell into another infatuation. Apparently little resulted from it except a poem he dedicated to her, "To the Maiden in the East," which he wrote after her departure in the autumn.

After Mary Russell, Henry stopped mentioning romance or young women in his journal except in an occasional mocking remark. Clearly there was no pressure in his family to marry. Two years older, John was still single; so were Helen, the eldest, and Sophia, the youngest. For that matter, many members of the family from the previous generation had remained single—Cynthia's sister Louisa and brother Charles Dunbar, Maria and Jane Thoreau, and many others. Henry would have stood out more if he had actually courted and married a woman.

"I WANT TO go soon," Henry muttered to his journal on Christmas Eve 1841, "and live away by the pond." The next day he wrote flatly, "I do not want to feel as if my life were a sojourn any longer. It is time now that I begin to live."

Halfway through his twenty-fifth year and more aware every day of fleeting time, he redoubled his focus on nature and literature. Carefully reading Chaucer, he noted his admiration for the poet's "sturdy English wit," his unadorned diction, and his seemingly unlimited sympathy for others. Always practicing his own expression, Henry turned a description of nature into a metaphor for the process of recalling it: "In memory is the more reality. I have seen how the furrows shone but late upturned, and where the field-fare followed in the rear, when all the fields stood bound and hoar beneath a thick integument of snow." He watched snow falling with the attention that Leonardo had devoted to water flow. He observed that distant flakes in a snowstorm seemed to quiver in the air, hovering like almost invisible birds, while closer to his eyes the flakes seemed to dive straight toward the ground. "So, at a little distance, all the works of Nature proceed with sport and frolic. They are more in the eye and less in the deed."

On the last evening of 1841, indoors in the cold beside a blazing fire, ecstatic with the love of the outdoors and of literature inspired by it, he wrote in his journal,

> Books of natural history make the most cheerful winter reading. I read in Audubon with a thrill of delight, when the snow covers the ground, of the magnolia, and the Florida keys, and their warm sea breezes; of the fence-rail, and the cotton-tree, and the migrations of the rice-bird; or of the breaking up of winter in Labrador. . . . I should like to keep some book of natural history always by me as a sort of elixir, the reading of which would restore the tone of my system and secure me true and cheerful views of life.

The end of the year inspired self-analysis, or at least self-observation. On a separate sheet, not in his journal, he scribbled playful autobiographical notes:

> I am about five feet 7 inches in height—of a light complexion, rather slimly built, and just approaching the Roman age of manhood. One who faces West oftener than East—walks out of

the house with a better grace than he goes in—who loves winter as well as summer—forest as well as field—darkness as well as light. Rather solitary than gregarious—not migratory nor dormant . . .

Then he went to bed, with 1841 behind him.

Chapter 15

NEAR TO THE WORLD OF SPIRITS

H ENRY WAS HAPPY in the new year, scribbling away in his room at the top of the stairs in the Emerson house. He read Walter Raleigh and listened to a music box. Downstairs, over the fire, he popped popcorn—a food he loved—for the Emerson children. He would arrive with ears of popcorn in his pockets, climb to the attic to retrieve the old brass warming pan, and slowly heat the corn over the big fire. Gradually the rattle of kernels changed to popping. When the pan reached its peak of fireworks inside, Henry would hold it in his firm patient grip above the laughing children seated on the rug and lift the lid as the popcorn spilled out and showered them. One night he noted in his journal that heating the kernels in a pan created "a more rapid blossoming of the seed under a greater than July heat."

He enjoyed these domestic evenings with the children. Finally named after several weeks without an official identity, little Edith was not yet three months old. Lidian had wanted to name her Lucy Cotton after her mother, but Emerson had resisted, still arguing that the child be named Lidian, which Lidian herself refused. Ellen was a charming and lively two and a half. Waldo was five and busier than ever, his father's pet and acolyte. Daily his grandmother taught his reading lesson and he was making progress in spelling. Waldo was curious about everything, picking up and deciphering each item in his father's study—magnet, globe, microscope. He loved tools and would walk around carrying pincers or a hammer. He liked to bring his share of wood for his grandmother's fire, and he was fascinated by the kinds of coal his father used in the study fireplace. Calm and grave, he would explore the barn and examine the hens' nests and survey the doghouse.

Now that Henry had lived in the Emerson household for a year, he and Waldo were fast chums. Firm and gentle and as serious as his young charge, Henry could whittle or mend toy guns and unsinkable boats that Emerson could never match. Henry helped Waldo with an ongoing construction project—a toy house, to parts of which the boy gave fanciful names such as the *coridaga* and the *interspeglium*. Waldo loved to blow the willow whistle that Henry had carved for him. Once when a storm rumbled nearby during his performance, he interrupted himself to exclaim, "My music makes the thunder dance!"

After ending 1841 with an ode to nature and natural history books, Henry began the new year thinking about the judgmental aspects of Christianity. "The practical faith of me belies the preacher's consolation," he scrawled in his journal. Happy in his poetic longings and his heresy, he wrote, "There is no infidelity so great as that which prays, and keeps the Sabbath, and founds churches."

NEW YEAR'S DAY 1842 dawned cold. It was a Saturday. At the Thoreau home that afternoon, John was stropping his straight razor, prior to shaving, when he slightly nicked his left hand. It was a tiny cut on the tip of his ring finger, barely slicing off a flap of skin that he simply pressed back over the slight wound and wrapped tightly with a small piece of rag. It didn't bleed much.

The cut caused John only minor inconvenience over the next couple of days. Then, rather than healing, it began to hurt again. John removed the bandage and found that while one side of the piece of skin had grown back to the rest of the fingertip, as he expected, the other side was mortified—had developed gangrene. Such changes were alarming, but he thought that probably the wound would heal.

On Saturday, the eighth of January, Henry was at home rather than at the Emerson house. Most of his family were ailing and needed tending. John's finger hurt enough that he couldn't help much around the house, so Henry did most of the work.

That evening John finally consulted a doctor. Most people turned to physicians only as a last resort, when despair convinced them to submit to the medical arsenal of calomel as a purgative, ipecac as an emetic, the laxatives castor oil and senna, and a regimen of molasses-and-sulfur (picturesquely called treacle-and-brimstone in England). A familiar sight around the village and countryside, tall, long-nosed Josiah Bartlett had practiced medicine in Concord since shortly after his graduation from Harvard Medical School in 1819, following in the footsteps of his near-legendary medical father. The junior Bartlett bragged that in all his years attending ill Concordians, only once had weather prevented him from reaching a patient, and that was when snow was so deep that his sleigh overturned every couple of rods. Even then, determined to proceed, he had unharnessed the horse and climbed astride its bare back—only to slide down across its rump and crupper as the horse floundered through belly-high drifts. Bartlett must have found this mishap humiliating, because he was a proud horseman, known for riding and driving at a horse's top speed. It was Bartlett whom Henry and John had gently refused two and a half years earlier, when he requested that they take his son on their river adventure.

Bartlett was a committed reformer who joined the Concord Social Club in 1822 and thereafter was involved in many local issues. In his everyday work, he saw the devastating effects of drink, which turned him into a crusader against its abuse, especially by laborers, among whom alcohol was considered good for a strong man. Too often he had watched hard-drinking patients succumb to disease or surgery that a healthy constitution would have overcome. In 1834 he had joined with his fellow physician Edward Jarvis—who, during the 1826–27 school year, had been Henry's teacher—to survey sales of wine, beer, and whiskey by every trader and tavern keeper in Concord. Drink was not an issue in the Thoreau family, certainly not with upright, gentlemanly John, who had even gone so far as to publicly sign a temperance pledge. He debated a long time before doing so, worrying about the loss of his own independence because he would feel bound by a public declaration of moral behavior. He wouldn't commit to the temperance stance until he felt he fully agreed with it.

On this day Bartlett removed John's bandage, examined the tiny cut, then cleaned and dressed the wound. Assuming that this would be the end of the matter, John started walking home in the cold winter evening. On the way he began experiencing acute pain in various parts of his body, some of it so strong he could barely make his way back to the big white Thoreau boardinghouse.

The next morning, Sunday, family friend Nathan Brooks came to get Henry at the Emerson house and reported John's horrifying new symptom: his jaw muscles were stiffening. By evening violent spasms racked his body. Everyone in the family knew what these symptoms meant. They presaged a disease that had tormented humanity as far back as history remembered—tetanus, or lockjaw as it was usually called because its symptoms included stiffening muscles of the mouth and throat. Constantly warring humanity had long ago recognized a link between battle wounds and the fatal convulsions that sometimes followed. Gradually people realized that sometimes an innocent mishap could have the same tragic result; centuries before Christ, Hippocrates recorded a death from tetanus that resulted from a minor wound to a finger. As recently as 1809, the Scottish anatomist and surgeon Charles Bell had painted a terrifying portrait of a tetanus victim in final spasm, with his head and heels supporting his arched body like the abutments of a bridge. From clenched toes and corded calves, the figure curved upward and back down to fists held close and a flung-back head grinning like a jack-o'-lantern. The Thoreau family may not have known, but surely Dr. Bartlett did, that with bitter irony tetanus often left its victims grinning. *Risus sardonicus*, the ancients called the rictus resulting from contraction of the facial muscles in death.

The family quickly arranged to consult a doctor from Boston, but to no avail. He told John that he would die very soon, that he wouldn't suffer long but that his death would be painful.

John accepted this warning without hysterics or even visible shock. But he couldn't resist asking quietly, "Is there no hope?"

The doctor had seen too many cases of lockjaw. Whatever caused it, like whatever caused so many other ailments, was unknown, invisible, and unstoppable. His reply was simple:

"None."

When he learned his fate, John quoted the words that Jesus uttered after Pilate's men came for him in the garden by the brook Cedron. After Simon Peter drew his sword and slashed off the ear of the high priest's servant, Jesus ordered him to sheathe his weapon. Then he asked the question that John Thoreau quoted: "The cup that my father gives me— Shall I not drink it?" John added quietly that he knew he was going to die, but that God had always been good to him and he would trust Him now.

Through his remaining few days of pain and fear, the family was impressed to find that John tried to be as playful and serene while dying of lockjaw as he had been while climbing Nawshawtuct Hill in search of Indian arrowheads. Henry saw glimmers of John's calm former self even in his brother's last delirium. Henry embraced John in death as he had in life. He tended his brother's every need for his remaining time.

After John bade farewell to his devastated mother and father, to tearful Sophia and Helen, he said to Henry, "Now sit down and talk to me of nature and poetry."

Henry sat beside his brother.

With the good humor that had made him popular in better times, John said through stiffening jaws, "I shall be a good listener, for it is difficult for me to interrupt you."

As Henry talked, delirious John smiled in a way that seemed to his desperate brother in this moment to transcend the endless suffering that plagued the world. Henry found himself sympathetically smiling back. Contorted in pain, John died early Tuesday afternoon, the eleventh of January, only ten days after nicking his finger and three days after the first symptoms appeared. Henry was holding John in his arms when he gasped his last choking breath.

ON WEDNESDAY MORNING, Henry returned to the Emerson house to pick up his few articles of clothing and other items. His family needed him at home. He told Lidian that he didn't know when he would return. She could see that Henry barely kept from breaking down, but she admired his attempt to be stoic and even, though unconvincingly, cheerful.

Lidian asked Henry if, when John first became aware of his fate, he had reacted with shock.

"None at all."

The funeral sermon was delivered by the Reverend Barzillai Frost of Concord's First Parish Church. In 1837, the year that Henry graduated from Harvard, Frost was ordained as a colleague of Dr. Ripley. Now, five years later, only a few months after Ripley's death, he would be preaching John's funeral. A graduate of both Harvard's College and its Divinity School, Frost was highly qualified, but his discourses inspired mixed emotions in Concord. In an address at Harvard's Divinity School, Emerson had parodied Frost: "The snowstorm was real; the preacher merely spectral." Frost was notorious for his unintentionally funny asides, which challenged the sober facial expressions of the congregation, as when he remarked during a sermon, "The Lord hath dealt graciously with this people this year. He has spared us from the pestilence that walketh in the darkness and the destruction that cometh at noonday. True, we have had some chicken-pox and some measles."

During the service, Frost recited some lines from a poem that John had written a few weeks before his death and given to Sophia.

Noble! the sympathetic tear!
Feeling we would not smother;
Knowest thou not that Jesus here,
Wept for a fallen brother?

Bid thou thy sacred grief to flow;
And while to man the tribute's given,
Thou shalt communion with the "Father" know,
Thy tear's a passport unto Heaven.

"Can it be possible," Frost asked from the pulpit, "that that face, which greeted us but yesterday in our streets, with such an open brow, and bright smile, we shall see no more on earth? . . . It brings us very near to the world of spirits. It makes our present possessions seem like shadows." It was a long-winded and discursive oration, in which Frost inflated every grain of John's character into material for a sermon. Yet Lidian Emerson considered the eulogy worthy of the admirable young man she had known.

At some point after their brother's death, Sophia was talking with Henry and mentioned John's affection for Ellen Sewall and his proposal to her on the beach at Scituate a year and a half earlier.

For some reason, Henry feigned innocence: "Did John love her too?"

He kept a lock of his brother's hair.

SOON THE ALREADY devastated Thoreau family had to face another crisis. Shortly after John's funeral, Henry's calm self-possession began to collapse. He sat staring into space, doing nothing, saying nothing. He didn't reply to questions. Although exhausted themselves, Sophia and Helen tried to help Henry, who seemed to be steadily declining. They led him outdoors to try to interest him in nature, but to no avail.

Then, terrifying everyone, Henry came down with the same symptoms that had forecast the death of John. When Emerson returned from a trip on Saturday the twenty-second, Henry seemed in the throes of lockjaw. No one knew what caused the disease— not where it originated or how it might be communicated, except that typically a cut was involved. But when a doctor examined Henry, he found no cut anywhere, not even a scratch. For two or three days Henry lay with muscles stiff and jaws clenched. Then the attack seemed to fade, as if he had survived it. But people did not survive lockjaw. Perhaps, the family decided, Henry's sympathy for John's pain had overwhelmed him in his loss. Just as he had imitated aspects of John's life—following him into teaching, studying

Indians, and proposing to the same young woman—so Henry imitated his death.

By the twenty-fourth of January, Emerson was describing the incident mostly in the past tense, adding cautiously, "You may judge we were all alarmed & I not the least who have the highest hopes of this youth. This morning his affection be it what it may, is relieved essentially, & what is best, his own feeling of better health established." Emerson went on to mention that he had been invited to a dinner honoring Charles Dickens, who had just arrived in Boston aboard the *Britannia* for a highly publicized tour of the United States. The young English writer's fifth novel, *Barnaby Rudge*, had completed serialization only a couple of months earlier in Dickens's own weekly periodical *Master Humphrey's Clock*. Then came the update on the children. Emerson reported an incident that had taken place on Monday night, when Waldo dictated a letter to his cousin Willie, thanking him for sending a magic lantern. "I wish you would tell Cousin Willie," he said from his bed, "that I have so many presents that I do not need that he should send me any more," and then he added, "unless he wishes to very much."

Then, as if the Thoreau and Emerson families had not suffered enough by losing John, little Waldo was struck with scarlet fever. Soon he had the sore throat, rash, and fever that characterized this scourge of small children, and on the evening of January 27, little more than two weeks after John's death, he lost the fight. Emerson thought the boy sighed his last small breath like a bird. Afterward, Emerson and Lidian and Mrs. Jackson wept and talked for hours. Then the others went away. Immediately Emerson began writing brief letters to family—his brother William, Lidian's sister Lucy, and others.

Needing to care for the baby and for two-and-a-half-year-old Ellen, Lidian sat up most of the night in the bedroom. With her husband sleeping elsewhere in the house, she took Ellen into their bed to comfort her. During the long dark hours, she felt that she was living two lives simultaneously, as scenes of each raced before her mind—one of her brief past time with lively, curious Waldo, and one of the long, empty-looking years ahead without him. So compelling were these painful visions that when daylight came and the others in the house stirred again, Lidian was surprised to find that only a few hours had passed since Waldo's death. Emerson was at his desk, writing to Margaret Fuller, "Shall I ever dare to love any thing again." Waldo's cold little body was still in the house.

But the Emersons' was the first generation to possess a new kind of memento after the death of a loved one—a daguerreotype. This brilliant new invention, which had been announced as recently as 1839 at a meeting of the Académie des sciences in Paris, was already being touted as a miraculous machine to preserve time. Originally exposures had taken hours or days, but over the last couple of years the process had been improved. A positive image, reversed as if in a mirror, was produced directly on a silver-iodide-coated copper plate, the result so sensitive to smudging that it had to be isolated under glass, inside a frame or a folding case.

Daguerreotype portraits still required excruciatingly slow exposures. Children posing for a photograph had to be coaxed into premature solemnity. The previous autumn, other friends and family members had been unable to talk the restless Waldo into sitting still long enough for the slow, boxy camera to capture his image. Only John had prevailed. At his behest that day at the photographer's studio, Waldo, dressed in a dark girlish smock with a light ruffled collar, had sat in a wooden armchair with his hands folded in his lap. Thus the Emersons could gaze at a framed oval daguerreotype of Waldo—his expression solemn and faraway, his hair parted in the middle with bangs combed sideways into temporary obedience. His sculpted thin lips, so like his mother's, had had to remain grave and still. Like the unrecorded movements of people strolling Paris boulevards as Daguerre took his early photographs, laughter was invisible to cameras, and even smiles faded while the inhumanly patient shutter waited for enough light to seep in. A person's likeness could be preserved, distilling memories into a sober gray portrait magically drawn with light, but the fleeting gestures—smiles, raised eyebrows, the sparkle of life—were lost.

BOTH HENRY AND Emerson turned to their journals for private exclamations of grief. On the twenty-first of February, after a trip to Providence, Emerson returned to a house that felt deserted. "Dear friends find I," he scrawled to himself, "but the wonderful Boy is gone. What a looking for miracles have I! As his walking into the room where we are would not surprise Ellen, so it would seem to me the most natural of all things."

Just before John died, Henry had been confiding to his journal excited hopes about the future. Now, on a completely different path than the one he had envisioned, his days aching with loss, his every thought carefully stepping around the hole where John had stood, Henry could only wish that there might be no such thing as past or present or future. He wanted to escape the relentless linear rush of time. "Why does not God," he wondered to himself, "make some mistake to show to us that time is a delusion."

On the second of March, Henry wrote his first letter in many weeks, to Lucy Brown, to whom he had given the bouquet wrapped in his poem "Sic Vita" four years earlier. He tried his Transcendental best to sneak past the reality of his grief to grasp a symbol. "I do not wish," he told her and himself, "to see John ever again—I mean him who is dead—but that other whom only he would have wished to see, or to be, of whom he was the imperfect representative. For we are not what we are, nor do we treat or esteem each other for such, but for what we are capable of being." Of John he wrote, "Soon the ice will melt and the blackbirds sing along the river which he frequented, as pleasantly as ever." Then he thought in similar terms about the loss of Waldo: "Neither will nature manifest any sorrow at his death, but soon the note of the lark will be heard down in the meadow, and fresh dandelions will spring from the old stocks where he plucked them last summer."

For weeks, Henry lay in bed and stared at the ceiling. His interest in the natural world, in the life of the village, in his family—all faded away. He read little and seldom wrote in his journal. Eventually he became aware of his numbness and, typically, he wondered whether other creatures were ever plagued with this kind of malaise. Did not their dull animal routines bore them? He thought about hens on their nests in a hayloft, perched atop an egg as if gestating an idea, day after day, night after night—just sitting there. Did they have thoughts enough in their primitive brain to distract them from such a mindless task? Or did they sink into an unfeeling ennui? Do hens, he wondered, sleep?

Such thoughts distracted him only briefly from the ache of loss. "Where is my heart gone," he wrote in his journal. It was a question without a question mark, because there was no answer; "—they say men cannot part with it and live."

His need for the outdoors was slow to return, as he spent day after day indoors, staring at walls, being cared for by his sister and mother. Finally, in mid-March, he went for a solitary walk in the woods. Beforehand, he tried to find a book about nature that he could slip into his pocket, but he failed to locate among the dry pages any observations that advanced into the forest even as far as his own thoughts. So he went out with only memories to accompany him.

The sun shone brightly. He saw old people sniffing the air after the long winter and young people working in the dark bare fields. Color was returning to the earth, in the veined green leaves of skunk cabbage peeking up from the swamp, in the cardinals dashing across the blue sky that was revealed as the wintry white clouds withdrew. For the first time in far too long, he felt aware of the world, and then gratitude for it washed over him. The sounds of life poured back into his ears—the wood-and-metal rattle of a shay on the road, the slurred whine of a phoebe repeating its name. A song sparrow, with one brown spot like a smear on a painter's smock, whistled grace notes and burst into liquid song. Henry heard a bluebird chortling and a robin belting out *cheerily cheerily cheerily*.

Alone at the pond, he admired the new form of a pine branch that had fallen into the water some time ago. Lathed by sun, wind, and current, it now lay clean and white in a new element, its upright former life forgotten.

Part 3

ECHO

Chapter 16

HAWTHORNE'S NEW BOAT

T HE SPRING OF 1842, shortly after the deaths of John Thoreau and little Waldo, found a tired and sad Emerson managing a different kind of family burden. His step-grandfather, the Reverend Ezra Ripley, had died the previous autumn. Death at the age of ninety did not strike his family as tragic, but to Emerson it seemed the end of an era. "Great, grim, earnest men," Emerson the former minister said to them in his journal, "I belong by natural affinity to other thoughts and schools than yours, but my affection hovers respectfully about your retiring footprints, your unpainted churches, strict platforms, and sad offices; the iron-gray deacon and the wearisome prayer rich with the diction of ages."

As one of Ripley's heirs, Emerson became unofficial agent of the Manse and surrounding property and soon needed to find tenants. The seventy-two-year-old clapboard building housed many of his own memories. After his return from a trip to Europe in 1833, he had resided with his mother for a year in Newtown before moving in with the elderly Ripley at the parsonage in October 1834. He lived there until he married Lidian the next year and they moved to Bush with his mother. During his year in the Manse he had written *Nature*.

In early 1842, Henry's friend Elizabeth Hoar brought the parsonage's virtues and availability to the attention of a close friend of hers in Boston—a talented young painter, Sophia Peabody, sister of Elizabeth Peabody who had worked at the Temple School with Bronson Alcott. Sophia was engaged to marry a writer named Nathaniel Hawthorne. On their first visit in May, Emerson greeted the couple-to-be when they came to the front door and raised the massive iron knocker adorned with a sphinx's head. Outside, the old house's white coat of paint had long since faded to a dismal gray, but indoors Hawthorne and Sophia loved the parsonage's high paneling and heavy beams. In Ripley's study, on the second floor above the dining room, the walls dark with generations of soot were typical of what they did not admire about the house. The room was rendered more glum by prints of dour divines who, to Hawthorne's skeptical eye, looked as if they had grappled with the devil until his satanic majesty had rubbed off on them.

Across narrow Monument Street, in front of the house, rose Poplar Hill, which in one direction provided a fine view of the village and in the other a view of the river and distant mountains. The field beside the house was known to have been the site of an Indian village, and arrowheads and shards of pottery could still be found there. Indoors, from the study's west window, Hawthorne could see—past the drooping willow that filtered light and brushed against the eaves and glass—Ripley's extensive orchard and the sparkling river. Hawthorne liked this haven's "accessible seclusion," the way their tree-shaded lane distanced the road and reduced carriages and wayfarers to irrelevance. Silently awkward with strangers, Hawthorne was not a misanthrope, but like Henry Thoreau he needed solitude. He had spent years in near-seclusion before meeting Sophia. He admired and worried over the human pageant from the margins, the same vantage point from which Henry disdained it. Until meeting Sophia, Hawthorne had been a solitary watcher, a man who fell silent in groups but loved quiet conversation with one or two friends. Yet here he was hopelessly in love. For the moment, at least, they filled each other's world and left no need or space for others.

They were pleased with the parsonage, and Emerson rented it to them for seventy-five dollars per annum. They needed a quiet hideaway in which Hawthorne could write and they could build a marriage and a family. Emerson needed a tenant but wanted an ideal one, and he thought that in Hawthorne he might have met his goal. A mutual friend observed to Margaret Fuller, "He seems pleased with the colony he is collecting."

Hawthorne was indeed a coup for Emerson's dream of an artistic community in Concord. Ever since the publication of his 1837 story collection *Twice-Told Tales*, Hawthorne's reputation as an American original had been growing. Even Edgar Allan Poe—a young but influential poet, critic, and conjuror of outré fictions—remarked when reviewing *Twice-Told Tales*, "Upon the whole we look upon him as one of the few men of indisputable genius to whom our country has as yet given birth." Although he complained about Hawthorne's frequent reliance upon allegory, Poe praised his imagination and style. Both writers were lauded for painstakingly crafting stories that built toward a single powerful effect, leading the creation of a new genre distinct from the rambling, discursive narratives of the eighteenth century. Although the first volume had not sold well because the Panic of 1837 led to the publisher's closing, a second volume of *Twice-Told Tales* had been published in late 1841, only a few months before Hawthorne knocked on Emerson's door.

Hawthorne also swore to himself that he would write another novel—*a* novel, as he said, because almost no one knew that he had also written the anonymous *Fanshawe*, inspired by his undergraduate years at Bowdoin College. He published it at his own expense in 1828, when he was twenty-four. Hawthorne kept a tight grip on his privacy, but about this not-at-all scandalous novel he was abso-lutely secretive, finally gathering up and burning every copy he could find. Not even Sophia knew he had written it.

On their wedding day, the ninth of June 1842, as the carriage from Boston trotted down the avenue of leafy green ash trees, the Hawthornes found the wheel tracks almost overgrown with weeds in the nine months since Ripley's death. An elderly white horse and a couple of cows wandered the path, noisily munching tall grass. The newlyweds found, however, that at Emerson's request a garden had been tilled and planted for them. They learned that Emerson had hired John Garrison, a Negro handyman who had worked for him before, and an odd young white man named, Hawthorne wrote in his journal, "Henry Thorow." It was one of Henry's first tasks out in the world following recuperation from his breakdown after John's death.

PHYSICALLY, HAWTHORNE AND Henry were antonyms. A trim hundred and fifty pounds at just under six feet tall, with luxuriant dark locks, Hawthorne was legendarily good-looking. When Elizabeth Peabody first met him, she exclaimed to Sophia, "You never saw anything so splendid as he is! He is handsomer than Lord Byron!" He had always been too shy to exploit his looks, but Sophia thought him a figure worthy of a classical marble. Hawthorne had been equally dazzled by her—a beautiful woman with chestnut hair and blue-gray eyes, who had been the object of masculine attention throughout her twenties despite health problems, including severe headaches. Soon she inspired an idealized character, a young woman named Alice Vane, in Hawthorne's story "Edward Randolph's Portrait": "She was clad entirely in white, a pale, ethereal creature, who, though a native of New England, had been educated abroad, and seemed not merely a stranger from another clime, but almost a being from another world."

Intellectually and philosophically, Henry and Hawthorne had more in common. In some ways, Hawthorne's bent was Transcendental. He thought in metaphors and sought to suffuse most phenomena with moral resonance. Preoccupied with sin and suffering, however, he was inherently less hopeful about the future and the prospects for social change than his new neighbor Emerson, and more hard-headed and realistic in his assessments of humanity. Like Emerson and Henry, he was preoccupied with reflections and shadows and echoes, with the oblique way that a scene's or incident's implications could evoke a greater creative or philosophical response than more explicit observations.

Recently he had experienced a vivid example of this propensity in himself. In Boston before his marriage, he had loved to stroll the Common and watch children play at the Frog Pond. Boys sailed accurately detailed schooners and pilot boats across the water, with one boy on the near shore and another on the far, like merchants separated by the Atlantic. At sunset, the Common became the meeting ground of young lovers, dandies in gloves and cane, girls rolling hoops, mothers holding the hand of a small child, and the occasional salty old tar who couldn't resist critiquing the authenticity of a toy clipper's draft or rigging. One sunset, Hawthorne watched a full-rigged man-of-war whose every rise on a swell or heel to the breeze seemed like that of an actual ship on the ocean. "There is something that kindles the imagination," he wrote at the time, "more than the reality would." A real ship would have been grasped immediately by the mind and filed away as a mundane artifact that lacked symbolic resonance. The Lilliputian mimicry of the toy ship, in contrast, was a representation, and thus evoked an absent ideal.

Haunted by his own family's past, Hawthorne had even created a different identify for himself. Just as David Henry Thoreau had turned himself into Henry David, Hawthorne modified his surname to distance himself from a notorious ancestor. He was born Hathorne, the great-great-grandson of John Hathorne, the son of an early settler in Massachusetts Bay and the only judge who never admitted regret for his role in the witch trials held in the early 1690s in Ipswich, Salem, and elsewhere in Massachusetts. Nathaniel Hawthorne may have changed his name to distance himself from his notorious ancestor, or he may have wanted to return to an earlier English variant of the name. Tracing his ancestry back to the dark early days of America's first European settlers, and every year celebrating the same birthday as the United States, Hawthorne at times seemed like a walking crossroads of American history.

Unlike Henry, who gloried in autonomy but admitted to loneliness, at least within the confines of his journal, and unlike Emerson, who often communicated with Lidian by means of notes carried from room to room by servants, Hawthorne saw the world through a romantic haze and felt himself now part of an indivisible couple. They had been secretly engaged since New Year's Day 1839, and as recently as the first week of June, Sophia had postponed the wedding because of one of her recurring illnesses. Despite her worry that health would prevent her from being the best possible wife for her dashing husband, finally they had married, in the parlor of the family's home and her sister's establishment, called Elizabeth Palmer Peabody's West Street Bookstore. The talented and dynamic Elizabeth was later business manager of *The Dial.* "We are as happy as people can be, without making themselves ridiculous," Hawthorne wrote to his sister a month later, "and might be even happier; but, as a matter of taste, we choose to stop short at this point."

This new secluded, romantic life was a world away from the exhausting and disappointing months in 1840 that Hawthorne had spent hoeing the barren soil at Brook Farm, where his thousand-dollar contribution earned him an assignment to shovel a mountain of manure. The months of backbreaking work in bitter cold, the meager provisions, the dissent among his fellows—all seemed like a nightmare now in this generous new life. Among his acquaintances, utopian dreams were discussed from lecture podium to dinner table and during long rambles through the woods in which dreamers hoped to found a just community. But Hawthorne had found his utopia on his own, with one other person—Sophia. The pleasures of the marriage bed had come as a glorious revelation to a man who had once bet a friend that he would remain a lifelong bachelor. "Would that my wife would permit me to record the ethereal dainties, that kind Heaven provided for us, on the first day of our arrival!" he exclaimed in the privacy of their shared journal. "Never, surely, was such food heard of on earth—at least, not by me."

Like the fictional Alice Vane in the story she had inspired, Sophia was a talented artist. With no reputation of her own yet, she had sold numerous impressive copies of famous works, to help feed Boston's post-Puritan appetite for artwork. Most of the Hawthornes' cheap furniture was ordinary maple, so Sophia made it colorful and unique by painting on it. A cherub cavorted on the dressing table; Venus rose from the washstand; Michelangelo's prophets and sibyls held court on the dining room wall. On the bed's headboard Sophia painted a striking copy of a seventeenth-century Roman fresco by Guido Reni—his famous *Aurora*, a parade of classically robed figures and chariot-pulling horses flying through the air, their saffron and coral hues heralding the arrival of the goddess of dawn above a sleeping blue earth. Years earlier, Thomas Carlyle's wife had sent a print of this very painting to Lidian Emerson as a wedding gift. Numerous glimpses of it had inspired Henry to begin a poem that he never finished, as a tribute to his favorite time of day: "The slumbering sea with the day's impulse heaves, / While o'er the western hill retires the drowsy night . . ."

Hawthorne settled into Ripley's study. They banished gloom with bright paint and a bronze vase of ferns; the gold-colored paper hangings would have struck Ripley as indecently cheerful. Hawthorne imagined old Ezra's ghost peering in the windows and moaning in confusion. He joked that perhaps posthumous outrage was behind the inexplicable sounds they heard around the house—an occasional clatter in the kitchen, a pounding like a workman's repairs in the study, even a piece of paper being crumpled near them in the bedroom as Hawthorne lay half asleep. Hawthorne's ragtag collection of books, mostly from discount-stall foraging, stood upright on the shelves. He was the first occupant of the study who did not write sermons. There Ezra Ripley had scrawled three thousand and Ralph Waldo Emerson had crafted his own secular sermon. At times Hawthorne felt that his fictions seemed light and airy beside the solemn thoughts whose memory lingered in the shelves.

On the last day of August, a wet Thursday, Henry rowed the green-and-blue *Musketaquid* up the river to the Hawthornes' house. Around him trees waded in floodwaters, their lower boughs dipping into the current, and the scarlet caps of cardinal flowers bobbed just above the surface on what had been the bank. Henry left his boat with a young man on the riverbank and walked up to eat dinner with the Hawthornes. After the pleasant and talkative meal, which included the first muskmelons and watermelons harvested from the garden that Henry had planted at Emerson's behest before the newly-weds moved in, Hawthorne and Henry strolled along the sopping riverbank. The boat was now on the opposite shore. Henry shouted to the man minding it, who rowed it back across the river.

Hawthorne and Henry climbed in. Henry rowed equally well with one paddle or two, and Hawthorne admired his calm and instinctive control. In reply Henry bragged that when Indians had visited Concord a few years earlier, he realized that without instruction he had hit upon an Indian-style method of paddling a canoe. But the rough little *Musketaquid* was not as graceful as a canoe.

To Hawthorne's surprise, Henry said that he wanted to sell the boat, apparently without mentioning that he and John had built it together. He asked only seven dollars. Hawthorne agreed, wishing that he could buy Henry's boating skills as cheaply.

The next day Hawthorne wrote at length about Henry in his journal:

> Mr. Thorow dined with us yesterday. He is a singular character— a young man with much of wild original nature still remaining in him; and so far as he is sophisticated, it is in a way and method of his own. He is as ugly as sin, long-nosed, queer-mouthed, and with uncouth and somewhat rustic, although courteous manners, corresponding very well with such an exterior. But his ugliness is of an honest and agreeable fashion, and becomes him much better than beauty. He was educated, I believe, in Cambridge, and formerly kept school in this town; but for two or three years back, he has repudiated all regular modes of getting a living, and seems inclined to lead a sort of Indian life among civilized men—an Indian life, I mean, as respects the absence of any systematic effort for livelihood.

On Friday, Hawthorne was picking up windfall apples in the orchard with Sophia and Louisa—the part-time servant they barely managed to employ—when he looked around to see Henry rowing across the hay field toward them. The swollen river had flooded the ground where men had wielded scythes a week or two before. Delivering the boat to its new owner, Henry floated above the earth, with the sky reflected around him in the brown floodwaters.

Hawthorne stepped into the boat. This sort of talent did not come naturally to him, although Henry assured him that if he relaxed the craft would move in whichever direction he willed. Hawthorne was skeptical. When pulling hard on two oars, he could propel the boat in approximately his desired direction. With one oar, however, switching it from side to side, Hawthorne failed so dismally that he was mortified to find Sophia watching on the bank. The enchanted craft lurched first toward one shore and then the other, pivoted as if to consider going upstream or down, then chose a third direction. Henry took over to demonstrate again. As soon as the oar was in his hands, the boat turned docile and obedient. Hawthorne thought perhaps it had yet to transfer its affection to its new master and decided that it was unlikely he would venture as far in this craft as Henry had. Recently Hawthorne had informed his journal, "A perfect pond-lily is the most satisfactory of flowers." He renamed the *Musketaquid* the *Pond Lily*.

Henry walked off homeward, leaving behind the boat in which he and John had rowed the Merrimack. Almost exactly nine months had passed since that ordinary morning when John nicked his finger while shaving. As the ache of loss receded, Helen had advertised in the *Concord Freeman* that she was opening a private school in Concord to teach young ladies piano, needlework, and painting. Apparently there was little interest, however, and she abandoned the idea.

AFTER HE BOUGHT the boat from Henry, Hawthorne experienced another powerful demonstration of his own imagination's response to nature. Over the next few weeks, as autumn crept in, Hawthorne spent less time rambling across Concord's wooded hillsides. In love with the new perspective brought to him by the *Pond Lily*, he spent his free hours on the water. On the afternoon of the seventeenth of September, less than three weeks after purchasing the boat from Henry, left alone after Sophia and her mother walked over to the Emersons', Hawthorne took the boat out by himself.

Rowing with difficulty against a quarrelsome northwest wind, he explored the north branch of the Concord. Every time he stopped paddling, the wind swept the boat around. Only in the shelter of a high wooded hill was he able to pause, because both the wind and current did. He passed a phalanx of aspens and elders leaning low toward the water as they marched down a high bank—"the Indian name of which I have forgotten," he later wrote in his journal, "although Mr. Thorow has told it to me." Vines wound around the trees. This stretch of the river felt as secluded and primordial as any that might have flourished before the arrival of Europeans.

Already some trees were wearing their autumn scarlet and gold. Now and then a leaf floated lazily down to the surface of the water and revolved slowly in the current. Trees cast deep shade except where sunlight angled through leaves. The scene was as beautiful as any that Hawthorne could recall, but when he glanced at its reflection he found it even more stirring. "I am half convinced," Hawthorne wrote in his journal, "that the reflection is indeed the reality." Somehow the mimicry was more what his spirit yearned for.

Chapter 17

A SKATING PARTY

H AWTHORNE AND HENRY got along well and soon became friends. The homely local boy taught the handsome author to watch for arrowheads—hidden stone splinters unearthed in plowing, crudely wrought in contrast to machined weapons but easily distinguishable from stones and earth. These relics romantically conjured for Hawthorne, as they did for Henry, a lost race.

Like Emerson and other advocates of Henry's talent and potential, Hawthorne tried to draw attention to the odd young man who could garden, boat, or write with equal facility. Hawthorne knew that Epes Sargent, an editor and playwright in New York— his drama *Velasco* had been admired by Edgar Allan Poe—was preparing to launch his own periodical, *Sargent's New Monthly Magazine*. "There is a gentleman in this town by the name of Thoreau," Hawthorne wrote to Sargent by October, finally spelling Henry's name correctly, "a graduate of Cambridge, and a fine scholar, especially in old English literature—but withal a wild, irregular, Indian-like sort of fellow, who can find no occupation in life that suits him. . . . He is somewhat tinctured with Transcendentalism. . . . The man has stuff in him to make a reputation of; and I wish that you might find it consistent with your interest to aid him in attaining that object."

In the autumn of 1842, Henry wrote to a friend about John's death, scribbled poems, and was elected, over his own feeble protests, curator of the Concord Lyceum, which meant that he would be responsible for attracting lecturers. He went to Alcott's to meet the English utopian Charles Lane. He had the satisfaction of seeing eight of his poems published in the tenth issue of *The Dial*—one of which, "To the Maiden in the East," he had written during his brief infatuation with Mary Russell. But few responded to Henry's poetry with applause. In November, he submitted more poems to Emerson, who found the same faults that he had often confided to his journal or to friends: slipshod meter, near-miss rhymes, a roughness like a wooden post with the bark left on. Henry was not interested in polishing his poems to a formal gloss; he wanted to get the idea down and take aim at his next poetic target. "Last night," Emerson wrote in his journal, "Henry Thoreau read me verses which pleased, if not by beauty of particular lines, yet by the honest truth, and by the length of flight and strength of wing; for most of our poets are only writers of lines or epigrams."

Whatever his opinion of Henry's poetic wings, Emerson rejected all of his new poems. At about this time, Henry became so despondent over his frustration with writing, and apparently over Emerson's ongoing criticisms, that he gathered many of his poems and tossed them into a fire.

THE WINTER OF 1842–43 was a cold, difficult time in Concord, with the thermometer sinking to its lowest point in recent memory. Sometimes Hawthorne wrote until dinner at two, then slogged through the snow to the Athenæum to read until dark, with a stop at the post office. He was working hard. In Philadelphia, James Russell Lowell and Robert Carter had recently founded an intellectually ambitious literary periodical called *The Pioneer*. Unlike many magazines, it emphasized new American writing, not reprints of European work. Its first issue, dated January 1843, published Edgar Allan Poe's feverish fantasy "The Tell-Tale Heart." Unfortunately *The Pioneer* survived for only three issues, but during its brief life it published two of Hawthorne's stories.

When Hawthorne wasn't writing fiction, he was filling his notebook with ideas and observations. Like Emerson and Henry, like so many other intellectuals of the time, both Sophia and Nathaniel were longtime diarists. They took turns writing in a large notebook covered in bright marbled paper, its spine and corners bound in red leather. Like Henry's journals, it was a volume built to last. Hawthorne's entries varied from detailed notes about his new surroundings to quick jottings of ideas as they passed through his mind, such as "A letter, written a century or more ago, but which has never yet been unsealed." He imagined someone picking up in the street a stray leaf from the book of Fate. "A stove," one brief note read, "possessed by the Devil." Soon he wrote a story narrated by the Concord town square's water pump. He tended to jot a note and add a remark along the lines of "What moral could be drawn from this?" or "It might be made emblematical of something."

Despite their hard work, the Hawthornes raced into winter like children. The first snowstorm found them in Sleepy Hollow just east of the square, where cut stalks of the summer's field of Indian corn lay buried under snow. The newlyweds slid down hills together, their laughter echoing from the pyramidal chestnut trees and the knotted arms of the oaks that surrounded the hollow on all sides.

The Concord's slow current froze quickly in winter, after flooding lowlands for miles, thus providing wide clean surfaces for skating. Ice-skating was as popular in winter as sleighing. At times both river and pond were covered with laughing skaters and the fields musical with the jingling bells of horse-drawn sleighs. In December, at the bottom of the Hawthornes' orchard, the often flooded meadow transformed into an Arctic sea. After a day in which Hawthorne wrote while Sophia sewed or painted or read, they would spend a cozy hour together in his study before dressing warmly and venturing out to cavort through sunset and into twilight. Hawthorne skated in a way that his adoring wife thought majestic, as if he lost his terrestrial shyness and acquired heroic grace. Wrapped in his fluttering dark coat, he cut nimble, sweeping curves away from her across the ice, only to glide back on whispering skates and circle her and dart away again.

Sophia herself liked to run and slide on the ice instead of skating. Often they saw other skaters, always boys or young men, never women. Few women skated. When Dr. Josiah Bartlett's wife's sister, Sarah Alden Bradford, visited Concord in the early 1820s, she impressed the locals by skating with energy and grace, but Concord women were slow to follow her daring example, at least publicly.

One afternoon Henry and Emerson joined Hawthorne for a skating party. Sophia watched from the window as they paraded by on the river. At home on the ice from countless forays since childhood, Henry led the way with an energy and abandon that Sophia found both impressive and ungainly. As if suddenly ecstatic, he cavorted in what she soon described to a friend as "dithyrambic dances and Bacchic leaps." Second in line was Hawthorne, gliding across the surface with his usual solemn grace, appearing to Sophia's eyes like a Greek statue propelling itself. Then came Emerson, seeming half asleep, tilting forward at the waist until his top half was horizontal, as if he napped by reclining on the air itself. Soon, exhausted, Emerson came indoors to rest, joining Sophia by the window. He said that her husband reminded him of a tiger or satyr whose energy might be the death of an ordinary mortal such as himself. He beamed a kind smile at her. "Mr. Hawthorne is such an Ajax, who can cope with him!"

★   ★   ★

EVERY YEAR HENRY was thrilled anew to find how quickly he could travel on the river's ice. He had come to know the transformed winter river—the marbled gray ice in the bays, the darker marbling where clear water pooled underneath. Where a crack crossed the surface, water sometimes oozed out and froze two or three inches thick in a space up to a few feet wide. Skating over these caused a jolt. After he got used to skates again each winter, Henry would soon recklessly race down even a foot-wide strip of ice between shore and water. He loved the freedom to follow the windings of a stream. He would whisper along on his skates and be surprised to reach a particular bend in the river or a tributary brook sooner than expected—with much less effort than trudging across snowy hills and through muddy bogs. Even brisk walkers on the shore seemed motionless while Henry flew across the ice. He felt as if he had winged feet, like Hermes.

Nor was this magical stage silent. The crack of the moving ice sounded one moment like aural chain lightning and the next like the call of a pigeon woodpecker—*a-week, a-week*. Once, as Henry skated across a stretch of river during a melt, a large area of ice forced up by the water settled on another section of ice, causing a crash and producing a small pond in the frozen river. Soon he learned that a couple of hours later, the next skater found the lines of Henry's trail across the ice, saw them vanish into water, and then was astonished to find them reappear on the ice at the opposite side of the melt.

Often Henry saw fishermen dragging a sled across the surface of Fair Haven Pond, leaving behind a hole surrounded by white chips of ice that bounced the sunlight like mirrors. From a distance, the tableau of pickerel fishermen seemed epic, even though they merely stood with their hands deep in the pockets of heavy cloth dreadnaughts and stirred their underwater thoughts. Every year, as soon as the ice was hard enough to withstand a man's weight, fishermen were out on the transformed water, even on Sundays. Heretically free himself on Sabbath mornings, Henry thought the fishermen performed their own kind of devotional, and he suspected that judgmental preachers dined on illicit pickerel come Monday.

One winter day, Henry was skating across the frozen surface of the pond when he saw ahead on the ice the vivid reddish-brown flash of a fox. Quickly he skated in its direction. When Henry slowed his pursuit, the fox sat on its dark haunches and barked at him in a way that made Henry think of descriptions he had read of young wolves. But the instant that Henry skated more quickly toward the fox, it leaped up and raced ahead at what seemed its top speed. Yet it never quite ran away. Experimentally, Henry stopped skating and waited. The fox also paused. It walked a dozen feet to one side, then sat down and aimed its black eyes and black-tipped ears at Henry and barked—a whispery nasal squawk most unlike a dog's bark, as well as quite different from the mechanical gekkering of cubs or a vixen's whine to her mate. Then it rose and trotted in another direction and sat down and barked again. It seemed held captive, a fixed distance away. But when Henry launched after it again, the fox was instantly up and running. Perhaps it enjoyed the game, too.

"Plainly the fox belongs to a different order of things from that which reigns in the village," Henry remarked to his journal the next day. "Our courts, though they offer a bounty for his hide, and our pulpits, though they draw many a moral from his cunning, are in few senses contemporary with his free forest life."

HENRY WAS INTERESTED not only in the act of skating but in the natural history and symbolism of ice itself. He wanted not only to read the language of bird tracks imprinted in snow, which were like a cuneiform tablet of events waiting to be deciphered, but to try to understand the snow itself, its varieties and forms, its behavior. He loved water, river and stream and pond, rain and its colder manifestations. He paid as much attention to bubbles in the frozen surface of Walden Pond in February as he did to its reflections of red maples in October.

His interest was scientific, visceral, and symbolic. He read widely in the discoveries of his time. The thrilling revelations of the eighteenth century had ranged from astronomer William Herschel's catalog of the impossibly vast cosmos above our heads to geologist James Hutton's theories about the formation of the impossibly ancient earth beneath our feet. The new science of crystallization had linked the growth of the eternal stones to the growth of ephemeral ghosts such as hoarfrost, and glimpses of such creativity and pattern in physics inspired poetic nature lovers from Goethe to Emerson. Even Emmanuel Swedenborg, the controversial Swedish mystic who influenced Emerson and Transcendentalism and thus Henry, had studied crystallization. Before his midlife veer into mysticism, during which he claimed that the Second Coming had already taken place but had been apparent only to enlightened souls such as himself, Swedenborg focused considerable attention on analogies in nature. In his first book, in 1721, he argued that the branching and budding of plants is echoed in the hexagonal shapes of ice, from frost to snow, as well as in how salt crystals grow out of water.

This kind of pattern was more than metaphor. It teased Henry with a glimpse of the laws of creation. Mathematical predispositions in matter itself offered what a Transcendentalist would immediately see as evidence of hidden connection and kinship throughout the cosmos. It was like Swedenborg's use of an ancient Stoic analogy, that nature in general worked much like a spider's web: "For it consists, as it were, of infinite radii proceeding from a centre, and of infinite circles or polygons, such that nothing can happen in one which is not instantly known at the centre, and thus spreads throughout much of the web. Thus through contiguity and connection does nature play her part."

In the first volume of the journal he opened after Emerson's prompt in October 1837, Henry had spent considerable time describing the effects of hoarfrost and other icy architecture. It was one of the first topics to which he turned. He painstakingly examined what appeared to be frozen mist on leaves, the rectilinear fissures of frozen mud below ice melting in a roadbed, even crystallized rhubarb in the bottom of a bowl he had left outdoors in the autumn. When he found a mosaic of channels in the ice of Swamp Bridge Brook, which ran behind Farrar's blacksmith shop on the edge of the village, he turned over a big section to find an upended city—Gothic steeples of mostly triangular prisms, with a more ancient civilization of ice below it. He found that every hole in a high bank near the Leaning Hemlocks on the Assabet River sported a phalanx of sparkling ice crystals. "In one place you might see minute ostrich feathers," he wrote, "which seemed like the waving plumes of the warriors filing into the fortress, in another the glancing, fan-shaped banners of the Lilliputian host, and in another the needle-shaped particles, collected into bundles resembling the pine, might pass for a phalanx of spears. . . . I tried to fancy that there was a disposition in these crystallizations to take the forms of the contiguous foliage."

He returned to this theme in his first published essay, "The Natural History of Massachusetts," which had appeared in *The Dial* in July 1842, half a year before the skating party with Emerson and Hawthorne. That spring, after the deaths of John Thoreau and young Waldo, Emerson had acquired most of a series of massive scientific studies of Massachusetts. Separate volumes by various authors surveyed invertebrates, quadrupeds, herbaceous flowering plants, fish, birds, reptiles, and insects. "By what chance or lucid interval or kindly overruling," Emerson had asked Margaret Fuller, "came our Legislature to give itself this bright vacation from Whig & Tory voting lists, from New Valuations, & Revised Statutes, and lend itself to be led for a time by the Boston Society of Natural History?" In April he assigned a review of this compendium to Henry, "explaining to him," as he told Fuller, "the felicity of the subject for him as it admits of the narrative of all his woodcraft boatcraft & fishcraft. Henry is quite unable to labor lately since his sickness, & so must resign the garden into other hands," and he added generously, "but as private secretary to the President of the Dial, his works & fame may go out into all lands and, as happens to great Premiers, quite extinguish the titular Master."

As if this writing assignment had been a prescription from a doctor, Henry used the scientific tomes to launch a fortifying expedition into his own worldview, incorporating journal entries and other reading beyond the books under review. Always he found thinking about nature as invigorating and nutritious as experiencing nature. He even opened the essay with a passage from his journal written on the last day of 1841, the day before John cut his finger: "Books of natural history make the most cheerful winter reading . . ." He borrowed other journal entries and even casually sprinkled his own poems throughout. Eager to encourage his disciple, Emerson let him get away with it.

Henry addressed crystals and ice in various ways. He began with a survey of the beautiful forms of hoarfrost that adorned winter windows at dawn—"crystal botany," he called this topic. "Nature is mythical and mystical always," he wrote, "and works with the license and the extravagance of genius." Henry's poetic sensibility was being fueled in part by science, by his determination to see his world as clearly as possible, even if he still yearned to assign each phenomenon a metaphorical resonance: "In some places the ice-crystals were lying upon granite rocks, directly over crystals of quartz, the frost-work of a longer night, crystals of a longer period, but to some eye unprejudiced by the short term of human life, melting as fast as the former." He expanded the idea through his growing sense of being surrounded by a world older than humans had first imagined, and even more mysterious in its natural functions than it seemed in fable and myth. Emerson's thoughtful gesture in assigning this review had distracted Henry from grief and helped him concentrate on intellectual work. And in the writing of it Henry drew closer to his instinctive goal of unifying his life and thought through words.

Chapter 18

STATEN ISLAND

H ENRY WAS BUSY in early 1843, but mostly with tasks he did not find satisfying. Halfway through his twenties, he was making little money and attracting almost no attention as a writer. Although he submitted a sheaf for Emerson's consideration, the pages of the eleventh issue of *The Dial*, published early in January, contained none of Henry's own poems—but then the preceding issue had included eight. The new issue welcomed only Henry's workaday translation of part of Aeschylus' *Prometheus Bound*, which Emerson had requested, as well as a compilation of another writer's work.

Emerson kept his library available to his protégé. Among the many Eastern texts on those shelves, Henry had found and enjoyed Sir William Jones's *Institutes of Hindu Law; or, The Ordinances of Menu . . . Comprising the Indian System of Duties, Religious and Civil.* It was such an ancient work that Menu was said to have been the son or grandson of Brahma. In July 1842, Emerson had launched in *The Dial* what he described as "a series of ethnical scriptures," for which he asked Henry to gather a bouquet of Jones's translations. Henry read German, French, Latin, and Greek, but not Sanskrit, so he did not attempt his own version. Like Jones's vast 1796 translation, Henry's nine-page selection, titled simply "The Laws of

Menu," presented Menu's thoughts in categories such as Temperance, Devotion, and Teaching. Henry's selections ranged from "The resignation of all pleasures is far better than the attainment of them" to "He must eat without distraction of mind." Under the heading *God*, Henry included an Emersonian exclamation: "Thus the man, who perceives in his own soul the supreme soul present in all creatures, acquires equanimity toward them all, and shall be absorbed at last in the highest essence, even that of the Almighty himself."

January did see the appearance of Henry's first essay to be published anywhere other than the *Dial*—"A Walk to Wachusett," in a year-old monthly periodical, the *Boston Miscellany of Literature and Fashion*, which survived for only one more issue. It described a four-day trek that Henry had made with Richard Fuller, Margaret Fuller's youngest brother and Henry's junior by seven years, who was on holiday from Harvard. Carrying strong walking staffs, Richard and Henry had wandered through the hop fields of Acton and Stow, crossed the shallow but rapid Nashua River and the misnamed Stillwater, and climbed Mount Wachusett, the tallest peak in Massachusetts until the mountains rose in the west beyond the Connecticut River. "No incidents worthy of note occurred during this pilgrimage," Richard wrote in his own notebook, but Henry turned the excursion into a Wordsworthian ode to the mythic nourishment of being outdoors. He filled it with vivid, joyful details: their splashing like children through every rill that crossed their path, moonlight bright enough through their tent roof to create an all-night twilight inside, auger holes patterning the trunks in a sugar maple wood. Unable to keep his mind in one track, reveling in his associative way of thinking, Henry alluded to writers from Homer to Samuel Johnson. Amid garnishes of his own poetry, he worked in a tribute to himself: "But special I remember thee, / Wachusett, who like me / Standest alone without society."

He was already making notes for an essay about walking in wintertime. He was discovering that he enjoyed using an outdoor ramble as a unifying cord on which to string his thoughts.

Nathaniel Hawthorne, who was growing fond of his new neighbor, critiqued the Wachusett essay in his journal, comparing Henry's writing to a lake's reflective ability:

> He is a good writer—at least, he has written one good article, a rambling disquisition on Natural History in the last Dial,— which, he says, was chiefly made up from journals of his own observations. Methinks this article gives a very fair image of his mind and character—so true, minute, and literal in observation, yet giving the spirit as well as letter of what he sees, even as a lake reflects its wooded banks, showing every leaf, yet giving the wild beauty of the whole scene;—then there are passages in the article of cloudy and dreamy metaphysics, partly affected, and partly the natural exhalations of his intellect;—and also passages where his thoughts seem to measure and attune themselves into spontaneous verse, as they rightfully may, since there is real poetry in him. There is a basis of good sense and moral truth, too, throughout the article, which also is a reflection of his character; for he is not unwise to think and feel, however imperfect in his own mode of action. On the whole, I find him a healthy and wholesome man to know.

In January, Henry received a package at the Emerson house, which he opened with Lidian watching. Richard Fuller had sent him a music box, probably as a thank-you for tutoring help on his Harvard application and other work. On its lid gleamed a romantic painting of Switzerland's mountain-ringed Lake Lucerne, which reminded Henry of the ponds around Harvard. The summer before, shortly after he met the Hawthornes, Henry had visited them with the express purpose of borrowing their own music box—only to have Sophia immediately suggest that she lend it to him. Now he had one of his own.

Henry was thrilled. Lidian thought she had never seen such childlike joy on an adult's face as when Henry opened the gift. He carefully wound it and they listened to its festive airs. Then suddenly Henry decided he must play it for his mother and sisters, and he rushed out to the Thoreau house. Lidian described the scene to Emerson in a letter, adding, "My heart really warmed with sympathy, and admiration at his whole demeanour on the occasion—and I like human nature better than I did."

THE WACHUSETT ESSAY, like Henry's contributions to *The Dial*, earned no money. The Thoreau family pressure for gainful employment must have been stronger than ever, now that John had been gone a year. In February, restless Henry wrote to ask Emerson to keep an eye out for employment for him outside Concord. He was not going to be able to survive on odd jobs.

Emerson received Henry's letter on Staten Island, where he was visiting his brother William, who was County Judge of Richmond Court. The father of three—the oldest a precocious and busy seven-year-old—William had an urgent personal interest in both education and child tending. Emerson suggested to his brother that the young firebrand of Concord, an experienced teacher, would make a fine tutor for Willie and might also be helpful with the other children, or at least with three-year-old Haven if not with baby Charley.

William agreed and Emerson brought home a job offer. By mid-March, Emerson was writing to his brother, "I have to say that Henry listens very willingly to your proposition. He thinks it exactly fit for him & he very rarely finds offers that do fit him."

Henry's mentor served not only as reference and agent; he even discussed each point with Henry and wrote up the details of the agreement in letters to William. "He says that it is such a relation as he wishes to sustain, to be the friend & educator of a boy, & one not yet subdued by schoolmasters. I have told him that you wish to put the boy and not his grammar & geography under good and active influence that you wish him to go to the woods & to go to the city with him & do all he can for him—"

Henry accepted, to begin his role as tutor on the first of May. Via Emerson, his brother and Henry worked out a deal: a modest but reasonable salary of one hundred dollars per annum, plus board and lodging; a room in which to study, one provided with a fireplace during cold months; and, unlike at Bush, no requirement of physical labor, because Henry feared that at the moment his health was not up to it. The loss of John, followed by a long bout with bronchitis during the winter, had prompted Henry to describe himself as "a diseased bundle of nerves standing between time and eternity like a withered leaf."

He asked for twenty dollars in advance, which Emerson offered to supply before his trip. Later he gave Henry seven dollars more for traveling expenses and advanced him a further ten against his stipend from William. Also Henry begged Emerson to ask his brother if he might need clerical help, and he promised to clean up his sloppy handwriting enough to accomplish it. Emerson conveyed the question, emphasizing that Henry wanted such extra employment only until he could "procure for himself literary labor from some quarter in New York." Henry was going to the big city with dreams of finally getting more of his words published.

WHEN HENRY'S FRIENDS learned to their surprise that he would be migrating to Staten Island, they responded with affection. Although Lidian Emerson said that she didn't want to have to get by without her assistant, she understood that in his mid-twenties Henry certainly needed both remunerative employment and experience in the larger world. Prudence Ward, Ellen Sewall's aunt, gave Henry a microscope to aid him in peering deeply into nature's secrets. Elizabeth Hoar brought him an inkstand and one of the newfangled steel pens, although she expressed misgivings about the latter, unsure if Henry preferred to write with a quill. "We have become better acquainted within the two past years than in our whole life as schoolmates and neighbors before," she wrote; "and I am unwilling to let you go away without telling you that I, among your other friends, shall miss you much, and follow you with remembrance and all best wishes and confidence."

A few months earlier, however, Elizabeth had confessed to Emerson, "I love Henry, but I do not like him." As Henry prepared for Staten Island, other friends were expressing similar doubts. Emerson waited until Henry's job was settled before warning his brother about the new tutor's personality: "I am sure no truer & no purer person lives in wide New York; & he is a bold and a profound thinker though he may easily chance to pester you with some accidental crotchets and perhaps a village exaggeration of the value of facts." He filed a similar complaint with Hawthorne, who wrote in his diary about a visit from Emerson: "Mr. Thoreau was discussed, and his approaching departure; in respect to which we agreed pretty well; but Mr. Emerson appears to have suffered some inconveniency from his experience of Mr. Thoreau as an inmate. It may well be that such a sturdy and uncompromising person is fitter to meet occasionally in the open air, than to have as a permanent guest at table and fireside."

One person who was disappointed to learn of Henry's pending departure was a new friend who was in the process of moving to Concord. Emerson had introduced Henry to Ellery Channing, a nephew of the prominent Unitarian theologian, in December 1840, and during Channing's later visits to Concord they had become friends. He had looked into renting various Concord residences, especially after marrying Margaret Fuller's sister Ellen in 1842. Spring 1843 found Henry supervising and assisting in work to make the Red Lodge, a small cottage on the Cambridge Turnpike, habitable for the Channings—everything from newly plastering around the chimney to moving the privy from behind the barn. In his mid-twenties, Channing was a poet of little renown but, in the eyes of Emerson and other Transcendentalists, great potential. Pampered as a child and gifted with supreme confidence in his own talent, Channing was notoriously self-indulgent and unreliable, but he and Henry were becoming steadily closer friends when he learned of Henry's departure.

On the evening of April 7, Hawthorne had just picked up his pen to write in his journal when Henry knocked on the door of the parsonage. Ten months into his marriage and still love-struck, Hawthorne was lonely but not particularly in the mood for company. A few hours earlier, Sophia had climbed into a wagon that carried her to the stage house for a journey to Boston to visit her sister Mary, who was about to marry. Previously, they had spent only one night apart, late in the fall when Hawthorne went on a two-day trek with Emerson and was thrilled to see Sophia upon his return—"the first time that I ever came home in my life," he commented to his journal, "for I never had a home before."

The past few weeks had been a difficult time. Sophia's pregnancy had ended in a miscarriage after she fell while cavorting on the ice. Their dream of having a child was lost, possibly forever. Only four days before Henry came to their door, they had stood together at a window of Hawthorne's study, peering sadly out at the world. Sophia took off her ring and scratched a melancholy reassurance on the window pane: "Man's accidents are God's purposes." Then Hawthorne took the ring and etched his name and the year and added, "The smallest twig leans clear against the sky. Composed by my wife and written with her diamond," as they watched the golden sun go down.

Now, always both reveling in solitude and inventing little symbolic gestures about his marriage, Hawthorne had thought to avoid conversing with others during Sophia's absence—but Henry's arrival wrecked this plan. Hawthorne was also sweaty and tired. After affectionately watching from the doorstep until Sophia's wagon had rattled around the curve of Monument Street toward the north end of the village near the courthouse, he had vigorously sawed wood to distract himself. Following his solitary dinner he lay down with a copy of *The Dial*, suspecting that its wordy pages would not prevent a nap. Thinking about Sophia's journey, however, diverted him, and he had given up and turned to his journal when Henry arrived to return a book and to deliver his news. Under his arm he carried like a child his beloved music box for the entertainment of the Hawthornes during his absence.

Hawthorne expressed his genuine happiness at Henry's prospects. Both were facing an urgent need for money. Naturally Henry was not earning much as an occasional surveyor or handyman. And despite Hawthorne's growing fame, and the eagerness of periodicals such as the *Democratic Review* and *Graham's* to publish his moody, elegant stories (and essays disguised as stories), he was receiving no payment for his work. Again and again magazines promised respectable payment and never sent it, no matter how many times the author begged or cajoled.

They discussed the likely spiritual benefits of Henry's move, then chatted about *The Dial* and Bronson Alcott. Hawthorne hated to see Henry leave, because he considered him, as he observed to his journal after his friend walked home, "one of the few persons, I think, with whom to hold intercourse is like hearing the wind among the boughs of a forest-tree; and with all this wild freedom, there is high and classic cultivation in him too." But he knew that Henry had not yet found his own path. He seemed to lack what Hawthorne thought of as the "guiding clue" that would weave together his interests and ambitions. Also, the young man lacked a position in the world, and for that matter simply needed greater experience of the cosmos beyond Concord and Walden Pond. And there was the matter of Henry's health. He seemed to be haunted by the Thoreau family curse of consumption. Perhaps a change of scenery from these boggy lowlands might improve his overall resistance and restore him to the level of energy he had demonstrated before his brother's death, little more than a year ago. Hawthorne wound and rewound Henry's music box until its charm paled.

A few days later, following a drenching rain that melted late snow and began breaking up the ice in the river, Hawthorne's servant announced that Mr. Thoreau had returned. Henry suggested that he and Hawthorne make an expedition in the *Pond Lily*, and Hawthorne agreed. He was fresh from a morning of unsatisfying writing and a trek to the village to find their post box empty despite Sophia's absence. He was restless because finally she was due back that night. Together he and Henry bailed out the boat's accumulated rainwater—as well as seepage from a persistent leak—and rowed up the river, where they climbed a muddy hill of melting snow and admired the view. The flooded Concord River looked like an ocean. Large cakes of ice were drifting clumsily downriver like barges, and Henry and Hawthorne boyishly floated back to the parsonage aboard one. The boat built by Henry and John clunked along behind it, empty.

★   ★   ★

"WANT A CAB, sir?"

It was the first sentence Henry heard as the big boat docked at a wharf on the southern tip of Manhattan Island on May 7, 1843. As he readied his bag and prepared to leap onto land, he ignored the many drivers calling from behind their muddied horses. He had journeyed with William Emerson's wife, who was ending a month-long stay with her brother-in-law in Concord. They were arriving later than scheduled, in the middle of a busy Sunday morning, because low tide had run their boat aground on the Thames River near New London, Connecticut. Near the dock was Castle Garden (originally called Fort Castle), a round, three-tiered fort of red sandstone. Finished in 1811, along with the similar Castle Williams on the northwest point of Governors Island half a mile to the south, Castle Garden featured the innovative design of enclosed gun placements, visible only as castle-like lancet windows slotted into the lower circle. Along with other regional forts, including one on little Ellis Island, they had been intended to guard the harbor against British invasion, but they did not see action during what was being called the War of 1812.

"You want a cab, sir!"

This driver was telling, not asking. With his face carefully expressionless—his usual defense—Henry ignored him, too. Hunched in dirty coats, the phalanx of cab drivers sat atop their carts, resting their elbows on their knees and holding whip handles pointed like compass needles at the self-conscious young man in his country duds.

"You want a nice cab, sir," confided a more courteous driver, and hazarded, "to take you to Fourth Street."

Apparently they declined and took the ferry to Staten Island. The Snuggery, the Emersons' house, turned out to be long and not tall, painted brown, with a garden including potted plants and a piazza around which grapevines flourished. Surrounded by woods, the house was halfway up a hill. When Henry faced northeast, he gazed across Upper Bay to New York City; northwest showed him Newark Bay and, closer, the busy ship-filled tidal strait that connected the two, the Kill van Kull—a name recalling the early Dutch settlement of New Amsterdam. If he turned southwest, he could see all the way across the bay to the north-pointing barrier spit of Sandy Hook, which protected the Lower Bay and the coast of Staten Island from Atlantic waves. One evening Henry climbed to the pinnacle of one Madame Grimes's house and, as he turned around in a circle, he could see almost the entire island.

Judge William Emerson ran his household on a tight schedule: breakfast at half past six, lunch at noon, dinner at five. "From 9 to 2 or thereabouts I am the schoolmaster," Henry wrote to his parents, "and at other times as much the pupil as I can be." He taught mathematics and Latin and at the latter Willie proved precocious. At times his brothers, three-year-old Haven and two-year-old Charles, joined the class, occasionally accompanied by the young son of a family across the street. Yet Henry's employment at the Snuggery turned out to be the least interesting part of his summer. He didn't dislike young Willie; nor did he find him particularly appealing. To his own parents, Henry described Mr. and Mrs. Emerson as "not indeed of my kith or kin in any sense—but they are irreproachable and kind." To Emerson he phrased it differently: "I do not feel myself especially serviceable to the good people with whom I live, except as inflictions are sanctified to the righteous." Immediately upon arrival, he fell ill and had to renounce some of his obligations for a few days.

Over the next weeks, as usual, Henry paid more attention to the world around him than to the people around him. Tutoring was simply a job; his real interests lay elsewhere. "There are two things I hear and am aware I live in the neighborhood of," Henry wrote to

Emerson two weeks after his arrival, "—the roar of the sea and the hum of the city."

The sea roared below the house. Henry loved the solitary beach, which seemed distant from any city. Skinny and quick and curious about everything outdoors, he prowled the shore like a sandpiper, past fishermen spreading their shad nets to dry in the bright spring sun, past long-tailed horseshoe crabs winding across the sand in their gleaming helmet-like shells. Here and there dead fish lay among flotsam and seaweed flung by the tide. Often the surf washed up larger creatures—the bloated, monstrous corpse of a pig or even a horse, their stench so rank it struck Henry as darkly luxuriant. He watched teams of grunting oxen splash in the surf as their drivers coaxed them to draw heavy boats out of water and across sand. Just offshore, clumsy fishing boats bobbed like toys, while beyond them sailing ships moved more gracefully until they sank below the horizon. "The sea seems very near from the hills," Henry wrote to Emerson, "but it proves a long way over the plain, and yet you may be wet with the spray before you can believe that you are there."

The hum of the city appealed to him far less. He claimed to be unimpressed by New York. He was disappointed with everything, he told Emerson, but then remarked in his provincial way that he had been disappointed before coming here. However, he added, "The crowd is something new, and to be attended to." During the 1830s, despite cholera epidemics and the return of yellow fever, despite the disastrous fire of 1835 and the financial crash two years later, the population of New York City had leaped to well over three hundred thousand. Henry clomped in his country boots down the mostly cobblestone pavement of wide and sunlit Broadway. In the block between Chambers and Warren Streets, wooden blocks laid a few years earlier as an experimental roadbed were already showing too much wear to make them a feasible alternative to time-honored stone.

Henry found himself surrounded by flocks of fashionable women. No doubt he found such proximity disconcerting; back at the Emerson house, the maids had noticed that Henry could not even walk past them in the kitchen without blushing. Here rainbows of parasols twirled in delicate hands. The thrown-back hoods of the women's colorful cloaks unveiled an intimate lining of a different hue. Every step afforded a distracting parade of satin or lace or silk—fluttering tassels and ribbons, peekaboo glimpses of stockings. Well-groomed young men of Henry's age boasted beards under their chin, along the neck and throat, and many had turned down their shirt collar in a recent fashion trend. Dandies would promenade on the steps of a hotel, generously providing tourists an opportunity to admire their finery. "It must have a very bad influence on children," Henry wrote to his mother, "to see so many human beings at once—mere herds of men."

Painfully missing the quiet paths of Walden, Henry slogged from office to office, from magazine to book publisher, yearning to find someone—anyone—who might dangle the carrot of potential publication. At the offices of the *New Mirror*, the *New World*, and *Brother Jonathan*, he was informed that they were already saturated with free contributions. The *Knickerbocker* claimed to be too poor to pay for anything. The *Democratic Review* cautiously expressed interest. Henry doggedly navigated the crowds, dodging a phalanx of gigs and shays, workaday hackney cabs, agile two-wheeled tilburies. Many private carriages were driven by coachmen, some of them Negro, a few actually dressed in formal livery like a military uniform. Hulking workmen carried or dragged blocks of ice, with insulating sawdust still clinging to its slippery surface, into rowdy taverns and dark basement-level oyster bars.

A year earlier, in the spring of 1842, Charles Dickens had walked these streets during his first visit to the United States. Having just turned thirty, Dickens was fresh from the triumph of his fifth novel, *Barnaby Rudge*, and was mobbed by Americans from his first appearance in Boston. He found New York City considerably less clean than Boston. He considered the Five Points area "in respect of filth and wretchedness" comparable to London's own dismal Seven Dials neighborhood, which Dickens had written about as early as his collection *Sketches by Boz* in 1836. He admired Wall Street, examined the Lower Manhattan jail nicknamed the Tombs, found the streets disappointingly quiet in contrast to London's, gawked at the almshouse and orphans' farm, and worried over house fires that reddened the skyline every night. He also wrote at length about a denizen of the streets with whom Henry also became familiar. Everywhere Dickens had gone, everywhere Henry went, the streets were populated with vagabond swine— ugly brown creatures with black blotches—that prowled the island as if they owned it. Skinny-legged hogs and portly sows and round little piglets sauntered alone, in pairs, and in parties of half a dozen or more. Their sparsely haired backs looked poorly upholstered. Many pigs showed battle scars—missing ear, abbreviated tail. Roaming far and wide, they grunted alongside beaver-hatted walkers and squealed out of the way of sporty high-wheeled phae-tons, and at sunset they could be seen migrating by the dozens toward wherever they slept.

Like the pigs, Henry wandered all over Manhattan. Desperate for cash, he even tried to sell a most unliterary periodical, *American Agriculturist*, door to door, once slogging through a drenching rain. Founded in New York City the year before and headquartered on Park Row, the magazine bore on its cover an optimistic montage of the fruits of modern husbandry—cows and pigs and sheep, crops from pumpkin to corn, and an arsenal of technologies such as steel plow, scythe, and watermill.

Henry watched ships disgorge hundreds upon hundreds of new immigrants. While waiting in quarantine on Staten Island for their ship to be cleaned, they stretched their limbs and peered westward toward a new horizon. In the city Henry saw sunburned immigrant families cooking their modest dinnera on the pavement. In his rambles he explored telegraph stations and borrowed books from the Mercantile Library Association. As usual, after a glance at a farm's soil, Henry walked away with an Indian arrowhead in his pocket. He attended a sermon by Lucretia Mott, a renowned anti-slavery and women's rights activist, where he admired the simplicity and sincerity of the service. Quaker women filing into the meetinghouse in their black bonnets and white kerchiefs reminded him of a flock of chickadees.

Helen wrote from Concord, asking Henry to help her locate a teaching position on Staten Island. Apparently he was unable to help, but he turned again to a poem he had written after John's death and mailed a copy to Helen on the twenty-third of May. "In place of something fresher," he added, "I send you the following verses from my Journal, written some time ago." The poem began with the age-old question of the grieving: "Brother, where dost thou dwell?" and a stanza later posed a question equally ancient: "Are not the fates more kind / Than they appear?" Near the end he wondered aloud "Where chiefly shall I look / To feel thy presence near?" and decided that the answer would be outdoors, along the brook, in the voices of the birds. He thought of John's agonizing pain in his last days and asked his spirit,

Is thy brow clear again
As in thy youthful years?
And was that ugly pain
The summit of thy fears?

Yet thou wast cheery still;
They could not quench thy fire;
Thou didst abide their will,
And then retire.

In June, Henry received an affectionate letter from Lidian. He took it to the top of the hill on the island and sat watching the sunset and looking down upon the ocean, where dozens of ships were heading out of the great harbor toward distant ports, and wrote an almost romantic reply.

You seem to speak out of a very clear and high heaven, where any one may be who stands so high. . . . The thought of you will constantly elevate my life; it will be something always above the horizon to behold, as when I look up at the evening star. . . . My actual life is unspeakably mean, compared with what I know and see that it might be. . . . What wealth is it to have such friends that we cannot think of them without elevation. . . . I send my love to my other friend and brother, whose nobleness I slowly recognize.

AT TIMES ON Staten Island, caught up in his teaching and his writing, Henry felt disconnected from nature, a step back from it. He encountered too many people, too many houses, too much noise. Then out of the very ground beneath his feet erupted like dragons' teeth a reminder of the mythical power of nature lurking behind everyday life. All over Staten Island—in field and lawn and cemetery—locusts crawled out of the earth and swarmed with biblical abandon. While walking around the island in the humid summer, admiring the redolent white magnolia blossoms and the waxy yellow cups of tulip tree flowers, Henry could see the locusts climbing shrub limbs, tangled in a dog's fur, snapped up buzzing in the beaks of chickens.

These weren't the annual crop of locusts whose thrumming buzz was part of the unheard music of summer. Those would not emerge until July. These were the seventeen-year periodical cicada—about half the size of the annual locusts, with huge red eyes and orange-veined wings that folded elegantly over their back. The young emerged from the ground a ghostly white but developed other colors within a couple of hours. After each molt, their hollow skins crunched underfoot and piled up at doorsills like snowdrifts. The locusts bored into twigs and killed them; by early July Henry could see clusters of twigs that from a distance resembled hanging chestnut blossoms. The locusts were loud, too, their buzzing *Pha-r-r-aoh—Pha-r-r-aoh* audible from well out on the water.

Like Rip Van Winkle, the Kaatskill man who slept through the Revolution in Washington Irving's 1819 story, the locusts had returned to find their world different. When the larvae went underground back in 1826, Henry was nine years old and John eleven; John Quincy Adams was president, only the sixth since the Revolution. Through six thousand sunrises, the insects had incubated in the soil beneath the feet of New Yorkers. When they reappeared in July 1843, John Tyler was the tenth president, having succeeded Ol' Tippecanoe, who died a month after his hard-won election, and Henry was turning twenty-six. Then the locusts were gone, not to return until 1860.

MEANWHILE EMERSON STROLLED his beloved Walden trails, watching the stirrings of railroad building with a skeptical eye. The Fitchburg Railroad was finally reaching Concord. Woods and fields were noisy with officious surveyors planting their red-flagged poles and triangulating their location with an elaborate tripod-mounted theodolite, its adjustable viewing tube balanced atop graded semi-circles of brass. A long-established instrument for measuring both vertical and horizontal angles, refined in the late eighteenth century, the theodolite had become crucial in surveying. To Emerson the surveyors' repeated calls of feet and inches became a constant song around Walden Pond. Elsewhere the railroad ties were already being laid in their unnaturally straight lines, including near Bronson Alcott's house on Lexington Road. Daily Emerson witnessed the railroad's need for trees: trees killed to make way for tracks, trees killed to shape into ties, trees killed to stoke forges, trees killed to fuel the trains themselves. It was unnerving, this dragon's ravenous appetite. And he found many of the Irish laborers an insult to his eye and ear.

When Emerson complained about the profanation of his Eden, Henry sat in a cornfield on Staten Island, dipping his pen into the portable inkwell that Elizabeth Hoar had given him, and demonstrated that daily encounters with the hungry poor in New York had—at least temporarily—softened his view of humanity:

> But no matter let them hack away—The sturdy Irish arms that do the work are of more worth than oak or maple. Methinks I could look with equanimity upon a long street of Irish cabins and pigs and children revelling in the genial Concord dirt, and I should still find my Walden wood and Fair Haven in their tanned and happy faces.

The Irish thronged Concord woods and town with their exotic accents. As they had done elsewhere in the railroad's progress along the eastern coast, the workers built rough shanties near the surveyed lines. While Henry trod the streets of New York City, surrounded by Irish laborers fresh from the old country in their near-uniform of dull trousers and long-tailed blue coats, Nathaniel Hawthorne observed their arrival in Concord with the railroad. As he strolled a path at Walden, disgusted by the bleak gash of the railroad's embankment, he came upon a makeshift village of these low huts. The Irish had built them under the spreading walnut and oak branches without clearing away trees. The huts had been slapped together with rough boards whose ends protruded haphazardly, and soil was piled against some of them almost to the roof, with weeds sprouting in these mounded burrows. A muddy hog snout poked from a ramshackle sty. Women washed clothing in wooden tubs, while whitened laundry fluttered above them from lines strung between trees. The huts were barely shelter from the elements, a place to steal enough hours of exhausted slumber to hold body and soul together while the workers hammered out the new path of commerce. Innocent of their future, children ran laughing through splashes of sunlight.

WRITING WAS NEVER far from Henry's mind on Staten Island. With introductions from Emerson and others, he met the theologian Henry James and the newspaper editor Horace Greeley. Henry and Emerson corresponded often about work. In early September, amid chatty news about Channing and Elizabeth Hoar and other mutual friends, Emerson asked for more Greek translations for *The Dial*. Then he mentioned that he had been meaning to send Henry's essay "A Winter Walk" to the printer for inclusion in the next issue, but that he had concerns about Henry's writing style. "I had some hesitation about it, notwithstanding its faithful observation and its fine sketches of the pickerel-fisher and of the wood-chopper, on account of mannerism, an old charge of mine,—as if, by attention, one could get the trick of the rhetoric; for example, to call a cold place sultry, a solitude public, a wilderness domestic (a favorite word), and in the woods to insult over cities, whilst the woods, again, are dignified by comparing them to cities, armies, etc." He added a significant remark: "By pretty free omissions, however, I have removed my principal objections." Henry accepted the changes and the essay was scheduled.

Henry informed his parents about everything from the price of pantaloons ($2.25 per ready-made pair) and how well his stockings were holding up to his opinion of the preaching of a young clergy-man. "I think of you all very often," Henry wrote to his mother in midsummer, "and wonder if you are still separated from me only by so many miles of earth, or so many miles of memory." He liked getting the news of lively events in Concord. A bank officer named Wyman had been charged with fraud, for example, and the attorney and statesman Daniel Webster had been retained in the case and was adding some celebrity to the Concord courthouse. "Methinks I should be content to sit at the back-door in Concord, under the poplar-tree, henceforth forever. Not that I am homesick at all,—for places are strangely indifferent to me,—but Concord is still a cyno-sure to my eyes, and I find it hard to attach it, even in imagination, to the rest of the globe, and tell where the seam is."

Autumn crept in and turned toward winter. Thanksgiving was the most revered annual holiday in Concord. Many heads of house-hold sought the largest turkey they could raise or buy or hunt. Plum pudding, cranberry sauce; figs and apples, nuts and raisins; mince, pumpkin, and squash pies—the hot, aromatic dishes kept coming, and leftovers lingered for days. Naturally Henry journeyed home from Staten Island to see his family for the holiday. Admitting to himself how much he had missed Concord, and how little he had enjoyed tutoring Emerson's nephew, and how little he had accomplished in the offices of New York City periodicals, he decided to quit this job.

He visited Staten Island again only to gather his clothing and books and returned immediately to Concord. In mid–December, Emerson wrote to his brother William, "Henry T. thanks you for the purse and says that the Pindar he will return through me, & says that he left nothing of any value at all in his chamber. You will please use your discretion with any matters found there."

Back home in Concord, Henry did not rejoin the Emerson household. He moved back to the Thoreau boardinghouse and again concentrated on pencils.

Chapter 19

FIRE

T HEY FORGOT TO take matches. Before they were far downstream, Edward Hoar and Henry discovered their oversight and stopped at the nearest house by the river—home of one of Concord's many shoemakers—to beg a match. In the fifteen years since the introduction of the lucifer match, the clever invention had improved a great deal. Now safer and more reliable, matches had become a staple of travel, vastly reducing the amount of time and energy devoted to fire building. After deciding that they wanted to live off the land like Indians on their brief boating expedition, the young men had packed few supplies other than fishing tackle. Quick to follow technological advances, however, Henry naturally adopted matches as camping equipment—and then forgot to bring them.

It was Tuesday, the last day of April 1844, five months after Henry's return from Staten Island and six weeks before his twenty-eighth birthday. A senior at Harvard, Edward Hoar was the twenty-one-year-old son of Samuel Hoar; brother of Elizabeth and Rockwood and George, Edward had known Henry for most of his life. His enthusiasm for natural history helped draw him to Henry, because both were passionately interested in the plants of the region. When Edward was young, he trekked the woods with Henry, who showed him how to fire his antique single-barrel flintlock even though Edward's parents forbade his carrying a gun.

Edward and Henry were ignoring Town Meeting Day in Concord. Able-bodied citizens were expected to debate and vote on such municipal issues as expense appropriations and motions for raising taxes. Instead, Henry had taken time off from making pencils and, while Edward was on holiday from college, the young men had set out to boat the sources of the Concord, planning to spend their nights sleeping on the riverbank or in a nearby farmhouse or perhaps in a country inn. They rowed south and southeast of the village, heading toward Fair Haven Pond. Thanks to recent drought, the river was shallow and its banks parched. They caught enough fish for their supper before Concord was out of sight. A few minutes later, where the river poured out of Fair Haven, which was southwest of Walden Pond with Adams Woods between them, they pulled the boat up to the eastern shore, which was warmed by afternoon sun in the west.

A good distance from the woods, Henry and Edward chose as a fire site a stump in a little recess on a hillside where scattered bushes were surrounded by long wiry grass. Last year's dry grass lingered around the stump's base like a straggly beard. Henry and Edward used their match to start a fire on the stump—and almost instantly the flame leaped to the grass around it. Caught off guard, both rushed to quench it, but nothing they threw on helped. Frantically they stomped the flames. One ran to get a board from the boat and slapped at the fire with it, but to no avail. Soon the flames were racing up the hillside, crackling loudly and leaping from bush to bush across the grass, which itself burned almost instantly.

"Where will this end?" Edward yelled.

"It will go to town."

Edward jumped in the boat and guided it toward town to get help. Henry raced toward the woods to alert the landowners and to rouse as many neighbors as possible. A veteran of campfires since childhood, he had never lost control of one before. This was a disaster. There was no telling what the fire would devour before it was stopped—if it could be stopped. Henry ran up the hill and through the woods as smoke climbed to the sky behind him. Emerging from the trees, he encountered a farmer who paused in driving his team only to ask where the smoke was coming from.

A breathless Henry explained.

"Well, it is none of my stuff," the farmer replied, and drove his team onward.

Henry started racing again. He had run two exhausting miles by the time he met one of the landowners in his field, and they immediately turned and ran back together to the woods. As they neared the flaming trees, they met a carpenter who was fleeing with a firm grip on his ax. The farmer ran back for more help. Spent to the point of collapse, Henry remained where he was, panting. He estimated that the fire now had a raging front a good half mile wide. It was being fueled not only by standing trees and brush but by countless stacked cords of firewood scattered throughout the woods like tinder, fuel that had been cut the previous winter and left to age.

Alone, he walked slowly through the woods to the highest promontory of Fair Haven Cliff and sat down on a rock to watch the fire, which was moving in his direction. Already the woods were burning more than a mile from where Henry and Edward had built their campfire. It was terrifying but also a spectacle, the flames devouring trees, the smoke climbing into the clouds. Struggling to distance himself from his shame and embarrassment and anger by renouncing his sympathy for the farmers and landowners, Henry asked himself, *Who are these men who are said to be the owners of these woods, and how am I related to them?* More than once, in walks with Emerson, Henry had expressed frustration with property owners' restrictions about their land. *I have set fire to the forest, but I have done no wrong therein, and now it is as if the lightning had done it.*

The fire bell in the village was clanging loudly. While Henry sat atop the hill as if in shock, villagers were running to help. Henry stood up and peered at the wall of fire, which was drawing nearer, beginning to climb Fair Haven Hill. Three confused passenger pigeons flew straight into the smoke. Squirrels ran from the fire as if fleeing a hawk. The woods were so dry that when the fire reached the base of a pine, it dashed up it like some mythic animal, igniting the bark and needles almost instantly, as if they were composed of gunpowder. The tree became a torch and shed fireworks.

Henry realized that soon the flames were going to surround him on the hill, so he went down a different way and rejoined the men fighting the monster. Amid the blinding smoke and heat, they labored for hours, digging the dry soil with shovels, hacking at the ground with hoes. They built backfires and chopped down trees until they created dry moats of treeless ground. Henry saw a man struggling to defend his stacked cords of firewood from this wild blaze and realized that it was the farmer who earlier had dismissed the fire as not his problem. Later the farmer Henry had led to the woods revealed how little he knew his property by asking Henry the quickest route back home through his own woods.

Henry went home, surrounded by the condemnations of his townsfolk but answering none of them. He tried to tell himself that many seemed almost invigorated by the battle with fire. Later he went back out. For hours that night, while all the other exhausted firefighters slept at home or drank in a tavern, Henry walked alone. His woods were a blackened battlefield. What had been pine trees were now trunks of charcoal. Here and there small flames still licked at stumps;

embers glowed in the burned needles and leaves on the ground. An irresistible morbid curiosity drew him back to the scene of the crime. In the wee hours of the spring morning he found himself working his way through the massacred woods to where he and Edward had foolishly built their campfire. There around the stump were the dressed fish they had been trying to cook—now broiled and charred.

"THE FIRE, WE understand," declared the *Concord Freeman* on the third of May, "was communicated to the woods through the thoughtlessness of two of our citizens who kindled it in a *pine stump*, near the Pond, for the purpose of making a chowder. As every thing around them was as combustible almost as a fire-ship, the flames spread with rapidity and hours elapsed before it could be subdued. It is to be hoped that this unfortunate result of sheer carelessness, will be borne in mind by those who may wish to visit the woods in future for recreation."

The demands of farming and firewood, and especially the construction of homes and more recently of the railroad, had left few trees standing in surrounding areas. Only around Walden had substantial tracts of woods remained in the Concord area. Thanks to Edward and Henry's carelessness—and Henry was the older culprit—more than three hundred acres burned and many of the trees left standing were irreparably damaged. The estimate of the number of stacked cords of wood destroyed by the fire climbed above one hundred, the value of which was estimated to range between $300 and $450. The estimate of total damage passed $2,000. Probably the only reason that Edward and Henry evaded prosecution was that Edward's father was the irresistible force of Concord government, the jurist and former senator Samuel Hoar.

In the same issue of the *Concord Freeman* as the news story about the fire, an advertisement appeared that applauded neighbors' efforts to control it: "Cyrus Hubbard and others, return their thanks to the citizens of Concord for their prompt and unwearied exertions in extinguishing the fire in the woods on Tuesday last." Hubbard was one of the men to whom Samuel Hoar was later said to have paid damage costs, and Abiel Wheeler was another. "Don't talk to me of Henry Thoreau!" one of Wheeler's daughters exclaimed later. "Didn't I all that winter have to go to school with a smootched apron or dress because I had to pitch in and help fill the wood box with partly charred wood?"

For months, as Henry walked through the woods or town, he heard people yell to him about the "burnt woods." He strode past with his usual rigid stoicism, but inside, beneath his mask, even below his guilt and shame, he felt an inconsolable grief over the loss of the woods. He was informed that some people now referred to him not as a ne'er-do-well or a curiosity—sobriquets he might wear with equanimity and even pride—but as a "damned rascal."

Chapter 20

A POOR MAN'S HOUSE

H ENRY HAD RETURNED from Staten Island with the prospect of becoming, like his father, a respected local businessman. Finally the Thoreau family was prospering. By 1844 the Concord-based firm of J. Thoreau & Son (sometimes identifying itself as Thoreau & Co.) was established as a maker of some of the finest pencils in America. Henry and his father had figured out that by varying the amount of clay mixed with the plumbago, they could produce pencils in a variety of hardnesses, "graduated from 1 to 4." They advertised "IMPROVED DRAWING PENCILS, for the nicest uses of the Drawing Master, Surveyor, Engineer, Architect, and Artists Generally." Some were marked S for Soft, H for hard, and so on, with extremes in the spectrum marked S.S and H.H. They produced red pencils as well.

"Henry Thoreau has made, as he thinks," Emerson wrote to his friend Caroline Sturgis, "great improvement in the manufacture, and believes he makes as good a pencil as the good English drawing pencil." He enclosed a packet of four drawing pencils as evidence. She replied, "The pencils are excellent. . . . I shall certainly recommend them to all my friends who use such implements & hope to destroy great numbers of them myself."

An advertisement in 1844 declared,

JOHN THOREAU & CO.,

CONCORD, MASS.

MANUFACTURE

A NEW AND SUPERIOR DRAWING PENCIL,

Expressly for ARTISTS AND CONNOISSEURS, *possessing in an unusual degree the qualities of the pure lead, superior blackness, and firmness of point, as well as freedom of mark, and warranted not to be affected by changes of temperature . . .*

J. Thoreau & Co. also manufacture the various other kinds of BLACK-LEAD PENCILS; *the Mammoth or Large Round, the Rulers or Flat, and the Common of every quality and price; also, Lead-points in any quantity, and plumbago plates for Galvanic Batteries. All orders addressed to them will be promptly attended to.*

After the disastrous fire he had helped cause, however, instead of a respected member of the community Henry soon became a pariah. For most of his adult life he had been looking for the ideal wooded or lakeside land on which to find solitude and concentration, and apparently the forest fire sped up his efforts. He was denounced so much around the village that he may have sought a sylvan refuge in part to escape censure or even reprisal.

Over the years, he had sometimes looked for a hut and sometimes for land on which to build a hut. "I only ask a clean seat," he had written in his journal as early as April 1840. "I will build my lodge on the southern slope of some hill, and take there the life the gods send me." Preoccupied as always with the way that etymology fossilizes ideas from the past, he wrote a few months later, "The rich man's house is a *sedes*—a place to sit in—the poor man's a *tectum*—a shelter. So in English we say a gentleman's seat or residence, but a poor man's house or roof." Identifying with poverty, and poor himself in worldly terms, he knew that in his own modest home he would feel like landed gentry.

He had made no serious move toward a home of his own, yet often he gazed longingly at sites that struck his fancy. "I have thought," he sighed to his journal in late 1841, "when walking in the woods through a certain retired dell, bordered with shrub oaks and pines, far from the village and affording a glimpse only through an opening of the mountains in the horizon, how my life might pass there, simple and true and natural, and how many things would be impossible to be done there. How many books I might not read!"

He became known in the region for his curiosity about each plot of land, as he cultivated acquaintance with all sorts of landowners. While nibbling a wild apple or discussing crop planting or the care of livestock, he interviewed farmers about the virtues and shortcomings of their own sites. In imagination he surveyed each plot, decided which few pines or oaks would need to be sacrificed to make room for a hut, or where he might plant an orchard or pasture a cow or provide chickens with scratching ground.

Each site had good points and bad. Used to imitating others, Henry considered building at Flint's Pond, where Charles Stearns Wheeler had built the shanty in which he and Henry spent some weeks in the summer of 1837, between Harvard's graduation and commencement. He found land he coveted near Flint's and sought permission but was denied. The orchard side of Fair Haven Hill— often called locally the Cliffs—looked promising, a half mile southwest of Walden Pond, on the bank of the Sudbury River. In Lincoln, about two miles southeast of Concord, lay James Baker's substantial farm on the eastern shore of Fair Haven Bay, and Henry considered renting or trying to buy land there.

He found one place he particularly liked, the broken-down old Hollowell farm, near Hubbard's Bridge on the western bank of the

Sudbury River, two miles from the village. The site had stayed romantically evocative in his memory from his young days on the river, when from his boat he could see no house, only a phalanx of red maples, but could hear a dog barking as if guarding something. As he considered the farm for a home, he decided he liked its seclusion, its tumbledown fences, and his awareness that there had been a long period between its last inhabitant and himself—the same reasons why it would have appealed little to others and been available for less money. A broad field between house and road kept passersby at a comfortable distance. In the gloomy orchard, the trunks of the tired old apple trees were overgrown with lichen that, Henry noticed, had been gnawed by rabbits.

Henry made a modest offer on the run-down plot of land, and the owner accepted it. Henry decided that he would leave the sad apple trees to their fate, permit the rocks to stay where they were in the garden, and not cut down the adolescent birches that had usurped the pasture. As he began to gather wood to build a wheelbarrow with which he could haul materials to and from the farm, he was certain that this secluded, dilapidated farm would repay many times his investment of attention.

But before Henry could pay over the money and receive a deed, the owner's wife talked him out of selling. He came to Henry and offered ten dollars to let him out of the deal. Henry released the family from their commitment without any charge and went his way, as poor as ever, but a little richer in experience.

He kept looking at sites and gathering ideas. In August 1844, he and Ellery Channing boarded an excursion boat to the Kaatskill Mountains, a hundred miles or so north of New York City, planning a walking tour that would cost them very little. On the Hudson River, they stood at the prow at night, admiring how moonlight caressed the mountains. Henry was wearing his usual urchin's garb.

A fellow passenger mistook him for a deckhand, cleared his throat a couple of times, and finally asked, "Come, now, can't you lend me a chaw o' baccy?" Henry was unable to help.

Later, among the raspberry and blueberry patches of a high mountainside, he and Channing lodged briefly in the home of Ira Scribner, a sawmiller on the Kaaterskill Falls, a 260-foot two-step waterfall in beautiful countryside in upstate New York. They were only the latest pilgrims to this site famous for inspiring writers and painters. The pioneer naturalist John Bartram had visited the falls almost a century earlier with his son, later writing up a brief account, "A Journey to Ye Cat Skill Mountains with Billy," that had become celebrated in the United States and Europe for its ode to an unspoiled Eden. Then Washington Irving set his 1819 story "Rip Van Winkle" near there, calling it "a region full of fable" although he had never actually glimpsed the area. Inspired by Irving's story, painter Thomas Cole first visited the falls in the mid-1820s and soon began producing paintings of the region and of Kaaterskill Falls in particular.

It was a shadowed perch where morning and twilight looked the same, where Baucis and Philemon might sit at their cottage door and unwittingly entertain Zeus and Hermes. The cottage itself, lathed but not plastered, was serenaded all day by crickets. This was the kind of divine hideaway that Henry dreamed about for himself. Long after he left the Kaatskills, it lingered in his mind.

"FRIENDS AND FELLOW citizens," Emerson began, "we are met to exchange congratulations on the anniversary of an event singular in the history of civilization; a day of reason; of the clear light; of that which makes us better than a flock of birds and beasts: a day, which gave the immense fortification of a fact,—of gross history,— to ethical abstractions.... The institution of slavery seems to its opponent to have but one side, and he feels that none but a stupid or a malignant person can hesitate on a view of the facts."

On the first day of August 1844, just before the Kaatskills excursion with Channing, Henry was witnessing Emerson's first public commitment to the abolitionist cause, on the tenth anniversary of the historic end of slavery in the British Empire's dominions in the Caribbean. The anniversary of this act was being celebrated in many parts of the United States, to add fuel to the abolitionist fire by demonstrating just how far America was behind its rejected mother country. The push toward abolition wasn't entirely moral; the revolution in industry and improvements in trade gradually made alternatives to slavery more palatable to businessmen. The empire's traffic in slaves had been abolished in 1808, although illegal traffic in human beings continued. Not for a quarter century was slavery itself actually ended throughout the empire. Under this sweeping and controversial act, which went into effect on the first of August 1834, slaves were turned into indentured apprentices, a program that was dissolved after four years. Even then exceptions were made for the East India Company's territories and a few other places, until as late as 1843, the year before Emerson's speech. Slaveholders were offered millions of pounds in compensation for their financial loss. "The sugar they raised was excellent," Emerson declared. "Nobody tasted blood in it."

For a month, the abolitionist weekly *The Liberator* had been promoting the anniversary celebration. This periodical was the pulpit of the legendary abolitionist William Lloyd Garrison, the founder of both the New England Anti-Slavery Society in Boston and the American Anti-Slavery Society in Philadelphia. Ever since its debut issue, on the first day of 1831, it had been the voice of a crusade. "I will be as harsh as truth," Garrison proclaimed, "and as uncompromising as justice." Arguing that slavery was a damned sin in the eyes of God, Garrison refused to actively enter politics because he saw it as the field of compromise. "I am in earnest—I will not equivocate—I will not excuse—I will not retreat a single inch—AND I WILL BE HEARD."

Garrison's life encapsulated the history of abolition. Pro-slavery factions fought him furiously. The summer after Garrison founded *The Liberator*, a slave named Nat Turner led a violent rebellion in Virginia, freeing slaves and killing their white masters. Garrison was one of the many abolitionists blamed for inciting the rebellion. The Georgia state senate offered a $5,000 reward for anyone arresting and successfully prosecuting under Georgia law "the editor or publisher of a certain paper called the *Liberator*," and similar bounties were placed on other abolitionists. Slavery had been illegal in Massachusetts since 1783, but in Boston in 1835 a nine-foot-high double gallows was built before Garrison's house to warn him and his colleagues. In Charleston he was burned in effigy.

The *Concord Freeman* advertised the August 1844 gathering as "a collation in the woods." To defray the costs of promoting the event and bringing in speakers, Henry's neighbors, visiting abolitionists, and others paid a quarter apiece to attend. The owner of Sleepy Hollow, a quiet glade whose oaks and chestnut trees often overheard public gatherings in warm weather, had granted permission for this particular assembly. Then, probably in response to the disapproval emanating from many local churches and other institutions—some of which claimed to stand outside politics, and some of which simply refused to oppose slavery, which after all was common in the Bible—he withdrew permission, leaving the organization with no venue. Shy Nathaniel Hawthorne stepped up to offer the lawn and avenue of his parsonage by the river. But the first of August pummeled the celebration with rain and wind, sending the crowd to the courthouse vestibule.

Over the last few years, Henry had joined with his family in becoming ever more passionate about the sin and blight of slavery. In May, his mother and both sisters had journeyed to Boston to lend their voices to the New England Anti-Slavery Society convention. They had even scandalously supported a resolution to "agitate for a dissolution of the Union." At an abolitionist gathering the following month, Cynthia had met Frederick Douglass, a former slave and one of the most powerful writers and orators on behalf of abolition. It may have been she who arranged for Douglass to speak at the upcoming Concord gathering on the first of August. Scheduled speakers included Douglass, Samuel J. May, and Emerson, but apparently Douglass did not show up.

On that rainy day Henry took it upon himself to get last-minute permission for Emerson to speak in the courthouse, and once he had done so, he scurried from house to house in the wet to alert his neighbors about his mentor's speech on this important topic. The usual public notice was the loud town bell in the steeple of the First Parish Church. For this radical gathering, however, the sexton refused to ring the bell, denouncing these shenanigans as "irresponsible." Nor were the Concord selectmen willing to exercise their option to order him to do so. Various abolitionists present were asked to go and ring the bell, but they couldn't muster the courage. Finally Henry himself ran to the steeple, grasped the rope firmly in his calloused hands, and kept the bell ringing until its peals drew a crowd.

The audience was mesmerized by Emerson's eloquence and also by his physical presence—the handsome face and sculpted lips, the famous dreaming eyes. He stood tall and slender, smiling benevolently on the crowd and the world. This was not Emerson in his abstract or contemplative style. Those who expected an intellectual disquisition on justice or freedom were surprised to find themselves deeply moved by a sermon on brotherhood. One observer, twenty-year-old George William Curtis—another former Brook Farmer who had settled in Concord—thought that Emerson's recent careful reading of the history of abolition, and particularly of the Caribbean triumphs, had lit a fire under him. Emerson spoke passionately for almost two hours, and by the end he held his audience so completely in his palm that there was a staring, respectful hush when he stopped. Finally applause ignited here and there, only to die out as inappropriate to the somber topic.

As the abolitionist movement gained force in the United States, and particularly in Concord, Emerson had grown more and more uncomfortable about his position of public silence on the topic. Like Henry, Emerson was nudged and inspired by the women around him. Lidian had long encouraged her husband to use his growing fame as an essayist and lecturer to address what she felt was the great moral issue of their time. But Emerson had been loath to join the fray. He hesitated in part because, despite Transcendentalism's insistence upon an individual's ability to triumph over circumstance, he considered Negroes distinctly inferior to himself and others of European ancestry. "I think it cannot be maintained by any candid person," he complained to his journal in 1836, "that the African race have ever occupied or do promise to ever occupy any very high place in the human family. Their present condition is the strongest proof that they cannot. The Irish cannot; the American Indian cannot; the Chinese cannot. Before the energy of the Caucasian race all the other races have quailed and done obeisance."

Gradually his opinion of Africans was improving, but he also disliked climbing aboard a bandwagon and was wary of the heady emotions stirred by the evangelical style of reformist speakers. In 1840 he had described the Convention of Friends of Universal Reform in Boston in terms that dramatized his distaste for movements and crowds: "Madmen, madwomen, men with beards, Dunkers, Muggletonians, Come-outers, Groaners, Agrarians, Seventh-day-Baptists, Quakers, Abolitionists, Calvinists, Unitarians, and Philosophers."

Yet he had long believed that slavery was an abomination, as he declared on the first of August. "There is no end to the tragic anecdotes in the municipal records of the colonies," he said simply, and provided examples that had been proven to Parliament—hundreds of slaves at a time thrown overboard to reduce a ship's weight while fleeing from a man-of-war, a boy forced to strip and flog his own mother for a minor offense. "Their case was left out of the mind and out of the heart of their brothers," he said of the slaves.

> The prizes of society, the trumpet of fame, the privileges of learning, of culture, of religion, the decencies and joys of marriage, honor, obedience, personal authority, and a perpetual melioration into a finer civility, these were for all, but not for them. . . . It became plain to all men, the more this business was looked into, that the crimes and cruelties of the slave-traders and slave-owners could not be overstated. The more it was searched, the more shocking anecdotes came up—things not to be spoken.

It became clear to those who had braved the rain for this cause that Emerson had abandoned his pose of philosophical distance and had rolled up his sleeves and joined the fight.

OVER THE DECADES, there had been many inhabitants of Concord for whom slavery was not an abstract concept, and a number of those took refuge near Walden Pond. In the last half of the eighteenth century, many former slaves and free black families eked out a scant living as squatters near the little-traveled road through the woods around the pond. Brister Freeman, who had been a slave of Squire Cummings, had planted the apple trees on Brister's Hill that Henry still enjoyed. Henry had seen his gravestone in the Lincoln cemetery—identified as "Sippio Brister, a man of color"—near those of grenadiers who died during the British retreat from Concord.

Squire Cummings left the country, and in doing so abandoned not only Brister but his sister Zilpah. Unlike many other women in her position, Zilpah did not seek a position as a meagerly paid servant, the common situation of freed slaves, which sometimes resulted in their laboring in the same position in the same household as before, with only nominal wages. Instead, Zilpah chose the precarious and dangerous path of independence. She did what Henry himself imagined doing—she built or rented a small hut in the woods near Walden and there contrived to survive on her own wits.

Naturally Zilpah had learned spinning while a slave. Living near Walden, she wove flax and wool with raw cotton that had been shipped from the West Indies. Wealthier Concord families kept a spinning room, in which they stored several cradles so that laboring former slaves could tend their own sleeping infants in their rags while spinning finer coverings for employers. Zilpah was known for her loud singing voice. Naturally, a woman living alone in the woods acquired the reputation of being a witch, and a local man claimed that he had once overheard her chanting over a boiling kettle, "Ye are all bones, bones!" During the War of 1812, one day while Zilpah was away, British soldiers on patrol torched her hut. Henry himself had seen only her hut's bricks grown over with weeds, but her spirit spoke to his own.

IN 1844 THE prominent factory owner David Loring, who had bought the Heywood farm west of town, beyond the Concord Academy and past the railroad station, began selling building lots.

Although not a mile from the bustling village, and alongside the tracks of the new Fitchburg and Boston railroad, the neighborhood seemed so distant and quiet it was nicknamed Texas. The actual Republic of Texas was often in the news, with discussion of annexation by the United States bandied about among Whigs and Democrats.

Cynthia Thoreau was determined that the family should build their own home. Despite her husband's doubts, she examined Loring's land, chose a lot, and personally measured out the site for the house. Although the area was a bit treeless for Henry's taste, Cynthia selected an otherwise appealing spot not far from the Concord River, with a pleasant view toward the southwest. In September they purchased the land. To finance construction, John Thoreau borrowed five hundred dollars from the Concord businessman Augustus Tuttle and signed a mortgage on the property. The whole family was present for the mortgage signing—John and Cynthia, Sophia and Helen, and Henry. Cynthia worked with a carpenter to loosely develop a blueprint for the house, although both demonstrated their ignorance by forgetting at first to include stairs.

Eager as usual to learn new skills, Henry was soon digging the basement for the house and lining it with stones. Together, he and his father built a square ordinary-looking home with a front door off center. Sam Staples, the local constable, conducted an auction of huts left behind by the Irish laborers on the Fitchburg railroad, and Henry and his father bought a couple. With the wood they built a shed near the house, which could serve as headquarters for their pencil business. Although he had always been considered clever with tools, this was Henry's first extensive experience in constructing a house.

Even as he was building for the future, some of his neighbors were abandoning their homes. Nearby Pittsfield housed the headquarters of the evangelist William Miller, who had been claiming for months that the twenty-second of October would be the end of the world, with the return of a triumphant Christ. All around Henry, some country people and townsfolk joined the Millerites—abandoning crops and livestock, closing shops, waiting for the Second Coming. Henry witnessed these events with fascination. Like the thriving utopian communities around Concord, this vast revival demonstrated a yearning latent in the breasts of his neighbors—a restless desire to transcend the limitations of society and mortality.

ONE DAY IN early October 1844, Emerson went for a ramble alone in the colorful autumn fields, naturally wending his way toward Walden Pond. Along the northeast shore, on a little rise above the pond's largest cove, he encountered a couple of men who were walking around appraising the land. It was an area Emerson was fond of, where he had strolled many times over the years—only a mile and a half from Bush and two miles from his old home, now inhabited by Nathaniel and Sophia Hawthorne. Pitch pines and hickories covered the slight rise, and he could see the pond down a narrow path between their trunks, a hundred feet away. The wooded far shore was half a mile distant.

Explaining that they were there to appraise and sell a field, the men invited Emerson's bid. He made an offer. Later he went home to tell Lidian that he had paid $8.10 per acre for eleven acres. The next day, he brought family along to explore his new property. The site was not isolated. Less than half a mile in any direction, a walker would encounter shanties owned by free Negroes and Irish laborers. Bordering the land was a three- or four-acre pine grove belonging to Hartwell Bigelow, owner of a tavern on Main Street. Emerson's companions pointed out that if Bigelow logged his woods, it would make Emerson's new land far less pleasant. So Emerson bought Bigelow's parcel as well, but at a considerably higher price—$125. To his brother he wrote that he was "landlord & waterlord of 14 acres, more or less, on the shore of Walden, & can raise my own blackberries."

No one knew Walden Pond better than Henry. He was familiar with every cove and hill and woodchuck burrow, the nest of every squirrel and the hunting ground of each red-tailed hawk. He knew this shore's life-everlasting and johnswort, its sumac and scrub pine, high blackberry vines and low creeping strawberries. After Emerson's purchase of the land, however, Henry must have looked at this spot with a different eye. The hut of his dreams had been a castle in the air, glimpsed like a mirage at Flint's Pond and Kaaterskill Falls and the Hollowell farm, but Henry had made little real effort to make the dream a reality. Emerson's purchase put a foundation under it.

Of Emerson's scattered acolytes Henry was the great man's favorite. He was used to asking favors of him and Emerson was used to granting them—and Henry had returned in kind, from carrying coal and tending children to plowing gardens and occasionally helping edit *The Dial*. He went to Emerson and asked if he might have permission to build a small hut on the new property. Naturally Emerson, who had listened to Henry's dreams of the ideal monk's cell for seven years, said yes. Because of the Irish laborers and the former slaves, as well as the indigent and shiftless who could be found in its quiet coves and banks, Walden Pond was not considered a place where a gentlemanly white man might live. But Henry did not think of himself as a gentleman.

"I SEE NOTHING for you in this earth but that field which I once christened 'Briars,'" Ellery Channing wrote to Henry from a trip in early March 1845; "go out upon that, build yourself a hut, & there begin the grand process of devouring yourself alive. I see no alternative, no other hope for you."

Henry must have agreed. Shortly after he received Channing's letter, amid occasional snow flurries but mostly sunny days, he started clearing enough of Emerson's land at Walden Pond to make room for a cabin. The ice was beginning to melt, creating a few open spaces, and the pond's surface looked darker than it had in months, because the thin ice had water under it. An early meadowlark whistled *see-yoo, see-yee-hee-heer*.

Just as he had borrowed the land, Henry began construction by borrowing an ax. It was his rule to return a tool in better condition than he received it, if possible, so he was not averse to borrowing. The Thoreau family must have owned felling axes for hewing trees. To square the timbers to frame a cabin, however, Henry needed a large broad ax, the kind that was being used by the Irish workers for squaring railroad ties. Its heavy head lent force when the ax was swung and its broad blade had a straight side for edging and a beveled side for wedging the blade into a log. He would have first marked the split line with a lighter ax and stood upon the log to swing the ax along the line, then rolled the log and repeated the procedure to get a full square timber. The same kind of ax could be used to cut flooring planks. The daily lumber work required strength and expertise, but Henry had a fair quantity of both, and his experience helping build the new Thoreau house came in handy. He labored for hours in the warm sun and at midday sat among the aromatic chips to eat his bread-and-butter lunch with hands redolent of pine resin. Apparently he had to return the broad ax before he was finished, because he did much of the later work with his narrow felling ax, cutting down the arrowy pines and hewing the timber into rafters and studs for the house.

He was in no hurry. On occasion someone who heard his ax might stop by to chat. It took him to the middle of April to finish the preparations, to cut enough boards and lay a foundation. The soil here was soft and pliable and he needed only a couple of hours to dig a cellar six feet square, during which process he unearthed a woodchuck burrow. His cellar had devoured the home of a neighbor, like a rich man's estate.

ONCE THE FITCHBURG railroad was completed through Concord, its builders moved on, following the new industry's insatiable appetite for trees and cheap labor. For a few dollars, the workers sold their slapped-together huts to locals who could use the lumber. The shanties bought by Henry's father now helped form the pencil business office next to their Texas Street house. Most builders reused whatever materials they could find, and Henry planned to do the same. During his rambles through woods and fields, consulting with landowners, speculating about possible sites, he had quietly assayed several huts.

An Irish railroad worker named James Collins owned a shanty that was better than most, and he was willing to sell. It was small, with a steep cottage roof and a single high window above the five-foot-high mound of dirt that covered the house's walls on three sides as if it had grown out of the earth like a dwarf's cottage in a fable. The roof was brittle and warped from baking in the sun, but its boards seemed stronger than the others.

Collins was away when Henry called to look over the shanty from within. A small flock of hens, alarmed by Henry's approach, squeezed under the door—there was no sill—and hid inside. Henry knocked and Mrs. Collins came to the door and invited him in. The single dirt-floored room was gloomy and dank, with a bare open hole for a cellar. The hut seemed to Henry like a good place to contract the ague. When his eyes adjusted to the darkness, he could see a chair, a stove, a bed, an incongruous duo of gilt-framed looking glass and silk parasol—perhaps from better times in the old country—and a quiet baby. A shiny new coffee mill, with its long-handled grinder, was nailed to an oak sapling. Coffee had gained in popularity in the United States ever since the high tax on teas had helped fuel the Revolution.

One of the window's two panes was missing. The cat broke it, Mrs. Collins explained. She lit a lamp and held it up to show off the ceiling and walls. "Good boards overhead," she said. "Good boards all around—and a good window."

James Collins returned and he and Henry settled on a price—$4.25 for the whole building. The family would be out by six the next morning. After Henry paid over the money, Collins warned him to arrive early and to expect trouble from lying scoundrels who might claim that Collins owed them rent or fuel costs.

Early in the morning Henry passed the Collins family on the move, complete with hens and looking glass and coffee mill. Driving a small cart, Henry went on to the hut. He began by drawing out the spikes, nails, and staples, putting aside those that were reusable. Gradually the pile of lumber in the cart grew. Then Henry varied his labor by driving the load of bent and splintery boards to the cabin site, where he spread them on the ground to bleach in the sun.

When he returned to the shanty, a small Irish boy told him that one of the Collinses' neighbors, an Irishman man named Seeley, had stolen the nails and staples that Henry saved. Although machined at this time instead of hand-made as they had been for centuries, nails were nonetheless valuable. Seeley himself wandered back to stand around watching Henry. There wasn't much work to be had, he said blithely. Apparently Henry didn't confront Seeley about his thievery.

★　　★　　★

AT DAWN ONE morning in early May, Henry arrived at the Hosmer farm. Edmund Hosmer was one of Henry's closer friends among the Concord farmers, a man he respected for his intelligence and level head. Awaiting Henry's arrival were Hosmer himself and his three older sons—Andrew, Edmund, and John. Hosmer's sons may have assisted in part because Henry specifically stated that he needed the strength of the young. More help came from young George William Curtis, who worked for the Hosmers. He found the cabin raising a pleasant diversion, although the previous autumn he had severely cut the joint of his right thumb when his hat fell off and in grabbing for it he swiped his thumb against the blade of a scythe.

Hosmer swung an ax up on his shoulder. With axes and other tools in hand, the group set off down the turnpike to Emerson's house and across fields and woods along the Walden Road to the pond. The Hosmer family knew and loved Henry. Aware that stormy weather might keep Edmund indoors, Henry would choose such days to drop by the farm. He and Hosmer discussed Scandinavian mythology until the listening children considered themselves experts in it. Sometimes they argued about such topics until the clock surprised them by chiming midnight, and now and then Henry went home and thought about the discussion and came back next day with a new argument.

The smaller children especially enjoyed Henry's appearance on their doorstep in his gray homespun, although their father felt that youngsters should mostly be seen and not heard, and Henry himself did not permit too great familiarity. He would read the *Canterbury Tales* to the Hosmer children, declaiming Chaucer's foreign enunciation, as in his portrait of the Squire: "'He koude songes make and wel endite, / Juste and eek daunce, and weel purtreye and write.' You can sometimes," Henry added in an aside to the children, "catch the sense better by listening than by reading." He also told them fanciful stories about his encounters in the woods with various wild animals, claiming that he knew a partridge neighbor that brought its brood to meet him. "The best part of an animal is its *anima*—its soul," he explained, "—but the scientists never get any further than its shell."

With the Hosmers, Henry arrived at Emerson's land beside the pond. Other friends joined them, including Bronson Alcott, brothers George and Burrill Curtis, and possibly Emerson himself. By nightfall Henry's house was framed and standing by the pond—fresh-looking white hewn studs, the straight lines of rafters and window like a sketch of a house, and the roof raised high and firm.

Chapter 21

FAVORED BY THE GODS

A S HENRY AND his friends were raising the walls and roof of his new home by Walden Pond, Nathaniel and Sophia Hawthorne were looking poverty in the eye more than ever before. Despite placing stories in prominent magazines such as John L. O'Sullivan's literary and political journal *The United States Magazine and Democratic Review*, despite his growing reputation, Hawthorne was almost destitute. Publishers casually guaranteed payment and casually sent excuses instead of checks. Meanwhile, when Sophia expressed dismay at the disreputable tears in her frock or in her husband's dressing gown, her husband joked that it was strange they had so little ready cash, considering that she was the holiest among them and he was a man of the largest rents in the country.

Their chief worry was for their one-year-old daughter, Una. After Sophia's earlier miscarriage, the Hawthornes had been astonished and thrilled by the birth of a healthy daughter. They named her after Spenser's personification of truth and the True Church in *The Faerie Queene*. Friends criticized this choice, and Hawthorne replied to one, "It is as simple as a name can be—as simple as a breath—it is merely inhaling a breath into one's heart, and emitting it again, and the name is spoken." Little Una was charming and talkative. As a baby she had grasped at shadows and splashes of sunlight, and she later she solemnly examined every picture in a book or her mother's paintings around the house. Hawthorne claimed that he was planning to publish her art criticism in one volume octavo. When Una first began awkwardly speaking, thanks to Bible stories she began saying aloud the name *Adam*. Then gradually she dropped the first syllable. She would sit quietly in a chair, pretending to read a book that her mother had given her, repeating softly to herself "'Dam, 'Dam, 'Dam."

Una's birth had brought her mother and father a new seriousness, and their money problems were constantly on Hawthorne's mind. "As for myself, who have been a trifler preposterously long," he wrote to a friend, "I find it necessary to come out of my cloud region, and allow myself to be woven into the sombre texture of humanity. There is no escaping it any longer. I have business on earth now, and must look about me for the means of doing it."

Following the surprise election in March 1845 of Andrew Jackson's protégé, the Tennessean James K. Polk, as president, Hawthorne turned his financial hopes toward the new Democratic administration. John O'Sullivan, editor of *The United States Magazine and Democratic Review*, which had published some of Hawthorne's stories, responded to pleas of increasing urgency from the Old Manse by asking Hawthorne, "What would you say to go out as a consul to China?" Hawthorne's close friend and his daughter's godfather, O'Sullivan was working on an essay, "Annexation," in which, while arguing for the annexation of Texas, he coined a new term for the United States' drive to conquer the rest of the continent west of the established states, which numbered twenty-seven after Florida's admission during the same month. He complained that other nations had interfered in this U.S. issue "for the avowed object of thwarting our policy and hampering our power, limiting our greatness and checking the fulfillment of our manifest destiny to overspread the continent allotted by Providence for the free development of our yearly multiplying millions." The term "manifest destiny" was soon embraced by proponents of relentless westward expansion.

Eventually Hawthorne's continued search for a job paid off. One day in May, while the man of the house was hewing wood in the shed, Sophia glanced out a window to see Horatio Bridge, one of Hawthorne's dearest friends and a fellow 1825 alumnus of Bowdoin College, walking into the yard with another man. She was fond of Bridge. Hawthorne had always credited him with early crucial encouragement in his fellow student's talent as an author, and he was a playful and good-humored guest. After ten years as a lawyer, Bridge had joined the Navy as a purser, after which Hawthorne called him "the Admiral." He was a trim, boisterous man with a long thin nose and large owlish eyes that opened wide when he was excited, as he clearly was now.

When Bridge saw Sophia he gallantly whipped off his hat and waved it. She lowered the window sash to greet them and Bridge introduced his companion—another Bowdoin classmate, Class of '24, named Franklin Pierce. In 1828, the year his father had become governor of New Hampshire, Pierce became the youngest member of the state's House of Representatives, serving as Speaker for five years, and he had since served in the U.S. Senate for five. President Polk, Pierce's close friend, had just appointed him New Hampshire's district attorney.

Sophia told them where to find her husband and soon they returned, smiling, with Pierce's arm around Hawthorne's waist, rumpling his old blue frock. They were there, they explained, to offer Hawthorne a position in the new president's administration, as Surveyor of the Custom House in Salem, Massachusetts, Hawthorne's hometown. Bridge was in a giddy mood, thrilled to deliver such a windfall of news. He blinked and smiled at Sophia and danced around the room and swooped in to kiss wide-eyed Una, who had not invited such tribute and who responded with royal hauteur. Sophia had heard about Pierce, about his affection for her husband—whom he offhandedly referred to as Nathaniel, she noticed, which was an intimacy permitted to few. Over the next hour he struck her as a natural gentleman, a man of honesty and refinement. Soon the three men strode to the village to dine and discuss the specifics of Hawthorne's new job in Salem. It might take a few months for the official appointment to be handed down from Washington, but the promise of it lightened spring days for the Hawthornes, after a long worrisome winter.

HENRY AVOIDED HAWTHORNE'S sort of crisis by dodging both romantic and financial commitments. Alone, he was building a tiny habitation on borrowed land. As he worked on his cabin, Henry optimistically planted crops in the field nearby, beside little Wyman Road that ran into the busy Lincoln road below Brister's Hill. The field had been sown with rye for so many years that a visitor thought the weeds themselves looked malnourished. Henry disagreed. The previous crops made his cultivation of the ground easier. He planted about two and a half acres of beans. Part of his plan for supporting himself on Emerson's land was raising crops for the Emersons. It was too large an area for his hoe, so he hired a man to bring a horse and plow, although Henry did some of the plowing himself. Up came the yellow blooms and dotted leaves of johnswort and the low yellow cinquefoil plants that so resembled strawberries except for their poor fruit that they were sometimes called "barren strawber-ries." In their place Henry planted a small amount of corn and potatoes and, most of all, many rows of white bush beans.

Early each morning, before even squirrels and woodchucks began their day, he started work barefoot, his toes planted in the gravelly yellow earth while it was still damp with dew. Gradually the sun warmed and dried the soil and began to blister his feet, at which point he reluctantly cleaned them and donned shoes.

One day a friend—a burly French Canadian named Alek Therien—walking by on his way to chop wood paused to advise, "If those beans were mine, I shouldn't like to hoe them till the dew was off."

"Ah," Henry replied, "that is one of the notions the farmers have got, but I don't believe it."

It took him so long to plant the rows that added up to seven miles of beans that the green shoots of the early ones were out of the ground before he finished planting the later rows. He had little rationale for raising far more beans than the Thoreaus and Emersons together could eat, but they had become part of his metaphor of self-cultivation. Because his garden abutted a busy road, and it was the only cultivated field among long stretches of woods, many travelers saw him at work in the early morning. Now and then he would hear someone jostling along in a gig exclaim to a companion, "Beans so late!" Often, amid the earthworms and cinquefoil roots in the quickly drying soil, he spied the barely artificial-looking facets of an arrowhead and reached down to scoop it up and drop it in his pocket, where he carried it as a talisman.

BY THIS TIME Hawthorne had known Henry for a couple of years. Like Emerson and others who knew the difficult young man, Hawthorne had gradually revised his opinion of him. On July first, several weeks after the visit of Bridge and Pierce, Hawthorne wrote a letter to Evert Augustus Duyckinck, who the year before had become editor of the *Democratic Review.* (Each issue of this periodical bore on its cover the motto "The Best Government Is That Which Governs Least," an idea with which Emerson was in agreement, as he remarked in his essay "Politics," which appeared in 1844 in his *Essays: Second Series*: "Hence the less government we have the better—the fewer laws and less confided power." Henry passionately agreed and soon adopted his own variation.) Duyckinck had launched a series of books and had asked Hawthorne's opinion of inviting Henry to contribute.

"There is one chance in a thousand that he might write a most excellent and readable book," Hawthorne replied," but added that he would not want to undertake the responsibility of nudging him to do so.

He is the most unmalleable fellow alive—the most tedious, tiresome, and intolerable—the narrowest and most notional— and yet, true as all this is, he has great qualities of intellect and character. The only way, however, in which he could ever approach the popular mind, would be by writing a book of simple observation of nature, somewhat in the vein of White's History of Selborne.

FOUR YEARS EARLIER, the Fourth of July had seen the Tippecanoe rally around the horse-drawn log cabin and the rolling campaign ball. The Fourth in 1845 saw Henry moving into his own home. The cabin wasn't finished, but Independence Day was too good a symbol to resist. The roof kept out rain, it was true, but chinks between the weathered, reused boards admitted wind and insects. Henry hid some of the crevices with decorations from the woods and pond: pieces he cut from patterned birch bark, blackberry vines, seed heads of goldenrod and sedge. There was no chimney. But the studs and rafters, the planed window framing, smelled fresh and clean.

The day was cloudy with the sun peeking through at times, the afternoon pleasant with a light breeze from the east. Henry

mounted a hay rig on a wagon to support his few pieces of furniture and drove it to the cabin. Vain about his spartan needs, he
had looked with scorn upon the wagon trains moving loads of
furniture and intimate belongings of wealthy Concordians. Some
of his furniture he had crafted himself—cutting and shaping the
wood, stretching the cane bottom of the bed. Besides his green
lift-top desk, he had a small three-legged table, with a chair for
each and a third for visitors. Jugs held molasses and oil. In his
rattling wagon he carried more utensils than furniture: two forks
and knives and one spoon, a pair of both andirons and tongs, a
wash bowl and a dipper, three plates, a single cup. For cooking he
had a skillet, a frying pan, and a kettle, and for shaving a three-
inch-wide looking glass. Naturally he took no clock. A woman
offered him a doormat, but he refused, claiming that it was too
much extra effort to wipe his shoes on it rather than on sod.
There were no curtains on the windows, just as there was no lock
on the lift-latch door. Henry's draperies were the woods themselves, his security a lack of valuables. Two windows brought in
the woods and sky until twilight, when they began to mirror a
young man reading Plutarch in Greek and writing in a journal or
polishing his flute.

Naturally Henry thought of how long Walden had haunted his
dreams. Many of the same pines stood together as they had when
he was first brought here as a small child. He had burned branches
from one of their fallen comrades to prepare supper outside the
cabin, where he would cook prior to completing a chimney and
fireplace. Pine cones that had lain on the ground during his first
childhood ramble here had opened and shed their seeds, which
had sprouted and grown into new pines to enchant a later
generation.

★   ★   ★

HENRY TURNED TO his journal with redoubled passion. The day after he moved into the cabin, he recalled the home of the miller on the Kaaterskill Falls, where he and Channing had stayed the summer before—the airy house itself, the Olympian view, a site "fit to entertain a traveling god," Henry wrote. "Could not man be man in such an abode? And would he ever find out this grovelling life?" He had high hopes for his new abode.

Always he returned to nature. "How symbolical, significant of I know not what, the pitch pine stands here before my door!" he exclaimed to himself on the seventh. "We are the subjects of an experiment how singular! Can we not dispense with the society of our gossips a little while under these circumstances?" He took stock of his crops and estimated that the woodchucks had nibbled clean an eighth of an acre. "This is the tax I pay for ousting johnswort and the rest," he wrote. But at least the beans would soon be too sinewy for the woodchucks to gobble.

He was deliriously happy during the first days at the cabin. Every morning he bathed in the pond while the night's mist slowly retreated into the woods. Unlike his neighbors, and despite his notoriously unimpressive clothes, Henry liked cleanliness, and he also felt that a daily baptism in his sacred pool kept him connected to its mysteries. Ten days after moving in, he sat indoors on a rainy day and felt not lonely but united with the world around him:

> What sweet and tender, the most innocent and divinely encouraging society there is in every natural object, and so in universal nature, even for the poor misanthrope and melancholy man! ...
> Sometimes, when I compare myself with other men, methinks I am favored by the gods. They seem to whisper joy to me beyond my deserts, and that I do have a solid warrant and surety at their

hands, which my fellows do not. I do not flatter myself, but if it were possible they flatter me. I am especially guided and guarded.

Finally he had a sanctuary, far enough from his parents' boardinghouse to hear no piano in the parlor below. Yet he was only a short walk from Mill Dam gossip, which he enjoyed in what he called "homeopathic doses." Each night Henry went to sleep in his own bed, listening to the crickets and bobwhites and owls, with the train's occasional dragon roar at the other end of the pond. Mornings found sunlight angling not across pine trunks but through the cabin's open door, warming not vegetable mold but the planed boards underneath his green desk. The pitch pines whose aromatic roots had slowed his digging of the cellar now rubbed their needled branches across the roof.

Chapter 22

DEATH ON THE RIVER

D URING THAT FIRST week after his move to Walden, not everyone in Concord was as happy as Henry. Less than a mile away from his cabin—almost to the Mill Brook and no more than two hundred yards from Emerson's desk—stood the almshouse, the Concord Asylum. It was not hidden. Painted red, it stood out against the trees and fields. Thanks to the almost constant screaming of an inmate named Nancy Barron, it stood out as well against the rattle of carriages passing on the turnpike and thrushes yodeling from the chestnut trees in the front yard. Emerson sighed to his journal that whenever he opened a window, he could hear mad Nancy scream. Her inarticulate lament rang in his ears and his memory—a reminder of a physical world of troubles anchored far below the celestial realm in which Emerson was comfortable. Barron's pain was the most vocal, but not the only such lament surrounding Henry's happiness.

On the evening of July 9, Nathaniel and Sophia and Una Hawthorne were at home together in the Old Manse. Ever since the visit from Horatio Bridge and Franklin Pierce in May, offering Hawthorne the job of surveyor in the Custom House, they had been in the midst of planning for their departure from this, their first home.

Following a knock, Hawthorne found Ellery Channing waiting at the door with darkness behind him. It was just past nightfall of a clear starlit evening, a few days past the new moon. Unlike Henry, Hawthorne didn't like Channing. "A gump," he had called him, and "little better than an idiot," in a letter to his wife the previous June. "He should have been whipt often and soundly in his boyhood," he fumed; "and as he escaped such wholesome discipline then, it might be well to bestow it now."

But these were unusual circumstances. Channing was there, he explained, to borrow the *Pond Lily*, which was needed for a search party. Young Martha Emmeline Hunt, a nineteen-year-old teacher, was thought to have drowned herself in the river that morning. Her parents, Daniel and Clarissa Hunt, lived farther down Monument Street, near Punkatasset Hill, so naturally the neighbors were form-ing a search party, and naturally Hawthorne would be expected to help. Friends had scoured the nearby woods, calling Martha's name, to no avail. He readily volunteered both the boat and, although his shyness and reserve must have made the gesture painful, himself. Either no one notified Henry, on the far side of Concord, or he chose not to leave his new cabin.

One of ten brothers and sisters, Martha was known in the village as an intelligent girl who had achieved an air of refinement and culture above her modest farm upbringing. She had distinguished herself with honors at a school in a nearby town, and was said to have been at her happiest during that time. Henry must have known this fellow teacher in a small community. At her young age she was already superintending a class at District School No. 4, with respon-sibility for sixty difficult students. Despite her well-known virtue and piety, however, and her much-admired quiet manners, she was plagued with melancholy humors and seemed to have no friends. The farmers who knew her family considered her uppity for not being satisfied to churn butter without complaint. Like Henry, she could often be seen walking alone in the woods. Martha resisted discussing her gloom with others. Her rough but supposedly well-meaning family had professed themselves unable to understand or help her. Although descended from early settlers of Concord, Daniel Hunt farmed with antiquated methods, had too few sons among his flock to help him, and barely kept his numerous children fed. The girls, especially, had few options, and Martha turned toward teaching as her way out.

In the darkness, Hawthorne and Channing pushed the boat into the water, Channing at the oars, Hawthorne maneuvering a paddle, and they set off downstream on the dark slow river. The almost still black water reflected the bright stars overhead. Some distance below the bridge, Hawthorne saw flickering lights and shadowy figures on the river bank—a crowd of searchers with lanterns and torches whose reflections danced on the dark water. He and Channing pulled the *Pond Lily* up to the bank and climbed out. Another boat was present. The searchers were gathered here because they had found Martha's bonnet and shoes on the bank, drenched with dew, and her kerchief caught in reeds by the shore. They assumed that, if she drowned herself in the river, her body must be near, because the Concord's current was sluggish and this was its deepest stretch. Their lanterns, held above the water, reflected in its black surface.

To continue the search, the *Pond Lily* took on board a stranger to Hawthorne, a young man in a blue frock coat. They also carried Joshua Buttrick, who had inherited the family farm in Sleepy Hollow, near the river not far north of town, in the hollow northeast of Punkatasset Hill—another neighbor of Martha's family. About Hawthorne's age, he was a general in the militia who liked to say that he found the smell of burning gunpowder exciting. The search party on shore included the general's relative David Buttrick;

a loquacious elderly carpenter; some people Hawthorne recognized and some he didn't; young George William Curtis; and even Martha's younger brother, William Henry Hunt. At fourteen, William kept his face from showing much emotion as he waited for news of his sister. When asked how many siblings there were, he calmly answered, "Ten."

As owner of the closest boat, Hawthorne found himself unwittingly at the center of the search party. They got into the boat without lanterns because they needed their hands for other work. Carefully Hawthorne steered them above the deeper water. Channing probed the depths with a long-handled hay rake, while Buttrick and the younger man used poles with hooks at the end. It was the kind of scene Hawthorne usually conjured rather than witnessed. For the villagers, it was a rare opportunity to glimpse the silent and reclusive author who had moved into Reverend Ripley's house, who was rarely glimpsed except in his garden in the morning or alone in his little boat. While the party on shore watched anxiously and occasionally shouted advice, Hawthorne guided the boat back and forth in front of the spot where poor Martha had left her bonnet and shoes. One of the men would catch his rake or hook on something, cautiously haul it up dripping into the lantern light, and find that what seemed at first to be drenched garments were in fact waterweeds. Both Buttrick and Channing thought at times that they had hooked the submerged body, but if so they were unable to dislodge it or pull it upward. Probably, Hawthorne thought, they were hooking sod that had slipped down from the bank.

Hawthorne took the boat past the party on shore one more time and, midway between the river's banks, turned it to float broadside. They drifted slowly downstream.

On the plank seat in front of him, the young man in the frock coat sat probing his hooked pole in the water. Suddenly it caught on something. "What's this?" he exclaimed. He tugged on the pole. "Yes, I've got her!"

To Hawthorne he sounded dismayingly like an excited fisherman. The young man bent all his strength on the pole and heaved upward, revealing in the faint starlight light-colored clothing rising to the surface, then the first undeniable glimpse of the girl's pale body. He pulled the corpse toward the boat, while the girl's limbs swayed stiffly in the water, until he could grasp her cold hand and draw her closer. He held on to her while Hawthorne steered the boat toward shore. Men waded out to help them, their lanterns revealing what had been barely visible in the starlit middle of the river. After eighteen hours in the water, Martha's arms and legs were already rigid—the legs only slightly bent and the feet close together, but her arms caught reaching forward in the act of struggling, her hands clenched in agony. Although her complexion was a terrible dark red, her hands were disconcertingly white.

"Ah, poor child!" exclaimed one old man who helped carry the body onto shore.

By the time Hawthorne and Buttrick and the young man were out of the boat, the others had placed the body under an oak tree. They huddled around it with their lanterns, horrified but fascinated, their shadows dancing around them as they spoke in low voices. Mary's eye socket had been torn, perhaps by the hooked pole that drew her corpse back up among the living. Her face was dark red. Watery blood streamed from her nose. Two of the men scooped water from the river and splashed it on the poor girl's face to stanch the flow of blood, but it wouldn't cease. The old carpenter, who in his long life had seen other villagers drowned in this peaceful river, confided authoritatively that the poor girl would continue to "purge" until they placed her in her grave, and that by morning her body would swell beyond recognition.

To Hawthorne's mind, always gnawed by religious symbolism, it seemed as if Martha's posture embodied an inflexible divine judgment rather than the grace he thought she must have sought in the next world. He imagined that she would keep the same heartbreaking pose in a coffin, that when her body decayed her skeleton would remember this horror and preserve it, that on Judgment Day her spirit would rise from the grave bent in this horrific mortal posture.

When the men tried to lower Martha's arms, they resisted, and if held down for an instant, when released they moved with ghostly autonomy back into their pose of supplication. One of the men even put his foot on the girl's arm to hold it down and force it into a normal position; but as soon as he moved, the limb rose to its former place. Surely, Hawthorne thought, when Martha stood by the river and dropped her bonnet eighteen hours earlier, had she foreseen a grotesque tableau of men stepping on her limbs she would have spared herself this posthumous indignity.

One middle-aged member of the search party, David Buttrick, could not bear the scene and fainted dead away. He was found insensible on the grass nearby and others bent to rub his limbs and hands to help wake him. Meanwhile everyone talked about the girl, her family, whether an inquest was needed, who might comprise it. The old carpenter remarked grotesquely that he would "just as lief touch dead people as living ones."

Some men brought two rails, laid broken oars and other boards across them, wrapped the girl's bent body in a quilt, and laid it on the makeshift bier. Everyone helped to either carry the burden or steady it while walking alongside. The body seemed to grow heavier as they trudged up the slight gradient of the hill from the river to the Hunt farmhouse, a long half mile under the distant uncaring stars.

Chapter 23

LIVING FIREWORKS

B EFORE HENRY EVEN finished building his cabin, he was not its only tenant. One day a wild mouse joined him for luncheon. Apparently its nest was under the floor, so it didn't have far to travel when it smelled food or heard the rattle of the paper in which Henry had wrapped it. Henry thought that perhaps it had never seen a man before. He sat quiet and still, letting bread crumbs fall to the bare pine boards, where the mouse moved from bite to bite, nibbling daintily, its big black eyes wary.

With a body about four inches long and a tail doubling its overall length, it was larger than a house mouse, its ears longer, its lighter belly fur continuing up the neck and chin to the mouth, where it met the gray-brown upper fur at the pink nose. At times it ran up a wall with little bursts of energy, like a miniature squirrel. Soon it was leaping onto Henry's shoes and, with a prickling of its tiny claws, racing up a leg inside his pantaloons.

Henry enjoyed the company and encouraged the mouse's visits. He wasn't surprised to find that it came readily for snacks, but gradually he discovered that it was willing to socialize for a less tangible return. During these warm summer evenings, Henry would sit in the cabin with the door open and play his flute. Soon the mouse would emerge from its secret home, venture away from the wall, and sit listening as long as Henry continued to play the same tune that first lured his tiny neighbor. It seemed, though, that when he changed tunes the mouse would flee. Henry wondered whether he shifted his posture in an alarming way or the mouse simply had finicky taste in music.

HENRY PARTICULARLY ADMIRED the migratory wild pigeons that frequented the woods around Walden—the pigeons that animated the woods and fields over much of North America, which he had admired and dined upon, including with John during their river journey. These birds were far more populous than doves. They traveled in vast flocks estimated to contain uncountable millions, and most people considered them an inexhaustible food source. Because they migrated, the Choctaw had dubbed them *putchee nashoba*, "lost doves," and the Narragansett *wuskówhàn*, "wanderers." Some English speakers called them passenger (meaning traveler) pigeons.

"How thick the pigeons are!" Alek Therien exclaimed one morning in mid-July. "If working every day were not my trade, I could get all the meat I should want by hunting—pigeons, woodchucks, rabbits, partridges. By George, I could get all I should want for a week in one day!"

The Scottish naturalist Alexander Wilson had written about these flocks in his monumental *American Ornithology*, which was published in nine volumes between 1808 and 1814. Boating down the Ohio River by himself in 1810, Wilson liked to rest his oars on the gunwales and gaze up at the endless wavering strands of migrating pigeons pouring out of Kentucky, heading toward Indiana Territory. One day Wilson went ashore to buy milk at a house he had glimpsed from the river. He was indoors, chatting, when a deafening roar blasted the house, quickly followed by the sky darkening in all directions visible from the windows. Terrified, Wilson thought a tornado was about to strike the house, but the homeowners smiled calmly and said, "It is only the pigeons." He rushed out to find a vast flock swooping low between the house and the high bank across the river.

Passenger pigeons had seemed inexhaustible ever since the first European settlements in the New World. William Wood wrote in his 1634 survey *New England's Prospect*, "I have seene them fly ... seeing neyther beginning nor ending, length, or breadth, of these Millions of Millions. ... Many of them build amongst the Pine-trees, thirty miles to the Northeast of our plantations; joyning nest to nest, and tree to tree by their nests, so that the Sunne never sees the ground in that place, from whence the *Indians* fetch whole loads of them." Not fickle eaters, passenger pigeons devoured beechnuts, acorns, huckleberries, chestnuts, Indian corn, even buckwheat. A roost floored with blue-black droppings indicated that the birds had been eating berries. Dead birds often revealed a crop full of acorns—even the huge ones from red oaks—that had been swallowed whole.

Henry was amused by the way they stretched their bronze neck to peer down at him, the neck feathers' iridescence when the bird moved reminding him of the interior of seashells. The pigeons would fly to a bough of white pine, their black-spotted blue-gray wings unfolding with a flutter as they perched, their silhouette tapering from plump breast to the tip of their long, white-fringed tail. He enjoyed the sudden rush when the birds appeared out of nowhere and raced in groups of two or three across his view. Sometimes Henry saw the pigeons as the color of weather-stained wood—their blue more mundane than celestial—and at a distance a larger flock appeared as a slate-gray blur. In fall they vanished, only to reappear on some brisk April day, or sometimes even in March, in flocks that dashed across the sky as one. Svelte in contrast to the fat pigeons that perched on Cambridge window ledges, they were also distinguishable at a glance from doves by their narrower body and more pointed wings—even when the pink breast of the male wasn't visible—and by their unusually fast, straight flight.

In the fields and woods around Concord, Henry could hear the flocks' chatter and keck at a distance. To discern softer notes, such as their tremulous coo, he had to creep closer. Many of the noises they produced didn't sound like birds, such as a harsh creak like two branches rubbing together. Early and late the pigeons were noisy, but in summer or early fall they were silent, roosting. In small flocks their wings sounded to Henry like a farmer winnowing after threshing— the airy flutter of chaff blowing away as grain fell to the earth.

HENRY NEEDED FEW tools to research the private lives of his wild neighbors. For birds and distant mammals he carried a looking glass, a simple telescope, protected by a case and hung in its own pocket. Identifying birds in the wild was difficult; he consulted Alexander Wilson's *American Ornithology* but could not carry along the bulky volume. His walking stick was notched to measure the depth of pond or snowfall. Instead of lugging a specimen box, as many naturalists did during the international enthusiasm for natural history that had been growing for decades, Henry carried home plants by tucking them inside his soft hat. When walking, he would sometimes gather a lock of the gray-green usnea lichen called old man's beard, or the shed husk of a cicada, and then would require a protective case for his trophies. Out would come his pocketknife as he stopped beside a birch, where he would carefully cut straight strips of bark and fold them into a box, which if small enough could be tucked inside his hat.

He wasn't always as quiet as an Indian on these walks. Channing observed that sometimes in the autumn Henry kicked through dry fallen leaves like a child. The noise sent animals scurrying, but he knew he would see them again tomorrow. Most of the time he moved quietly, deliberately, and he could often be seen standing still for several minutes or longer as a chipmunk or moth overcame its fear and circled closer. Disregarding fashion, he still wore grayish-brown clothes that helped him blend into the woods and fields.

He loved insects—the alchemical metamorphoses within a chrysalis, a skater bug's faithful walk on water, a mourning cloak butterfly with its yellow-bordered and blue-spotted wings and its spiny red-flecked caterpillars, a honeybee lurking in the spathe of a skunk cabbage. The uneven gray globe of a wasp's nest, like an Oriental paper lantern hung swaying from a branch, could entertain him for many minutes.

Always fascinated by fish, Henry knew the dozen or more species common in the ponds and creeks of Concord. "Unlike ours, the element in which they live," he wrote, "is a stream which must be constantly resisted." He once caught a stately pickerel that had swallowed one of its kin surely half its own size, with the other fish's tail protruding from its mouth—although, when Henry cut it open, he found the victim's head already digested within the aggressor's stomach. A few years earlier he had written in his journal, "How many young finny contemporaries of various character and destiny, form and habits, we have even in this water! And it will not be forgotten by some memory that we were contemporaries. . . . For they are to be understood, surely, as all things else, by no other method than that of sympathy." He saw fish in water as analogous to birds in air: the rapacious pickerel as hawk, the homely bream a kind of sparrow. "The pout is the owl," he wrote, "which steals so noiselessly about at evening with its clumsy body."

He stood in Walden Pond and stroked bream as if they were pets as they lingered near the shore above their shallow nest.

Bream deposited their spawn on weeds and on the sandy bottom of the pond, along the sunny side of a hollow usually about six inches deep and two feet across. Henry sometimes found a couple of dozen nests close together along the shore. This fish would hover protectively over its gelatinous mass of eggs, refusing to flee. As a consequence, when approached with care, it would permit Henry to caress its back and—slowly, gently—to close his fingers about its body and lift it from the pond, with its delicate fins sculling air instead of water. Then he would gently return it to its native element.

LIVING IN THE Walden cabin gave Henry more opportunities to enjoy the drama of moonlit nights. In the dark, armies of grain filled the fields to the river's edge, their heads nodding in the breeze. Oxen slept in fields, reclining like the Sphinx. Now and then Henry would meet another villager abroad—a farmer who offered him a ride or a boy who had set a pail down in the road to stone a bird—but mostly he walked alone.

Emerson thought that Henry had mastered the art of going anywhere he wanted to, on land or water, like an animal. He stepped across boundary lines as if he didn't know they existed. Often he crossed a wood lot or field during the night, when its owner was sleeping. Emerson declared that Henry knew what was on a farmer's land even when the farmer himself did not. Seldom did a landowner complain that Henry was trespassing. When one did, however, Henry might come by with a gift—a shrub or bag of fruit or bouquet of wildflowers. He didn't mention that he harvested the bribe from their own land.

Different sounds occupied the hours of darkness. Aside from spring peepers and the frog known locally as the dreaming frog, Henry noted that he once heard fifteen whip-poor-wills speaking from different directions at once. Partridges drummed. Now and then a cuckoo squawked a strangled call or a sparrow chirped as if in its sleep, while owls asked their endless questions from the woods around the cabin. He recalled a line from an ancient Hindu epic, the Harivansa: "An abode without birds is like a meat without seasoning."

Night also offered his only opportunity to glimpse a favorite animal. As much as he enjoyed the sight of butterflies flitting about the grassy meadows of Concord, he thought they couldn't compare with the magic of fireflies. What kind of literary fairyland offered the living fireworks he could see around him every night? He would glimpse a firefly low near the ground with another flying toward it, but in rushing up to watch he would see only that the lower one perched atop a blade of grass before his approach made them both douse their lanterns. Patiently he kept watching. Soon the lower firefly turned on its light again, reminding Henry of a maiden lighting a lantern in a castle turret to signal her lover, and then climbed down the grass stem.

Overhead gleamed the stars. Distant smaller suns merged into a blurry crowd, but before them, in the foreground of his imagination, the larger stars shaped themselves into constellations and thus into their myths: sinuous Draco, the vain queen Cassiopeia, Orion whose shade Odysseus met in the underworld. Henry could not separate mythology from nature. Lying beneath the constellations— gods and stories in the sky—inspired a feeling akin to reading Virgil and Homer.

At night, Henry became convinced, he inhabited his body more fully than in daylight. No one thought him strange. He was not awkward. No one yelled "Woods-burner!" Walking across a hillside, he would find himself amid a warm stratum of air, like Atlas strolling through atmospheres—and, rich in time, he would follow the warmth. He considered it a gift from the gods, this innocent delight in living. If Henry dug a few inches into sand, he found it still warm from the afternoon's sunlight, and he would sculpt a hollow with his hand and lie down in the warm earth, gazing at the stars.

Chapter 24

LUNCHEON AT THE CABIN

"HENRY T. HAS built him a house of one room a little distance from Walden pond & in view of the public road," Prudence Ward wrote a friend. "There he lives—cooks, eats, studies & sleeps & is quite happy. He has many visitors, whom he receives with pleasure & does his best to entertain."

His visitors included family, of course. Many Saturdays found his mother or sisters walking to the pond with a basketful of baked goods and other treats. It was less than two miles along the railroad right-of-way from the Texas house to Henry's cabin. He continued to accept supper invitations from friends, including Bronson and Abigail Alcott, at whose home he played with their four beautiful daughters. The bookish one, dark-haired Louisa May, was thirteen and especially fond of Henry. As he had been doing for years, Henry also dined frequently at the Emersons' house, where he played with their young son Edward, who reached his first birthday in the summer of 1845, when Edith was four and Ellen somehow already six years old. Waldo had been gone almost as long as Edith had been alive.

His former student George Keyes, who had particularly enjoyed Henry's natural history classes, came to visit him at Walden and found him pleasant and welcoming. George brought other boys along, and Henry showed them favorite recent discoveries in the nearby woods. George Frisbie Hoar, Henry's former student and the brother of Elizabeth, entered his senior year at Harvard in 1845. During winter holidays he trekked around Walden with Henry and visited the cabin. George was one of the boys who had called Henry "Trainer Thoreau" for his military bearing back in his teaching days, but he enjoyed Henry's company and was willing to serve as auditor to Henry's usual habit of thinking aloud without expecting a balanced conversation. Once Henry complained to George about the unrealistic brevity of the biblical span of history. Using as his example one of Concord's elder citizens, he exclaimed dismissively, "Why, sixty old women like Nabby Kettle, taking hold of hands, would span the whole of it!"

Henry made it often to Edmund Hosmer's farm, to dine amid his gaggle of children. On some Sunday afternoons, Hosmer would herd his family to the pond to visit Henry. The host sat at his green lift-top desk and Hosmer in a chair facing him. With the brick fireplace to one side of them and the open door to the other, the children climbed up on Henry's simple cot and sat in a row with the window light coming in over their shoulders and the smallest girl dangling her feet above the floor.

On the paths, Henry showed the Hosmer children nests hidden under leaves or led them to vines heavy with ripe berries. Sometimes he introduced them to animals, having made the children promise beforehand to sit still and quiet throughout an animal's visit. He would whistle and a woodchuck or squirrel would appear, or even birds. Now and then Henry took the children out on the pond in his boat, telling stories about the Indians who used to live there, interrupting himself to identify the kinds of lilies or point out a rare flower.

Once the children asked why he didn't shoot the birds to collect them.

"If I wanted to study you, would I shoot you?" he replied. He was grateful for his childhood experience with rifle and shotgun, but he seldom carried one nowadays. "A gun," he explained to the children, "gives you the body only, but the field glass gives you the bird."

Henry was fond of small children and was known for his willingness to play along with their games and for his ability to craft miniature bows and arrows. He happily led expeditions to find the most delicious chestnuts and huckleberries, and he could lead the way to spots where cardinal flower bloomed as red as its namesake. He took the children out in a boat and showed off pond lilies and demonstrated how to charm fish.

Henry responded unpredictably to his neighbors. When he saw lonely, deformed Bill Wheeler hobbling into town on stubs of feet, or chanced across him snoring in a rude shelter of hay piled over a makeshift frame, rather than expressing pity or disgust, Henry claimed to wonder if he was crossing paths with a silent philosopher. Although Wheeler was seldom seen in the village except on a festive military day, and he traded the few chores he could manage for ale, impressionable Henry found himself wondering if those who struggled through the world with even less than himself might be secretly blessed.

WHEN HE WASN'T walking the paths or boating among the water lilies, Henry would sometimes finish his morning dip in the pond—he bathed every day until cool weather set in, around mid- to late September—and sit in the open doorway of the cabin from dawn until midday, reveling in solitude. The woods were never silent, merely quiet despite the whack of ax against tree trunk. Only when a wagon rattled on the highway or the train shrieked from the tracks did Henry realize how much time was passing as he mused.

When the cabin floor had accumulated enough dirt to require attention, Henry started cleaning early in the morning. He carried each item of furniture out onto the dooryard grass, under the hickories and pines and chestnuts, where he found that in this natural living room each looked new and interesting again. Instead of removing the inkstand and paper and books from his table, he carefully picked up the whole array and carried it outdoors, settling the table's three splayed wooden legs down amid sumac sprouts and prickly pitch-pine cones and even more prickly chestnut burs.

No wonder we carve vines and nuts on our furniture and dwellings, Henry thought, looking at the furniture outdoors; they used to stand amid such natural architectural flourishes. He dipped a bucket in the pond, carried it up the little rise to the cabin, and dashed water on the wooden boards of the floor. Then he sprinkled hard white sand from the shore and used the broom to scrub and then to sweep the wet sand out the front door. The morning sun poured onto the boards through the uncurtained window and open door, and soon they were dry again and ready for the furniture's return. And yet, Henry thought, the bed and chair and table seemed as glad to be outdoors as children and as reluctant to go back under a roof.

IN EARLY SEPTEMBER 1845, with the first young maples already turning scarlet on the opposite shore, Henry invited his childhood friend Joseph Hosmer Jr. to come and see his new home and while away a Sunday at the pond.

Before Joseph arrived, Henry cooked a pot of his field beans and caught and cleaned some hornpout, an abundant freshwater catfish. Among a catfish's signature cluster of whiskerlike barbels around its mouth, the pout had two long ones that did indeed look like horns curving above and in front of the eyes. Henry saw the slow-moving, bottom-feeding pout as bullies, always itching for a fight. Every other one he caught had terrible scars across its body, often with the skin torn off in a bloody gash. Each spring, dense schools of the oddly whiskered fry lurked like a dark cloud near the shore of both river and pond. Sometimes, when wading among them, Henry estimated that he could see up to a thousand in a school. Pout were easy to catch with almost any bait, even kernels of corn. Usually he caught them—sometimes as many as three or four at once, and a squirming eel thrown in for good measure—with a tangle of worms on a thread, which would get caught in their fierce teeth as they fought for the prize. For half an hour after he cut off their heads, their mean-looking mouths would pantomime speech.

Joseph Hosmer knew that Henry was a newcomer to home building—his only experience had been in helping his father build the new Thoreau home the year before, and in helping out there and at the Emerson house—so he was impressed with the cabin's carefully thought out proportions and the level of Henry's craftsmanship. Clearly Henry was proud of it, and he was not one to hide his satisfaction with his own performance. On the outside, boards were carefully feather-edged and overlapped, making the hut secure against rain and wind—or it would be draft-proof, once the battening boards and plaster completed the interior. Now the rough brown boards showed many knots and let in the breeze. Not that Henry wanted a polished look; he had deliberately left the bark on the rafters, where he could reach the garret by standing on a stair. His rolled tent reclined up there.

Without curtains, the cabin wasn't dark indoors. Joseph watched as Henry opened the trap door in the center of the floor, which revealed that the cellar was shallow enough that even short Henry could have reached down and touched its earthen floor with his corn-husk broom. Henry had left some branches on the tree trunk he used as king post—the cabin's main support—and, like sailors going belowdecks, Henry and Joseph stepped down the trunk into the former home of the woodchuck. The layers of earth were visible in the bare walls—roots and pebbles and burrow hollows at the top, darker soil below, down seven feet to a six-by-six floor of fine sand, deep enough to protect potatoes from winter cold. Shelves were merely indentations in the earthen sides; the firm soil made it unnecessary to secure the walls with stones. The couple of hours Henry had spent in digging the cellar reminded him that in most places he had read about, people dig into the earth for a more tolerable temperature. In his constant comparison of humans to other creatures, it occurred to him that a house is a kind of porch above a burrow.

The chimney was unfinished, which explained the most surprising aspect of the day for Joseph—Henry's method of preparing a meal. He cooked in a fire pit that reminded Joseph of a clambake on a beach. The pit was beside the house, a hollow in the soil lined with stones and fueled with both polished-looking driftwood from the pond and rough-barked dead branches from the surrounding woods. As the fire died down, Henry added pond water to meal in a bowl and spread a layer of it to bake on a thin stone in the embers. It had to be spread thin or its surface would burn before its interior cooked.

Henry had baked various kinds of bread in this outdoor oven. First he tried hoecakes, which he cooked not on the flat steel surface of a hoe but on a shingle or a piece of board left over from house building. A heated pine board, however, tended to impart an unpleasant piney flavor to the meal, and also bread cooked in this way often wound up smoked. Unsatisfied, Henry had read what he could find on the history of bread baking, looking as usual for the most primitive and natural method. He experimented with different flours. Eventually he settled upon a mixture of Indian corn meal and rye flour. Indian corn meal was a staple of most diets in the region—especially as mush or hasty pudding, boiled and eaten with molasses or milk. In William Wood's *New England's Prospect* from 1634, Henry could read that when Indians traveled a long distance, they carried nocake, Indian corn parched in hot ashes, dusted off, beaten to a powder, and transported in a leather knapsack.

At first Henry regularly brought leavening yeast from the village, keeping it in a bottle, although now and then during his walk back to the cabin its volatile fermentation would pop the cork and spill the contents in his pocket. Then one day he scalded the yeast and decided to try his bread without it. Despite warnings that unleavened bread was unwholesome and would deplete his energy, he discovered no ill effects and began to regularly bake without yeast.

In preparing lunch for Joseph, only after the bread was done did Henry remove from the embers the thin stone with the meal baking on it. He wrapped some of the hornpout fillets in wet paper and left others bare, seasoning them only with salt. He placed them directly on the hot stones that circled the fire, where they soon began to sizzle. Joseph saw unleavened bread as unnecessarily harking back to the Old Testament, and he wasn't impressed with it, but the salty, tender fish were delicious, and with the beans and corn made for a surprisingly good meal. As a memento of the occasion, Joseph wrote up the modest menu in English and his multilingual host copied it in Latin, French, and even Greek.

HENRY ENCOUNTERED OCCASIONAL strangers in the woods. Once, on a lonely stretch of the road that led from village to pond, he came upon a worrisome scene. A young woman walking homeward alone had been stopped by two young men driving a horse and wagon. Apparently they were about to entrap her. It was reported that Henry marched the men to the village and turned them in to the authorities, which probably meant Sam Staples, the former bartender who had become constable. One Sunday, two young women knocked at the cabin door and asked for a drink of water. Henry replied that he had no cold water, but he would lend them his dipper, which they accepted and carried toward the pond. They never returned. Later Henry fumed in his journal, "They were a disgrace to their sex and to humanity. Pariahs of the moral world. . . . They will never know peace till they have returned the dipper. In all the worlds this is decreed."

Other encounters were more pleasant. On one Sunday morning in mid-July, Henry's solitude at the cabin was interrupted by the arrival of five railroad construction men, who, in their burly outdoorsy figures massed in his hut, reminded him of the Lestrigones, Homer's tribe of cannibalistic barbarians. They were curious about the little house and its inhabitant, and Henry explained how he came to be there.

"Sir," said the youngest man politely, "I like your notions. I think I shall live so myself. Only I should like a wilder country, where there is more game." Henry thought this handsome young fellow resembled a Greek sailor as he explained that he had had some experience of rough living, having dwelt among the Indians at Apalachicola, Florida. As the group departed, the young man added, "Good day. I wish you success and happiness."

In the woods around Walden, Henry often encountered Alek Therien. The big woodchopper was in his mid-thirties, although Henry thought him younger, a rough but intelligent man so strong he could dig fifty postholes in a single day. Henry loved Therien's way of talking. Sometimes, when he sat on a log and opened his tin pail to eat lunch—which once was a woodchuck his dog had killed—chickadees would settle on his arm and jiggle down to peck at the potato he was holding. Therien would laugh and say that he liked having them around.

Henry thought of Therien as one of the happiest people he knew. "By George!" Therien would exclaim, resting on his ax and looking around at the woods. "I can enjoy myself well enough here chopping. I want no better sport." Once, when someone—probably Emerson, who had hired Therien to chop and saw wood—assumed that Therien, too, would want the world reformed, the Canadian chuckled in surprise at such a question and murmured, "No, I like it well enough."

As overture to some moral advice he wanted to dispense, Henry once asked Therien if he was satisfied with his life. The woodchopper was too wise to fall into this trap. "Satisfied!" he exclaimed. "Some men are satisfied with one thing and some with another. One man, perhaps, if he has got enough, will be satisfied to sit all day with his back to the fire and his belly to the table, by George!"

Late one day, Henry ran into a well-off landowner who was driving a pair of cattle along the Walden road—heading, Henry figured, for the slaughterhouses in Brighton. The farmer asked Henry how he could bring himself to abandon the comforts of civilized life. Henry replied that he was sure he liked his rustic new home passably well. Later, he thought about the farmer trudging on through the mud toward morning, to exchange the cows' lives for money, while he himself lay in his warm bed in the woods, listening to the owls ask their ancient questions.

THAT AUTUMN, EMERSON invited a number of friends to congregate at Bush every Monday evening throughout the upcoming winter, to discuss ideas that preoccupied them. Henry strolled over from his new home by the pond. The scholarly and likable former Brook Farm member George Bradford, who was staying with the Emersons, had only to walk downstairs. Naturally Alcott was included. Channing was to be a corresponding member, through his recent connection with the New York *Tribune*. Farmer Edmund Hosmer was there, and so were two young men who had helped raise Henry's cabin back in the spring—Burrill and George Curtis. Hawthorne, always listening more than speaking, sat quiet and still under Emerson's portrait of Dante. His dark suit and dark hair, with his face in shadow, made him seem mysterious, as did his calm silence.

They were an unlikely mix. Hawthorne did not share Emerson's high opinion of Hosmer's intelligence and couldn't stand Channing. Curtis was skeptical of Alcott. At the first gathering, the men didn't speak much, although Emerson beamed smiling encouragement at them. Most were not gifted with social grace. George Curtis, amused by the gathering of oracles but eager to nibble any crumbs of wisdom that might fall from this Olympian table, thought that the silence asked cheekily, "Who will now proceed to say the finest thing that has ever been said?" Finally Alcott, in his deep melodic voice, dropped into the quiet an epigram reminiscent of his "Sayings" in *The Dial*, and after a minute Henry responded with one of his detailed monologues. Afterward Curtis could recall neither Alcott's remark nor Henry's reply. Then silence reigned again except for the thinkers' horselike munching of russet apples that Emerson had provided to fuel thought. Gradually night fell and the room grew dark.

This pattern recurred on a few successive Monday evenings. Eager and lucid in private conversation, lively and compelling on the lecture platform, the men were unable to relax and merely talk. George Curtis thought the problem lay in the tension inspired by the need to shine. Soon the gatherings ceased.

Chapter 25

MY MUSE, MY BROTHER

"WHAT ELSE IS there in life?" Henry replied when Ellery Channing remarked upon the fiery curiosity that animated his friend from dusk to dawn. Increasingly, as Henry's thinking turned more scientific and factual, he wanted to measure and record the actual Walden, its real creatures and phenomena, not merely let his imagination play over them or his philosophy find them satisfyingly metaphorical. "I wish to meet the facts of life—the vital facts," Henry insisted in his journal after moving to the pond, "which are the phenomena or actuality the gods meant to show us—face to face, and so I came down here. Life! who knows what it is, what it does? If I am not quite right here, I am less wrong than before."

Early in 1846, Henry spent much of his time on a new project. In late winter but before the ice could break up, instead of skating, Henry walked every stretch of the pond's firm surface. He bored holes in the ice to learn Walden's deepest point, as well as to measure its other characteristics. He had decided to plumb Walden's depths not only metaphorically but also literally. All his life, he had heard people casually describe Walden Pond as "bottomless." This was not an uncommon claim; nearby Sudbury had two ponds, Pratt's and Willis's, that were of unknown depth and thus dubbed bottomless.

To reach Walden's depths he used a simple cod line bearing a one-and-a-half-pound stone, with which he took more than a hundred soundings. He was used to this kind of tedious manual work. He could easily discern when the stone lifted from the bottom and began to rise, because it was much heavier when resting on the mud or sand than when the water got under it and helped support it as it rose. From nineteen feet in one spot and seven in another and eighty-eight in another, he plumbed and noted, measured across its length and breadth, into each little cove. The greatest depth turned out to be only one hundred and two feet, which was unusual but not unheard of. In its center, the pond's bottom was surprisingly flat for an area of several acres.

First he mapped the pond at ten rods to the inch. A rod could measure either distance or area; one rod measured sixteen and a half feet or an area of thirty and a quarter square yards. Finally he drew a full plan with a scale of 1:1920, forty rods to the inch. He also measured Walden from other directions, employing his surveying chain and compass. With a circumference of 1.7 miles, the pond comprised an area of 103 rods or 61 acres. Its longest distance, from east to west, was 175.5 rods or roughly 2,900 feet, not much over a half mile. In horizontal cross-section, the pond did not look as deep in proportion as Henry had expected, more like a shallow plate than a deep cup. He imagined that the ocean, should it ever be mapped, would also turn out to be relatively shallow in proportion to its great expanse.

As Henry went about his arcane and unpaid task, the bubbled and marbled ice, which he noted had an average thickness of sixteen inches, creaked under his boots. Water-wise folk knew that however solid and strong a frozen pond looked, a surveyor's level on its surface would bob too much to be accurate. During this survey, Henry set a graduated staff in the ice, walked a rod away to the shore, and measured it several times through his surveyor's level. Although the ice seemed attached as if soldered to the bank, it subtly bobbed as much as three-quarters of an inch. Henry imagined that some day machines would be able to detect undulations in the earth itself.

This careful measurement of Henry's sacred place excited his increasing interest in the poetic aspects of natural history. He diverged ever more from the Platonic thinking of his mentor and other Transcendentalists every time he carefully assessed some aspect of the natural world and found that in doing so his joy was not lost in dry statistics, but rather fueled by clear-eyed contact with the potent earth.

As Henry enjoyed his new home in early 1846, some of his friends were preparing to leave theirs. "We have authentic intelligence," wrote Sophia Hawthorne to her mother in late March, "that my husband is nominated, by the President himself, for Surveyor of the Custom House. It is now certain, and so I tell it to you. Governor Fairfield wrote the letter himself. The salary is twelve hundred dollars." It turned out to be a thousand, but that was far better than empty promises from magazine editors. Hawthorne's new full title was to be surveyor for the district of Salem and Beverly and inspector of the Revenue for the Port of Salem. Their excitement was tinctured with melancholy. As they had long known and been preparing for, they were about to have to flee their newlywed oasis, cast out by poverty. Thinking ahead to busy days at a city job, Hawthorne realized that soon his writing would have to blossom from the occasional cadged hour of free time.

Henry, in contrast, was rich in time if in nothing else. One of his goals while living at the cabin was to concentrate on his writing, and he had big plans to turn his notes and journal entries about the river trip into a book. He was twenty-nine years old, and that voyage in the summer of 1839 was now almost seven years in the past. At a distance of three and a half years, John's death was far enough behind him to enable Henry to think about his last great adventure with his brother without merely aching with loss.

Expanding beyond his models, which ranged from Hakluyt's *Voyages* to Goethe's *Italian Journey*, he merged time periods, blurred chronology, highlighted or excised events. Goethe's vital vision of landscape, his half-scientific and half-poetic view of plants, filtered into Henry's pages. Inevitably the rivers became the stream of time and the vehicle of self-discovery. Even though he wanted to structure the book around the actual events of the trip, Henry gradually decided to merge the two weeks into one, seven chapters of one day each. After all, one week they had spent trekking the countryside, with their boat moored near Hooksett, New Hampshire. His journal entries, preserving his immediate response to life, had to be developed and integrated into the text. Usually they didn't analyze adventures so much as respond to and play with them, wedding detailed description to a fireworks display of allusion. He began his smaller writing projects by surveying his journal for choice morsels that might add up to a meal, and he chose the same method for his first book, returning to these lively pages for the raw ore.

He copied into a separate volume his notes about the river trip. As he had with much of his writing, such as the essay on the volumes that gave him an excuse to write "The Natural History of Massachusetts," Henry ranged far afield from his original topic. In his first book, as in the voyage it described, he pulled ashore at every bend in the river that looked interesting, explored the bank, ventured into the forest, then eventually got back into the boat and rejoined the current of the voyage. He brought in memories, random thoughts and asides, even poems.

Although he was preserving the memory of his last big adventure with his brother, Henry didn't identify John or bring him to life as a vivid character. John appeared in some scenes as Henry's unnamed fellow traveler, but he haunted the edges of the story. Perhaps inevitably, working with memory and grief, Henry crafted the story into a voyage through time as much as across distance. He changed the title from *An Excursion on the Concord and Merrimack Rivers* to *A Week on the Concord and Merrimack Rivers.* He wrote a dedicatory quatrain that ended, "Be thou my Muse, my Brother—."

IN EARLY JUNE, Hawthorne's new story collection, *Mosses from an Old Manse*, was published, and was eagerly read in Concord. The two gold-stamped volumes brought together most of the stories he had written while living in the Ripley house—"The New Adam and Eve," "Drowne's Wooden Image," "The Artist of the Beautiful," and many others, as well as reprinting older tales such as "Young Goodman Brown."

Ellery Channing reviewed the book in *The Harbinger*—a merger of two earlier progressive journals, this one proclaiming itself "Devoted to Social and Political Progress" and published at Brook Farm as of a year before. Although Hawthorne had been a founding resident and shareholder at Brook Farm, *The Harbinger* hadn't critiqued his work until now. In his florid way, Channing insisted that Hawthorne was "baptized in the deep waters of *Tragedy*. . . . His feet have been blistered on the wide sand deserts which human crime has swept over the Eden of primeval innocence."

Edgar Allan Poe had a different point of view. Years earlier, through a mutual acquaintance, Poe had invited Hawthorne to contribute to his proposed journal *The Stylus*, but Hawthorne replied that he had "no more brains than a cabbage" at present and would try to write something soon. The journal, like many of Poe's dreams, never became a reality. A few months after publication of the first volume of *Twice-Told Tales* in late 1841, Poe had praised Hawthorne's imagination, declaring him "original at *all* points." Hawthorne had himself sent Poe a copy of the book and praised Poe's fiction, but he had recklessly added the comment, "I admire you rather as a writer of Tales, than as a critic upon them." In response to either Hawthorne's book or his letter, Poe reversed his opinion and declared about the author of the new *Mosses*, "he is not original in *any* sense." He complained of Hawthorne's monotonous tone of voice and his reliance upon allegory. Then Poe worked in a vivid denunciation of the whole Transcendentalist crowd: "Let him mend his pen, get a bottle of visible ink, come out from the Old Manse, cut Mr. Alcott, hang (if possible), the editor of 'The Dial,' and throw out of the window to the pigs all his old numbers of the *North American Review*."

In his introduction, "The Old Manse," Hawthorne wrote an elegiac tribute to how his beloved home had lured his muse during the productive first few years of his marriage and move to Concord. Then he added a tribute to a certain friend's arcane talents:

> Here, in some unknown age, before the white man came, stood an Indian village, convenient to the river, whence its inhabitants must have drawn so large a part of their subsistence. The site is identified by the spear and arrow-heads, the chisels, and other implements of war, labor, and the chase, which the plough turns up from the soil. You see a splinter of stone, half hidden beneath a sod; it looks like nothing worthy of note; but, if you have faith enough to pick it up—behold a relic! Thoreau, who has a strange faculty of finding what the Indians have left behind them, first set

me on the search; and I afterwards enriched myself with some very perfect specimens, so rudely wrought that it seemed almost as if chance had fashioned them. Their great charm consists in this rudeness, and in the individuality of each article, so different from the productions of civilized machinery, which shapes everything on one pattern. There is an exquisite delight, too, in picking up, for one's self, an arrow-head that was dropt centuries ago, and has never been handled since.

Only four years had passed since Henry had taught Hawthorne to see arrowheads, and Hawthorne had reached different conclusions about the importance of Indians. In his introduction, he went on to conjure an Indian village from these relics and shards, to see visions of wigwams on his lawn. "But this is nonsense," he exclaimed, and reminded himself that his preface was supposed to be about his house. Then he came back to a reminder of how much he , like the Transcendentalists, often valued his daydreams over the reality that inspired them: "The Old Manse is better than a thousand wigwams."

More interested than ever in the people who trod these paths before Europeans arrived, Henry disagreed. He needed this sense of an ancient past surrounding him. It sparked his imagination and validated his impatience with his own era. "Even time has a depth," he wrote in his journal on July 6, "and below its surface the waves do not lapse and roar."

FINALLY CREATIVE ENCOURAGEMENT came to Henry from the person whose opinion mattered most. One hot afternoon in early July 1846, he and Emerson sat down together on the riverbank, in the shade of an oak, and Henry read a substantial portion of the scribbled river journey manuscript to his mentor. Henry liked to hold forth in a monologue, and reading aloud to friends provided him with an ideal captive audience. While the river flowed quietly past them, Henry conjured the story of his adventures on it. By turns lyrical, argumentative, and mock-heroic, the book moved like the river itself, offering a new view with every page.

Emerson was impressed. He found the story lively and invigorating, at times even profound. After years of striving for the master's approval, after burning many of his poems following Emerson's critique of them, finally Henry had the satisfaction of hearing unstinting praise. No doubt much of the material was already familiar to Emerson. Henry had piled into his narrative many older fragments of writing that had been heavily influenced by Emerson— observations about books and reading, journal entries, rants about society's strictures and inconsistencies, and a vast array of quotations by his predictable companions Homer and Pindar, as well as a range of English poets such as George Herbert and Francis Quarles. Emerson wasn't merely flattering his eager pupil with kind words. A few days later, he wrote to a friend that Henry's book was "pastoral as Izaak Walton, spicy as flagroot, broad & deep as Menu."

In the text Henry quoted Emerson himself, both by name (for "Of Syrian peace, immortal leisure") and under the transparent description "a Concord poet": "By the rude bridge that arched the flood . . ." Henry invoked the battle poem early on, as he and John sailed past the battleground and bridge, past the Manse that had then housed Ezra Ripley and had since harbored the Hawthornes. A melancholy tone often crept into the river story, as when Henry quoted part of George Herbert's poem "Vertue":

Sweet day, so cool, so calm, so bright,
The bridall of the earth and skie:
The dew shall weep thy fall to night;
For thou must die.

ONE DAY THAT summer, Henry's childhood friend Benjamin Hosmer—who on that long-ago day had brought down a bull with a thrown rock—walked the seven miles from Bedford to visit Henry at his cabin in the woods. He went home disappointed. The summer before, Henry had welcomed Ben's brother Joseph when he came for a luncheon of beans, unleavened bread, and hornpout fillets. Yet Ben went home and reported to his little brother Horace, who was now sixteen, that Henry not only received him coolly but even remarked at one point that he had no time nowadays for friendship.

Offended on his brother's behalf, Horace thereafter met Henry's distance with his own family pride. At times Henry seemed to others in the village to be in his own world, walking with his eyes on the ground, not greeting some of those he passed. Now Horace behaved the same way when they met, refusing to look up or say hello, and he and Henry crossed paths in silence.

Chapter 26

A NIGHT IN JAIL

ONE WARM EVENING late in July 1846, a couple of weeks after Henry turned twenty-nine, he closed the door of the cabin and walked away from Walden toward town. He was headed into the village to pick up a shoe that he had left for repair at the cobbler's, so that he could wear it on Fair Haven Hill the next day while guiding a huckleberry party. He walked past his garden, in which much of the squash, tomatoes, beans, potatoes, and corn had been killed by the previous month's unseasonable frost.

He didn't make it to his destination. Along the way, he ran into Samuel Staples, the constable and recently retired tax collector. Henry liked Staples, thought him an honest and gentle and well-meaning fellow who didn't abuse his power over lawbreakers. He was a popular man in Concord. In 1832 Staples had moved to town from Mendon, near the border of Rhode Island. He had one dollar and three cents in his pocket and immediately spent the three cents at Bigelow's tavern—which, he insisted, gave him strength for the struggle ahead. Since then he had become known for his industry, honesty, and versatility. Before becoming local constable, a job he had begun three years earlier, Staples had been a carpenter and an auctioneer, as well as barkeep—and for a while manager—at the Middlesex Hotel. The hotel's owner, Thomas Wesson, was his father-in-law; in 1839 Staples had married Lucinda Wesson, with Emerson officiating.

Concord hired its tax collector by taking bids. In 1842 Staples had been handed the job in response to his low bid: the city would pay him only one cent on each dollar of taxes collected. By 1845 his fee had crept up to one and a half cents per dollar. In early 1846 Staples retired and the new tax collector, Addison G. Fay, won the job with a bid of one and a quarter cents. Legally, the outgoing tax collector was required to furnish the amount of missing tax funds— which may be why Staples finally came after Henry.

He had warned Henry several times that he could not continue to ignore his poll tax without legal repercussions. Henry knew that Staples possessed a warrant for his arrest; Staples hadn't served it yet because he knew that he could find the young man whenever he wanted to. On this day he told Henry his time was up to meet this legal obligation.

"I'll pay your tax, Henry," sighed Staples agreeably, "if you're hard up." In 1843 he had arrested Bronson Alcott for not paying his poll tax—without offering to pay *his* bill. Samuel Hoar had paid Alcott's tax because he thought the educator's arrest an affront to the town's reputation. Protesting a war by refusing to fund it was not an uncommon pacifist action, but Alcott had been deliberately reject- ing the government's right to take any percentage of his property for any reason. (Less than a year later, Charles Lane, the English- born founder of the utopian community Fruitlands near Harvard, was arrested for rejecting the poll tax.) Early the previous May, Staples had threatened Alcott with selling his land to settle his again unpaid tax. Staples had a higher, more affectionate opinion of Cynthia and John Thoreau's son, and was inclined to be generous.

Henry explained that his opposition to the poll tax's contribu- tions to governmental policies he opposed was a matter of principle and that he had no intention of paying. Patiently, Staples said he was willing to argue with the selectmen himself, to get them to reduce the accumulated total of back taxes, which could not have exceeded several dollars. Still Henry refused.

The constable asked what Henry expected him to do about the morality of the situation.

Resign, said Henry.

"Henry, if you don't pay, I shall have to lock you up pretty soon."

"As well now as any time, Sam."

So Staples told Henry to come along with him to the jail. He escorted Henry through the almost treeless outskirts of the village, past the poor farm and poor house, past the house at the corner of Walden and Sudbury Roads where the Thoreaus had lived back in the 1820s, and finally across the Mill Dam itself to the Middlesex County Jail. It was off the Common behind the Middlesex Hotel, nicknamed the jail tavern, which had just been rebuilt after a fire the year before. Besides trying to build a life in resistance to conformity and government, for years Henry had been thinking about the moral ramifications of the dour jail. He had watched the gathering of prisoners every few months for court sessions—the Supreme Court in March, with the Court of Common Pleas following in June and then again in September. Eleven years before, as a Harvard junior in September 1835, Henry had written an essay—a pro or con "forensic" on an assigned topic, required for the upperclassmen—entitled "The Comparative Moral Policy of Severe and Mild Punishments." It thoughtfully considered incarceration: "The end of all punishment is the welfare of the State,—the good of the community at large,—not the suffering of an individual. . . . So far only as public interest is concerned, is punishment justifiable,—if we overstep this bound, our own conduct becomes criminal."

Because Concord was a shire town, one of the seats of county government that hosted court sessions and had to accommodate prisoners transported for all sorts of crimes, its jail was larger than that in most towns its size—a three-story stone building, roughly sixty feet long and half as wide. It had been erected in 1791 to replace the earlier wooden jail that had famously housed Scottish Lieutenant Colonel Archibald Campbell during the Revolution. Campbell—colonel of a Highland regiment, as well as Member of Parliament—had marshaled his troops toward a rescue of Sir Henry Clinton, who was battling General Washington's army in Boston; but Campbell found Clinton already defeated and soon found himself residing in the Concord jail. It had also been the temporary abode of Henry's Tory great-uncles, Simeon and Josiah, during the same period.

This later jail's walls were built of split granite, the stones two to three feet thick, with heavy wooden doors a foot thick. Surrounding the yard behind the jail was a ten-foot-high brick wall, in which here and there were mounted iron rings to which felons or maniacs could be chained. Most of its temporary inhabitants, however, were not considered violent. When Staples brought in Henry, some of the prisoners were standing around the doorway in their shirt-sleeves, enjoying the mild evening air and gossiping.

"Come, boys," said the former barkeep, "it is time to lock up."

As Henry was led to his own cell on one of the upper floors, he could hear the footsteps of the other men and the clang of their cell doors, the noises echoing off the hard unfurnished walls and floors. Henry noticed that the cell door had a narrow rectangular slot in it. His cellmate, according to Staples when he introduced them, was "a first-rate fellow and a clever man." Staples closed the door and left.

★   ★   ★

As CONSTABLE, STAPLES arrested Henry for nonpayment of previous years' tax, including that of 1845—just as he had arrested Alcott in 1844 for failing to pay his 1842 tax. Henry had not resisted paying his highway tax; he felt it was the duty of a good citizen and certainly he used the highways. An educator himself, he had also not neglected school taxes.

Six years before, however, in 1840, the state had sent Henry a tax bill on behalf of First Parish Church in the center of town, the church to which his father and some others in his family belonged. Massachusetts commanded Henry, along with every other citizen of Concord, to pay a certain amount toward the support of Reverend Ripley. Henry was furious. Priests weren't taxed to support schoolmasters, he thought, so why should it be the other way around? If the church could submit its tax bill to the state, why couldn't the lyceum? Henry refused to pay. Someone else paid the church tax bill for him, but he was encouraged to deliver to the town clerk a signed official note in January 1841: "Sir, I do not wish to be considered a member of the First Parish Church in this town." After this public statement, the government dropped the matter.

During the same six years, Henry had also refrained from paying his annual poll tax. Sometimes this was called a head or capitation tax; *poll* meant head, just as to poll a cow meant to cut the horns off a young cow's head, and beheading a plant or tree was called polling. In 1780, immediately after the war with Britain, the Massachusetts constitution had renewed the poll tax, a well-established source of revenue assessed upon every adult rather than by income. Not that the tax was levied evenly. "Ministers of the Gospel, and Grammar School-Masters," declared the 1784 Tax Act, "are not to be assessed for their polls and estates," and it pronounced the faculty, administration, and students of Harvard free of the tax burden. Bowdoin, Williams, and Amherst were added later, but an

1829 revision to the code removed all these exemptions and restored colleges to the ranks of taxpayers. Tax for minors was assessed on their parents, and exemptions on account of infirmity or even poverty were left to the assessors in each region. "Each taxable person in the town," read the law, "where he shall be an inhabitant on the first day of May in each year" must pay the poll tax. "The whole poll tax assessed in any one year upon any individual for town and county purposes, except highway taxes, shall not exceed one dollar and fifty cents." Five-sixths of county revenues were to come from property taxes, with the remaining amount to be raised by the poll tax.

Fiscal policy in general, and the poll tax in particular, had been a stormy political issue in Massachusetts for several years, at least since the Panic of 1837. The virtues and vices of poll and other taxes were bandied about in every election campaign, with each side threatening disaster if their own agenda was resisted. Yet little change was taking place while Whigs and Democrats seesawed. Henry encountered these topics everywhere. Tax reform had been a fierce issue among abolitionists for years, in the writings and speeches of *Liberator* founder William Lloyd Garrison and many others. During 1844 and 1845, as abolitionist resistance to taxation had heated up even more, Henry's family had attended more and more to such issues.

THE CELL WAS brightly whitewashed and even spacious, at least to someone who lived in a lakeside hut. The shutters of the two barred windows were inside the iron grate and open, letting in the domestic sounds of the village—the tolling of a church bell, the rattle of carts driving by, the clank of cooking pans in the kitchen of the Middlesex Hotel next door. The other man showed Henry the cell's few amenities and pointed out a peg on which he could hang his hat. Henry thought it the neatest apartment in town, its daunting whiteness surpassing even his cabin's simplicity.

Naturally Henry's cellmate asked him how he happened to be in jail, and Henry recounted his story. Then he asked for the biography of the other man, who had been in jail three long months already awaiting trial—although he felt that free room and board were not exactly a burden, considering that he was treated well and left alone.

Henry asked why he was there.

"Why, they accuse me of burning a barn," his cellmate replied, and not surprisingly added, "but I never did it."

Henry pieced together the disjointed story and concluded that probably his new friend had been ending a drunken binge in a barn, smoking a pipe among his straw bedclothes, and had gone to sleep and caused a fire that burned the barn. He was lucky to escape alive. As a reviled accidental arsonist himself, Henry may have felt sympathy for his cellmate's plight.

Meanwhile other people were getting involved in Henry's arranged symbolic drama, without his awareness or consent. When Mrs. Thoreau learned of Henry's arrest, she hurried to the jail to confirm it, apparently without seeing Henry in his upstairs cell. Then she walked over to the Square, to the home of her sisters-in-law, Misses Maria and Jane Thoreau. After dark, one of them, probably Maria, emerged from the house—with her head covered by a shawl—and strode to the jail. Sam Staples was out running an errand in the village, but his young daughter Ellen was there.

The veiled woman handed the girl money, explaining, "To pay Mr. Thoreau's tax."

When Ellen told her father at home, Staples had already taken off his boots. He decided that a night in jail was exactly what Henry seemed to want, so he might as well get it.

Legally, Henry ought to have been released immediately—or should not have been arrested in the first place. The law required that authorities unable to collect delinquent tax must "find suffi- cient goods upon which it may be levied" before they could "take the body of such person and commit him to prison, there to remain until he shall pay the tax and charges of commitment and imprison- ment, or shall be discharged by order of law." But Staples was not well versed in legal matters, and his Concord neighbor had contrived his own arrest to make a statement.

The two prisoners in the cell spent most of their hours until bedtime staring out through the bars, one man at each window. Henry found himself a witness to everything that happened at the Middlesex Hotel. He realized that if he stayed in jail for long, he would spend most of his time watching the parade of gloriously unjailed life go by. But he also fidgeted around the cell, reading every pamphlet that had been left behind. In the course of the evening, Henry was shown where one of the iron bars had once been sawed off and where former prisoners—actual felons—had escaped. His roommate also introduced him to a collection of handwritten verses by prisoners, including some by a group who had been caught trying to break out.

At last Henry's roommate showed him which bed he was to occupy and retired to the other himself, leaving Henry to trim the lamp when he was ready.

For a while, Henry couldn't go to sleep because the man in the cell below, apparently a drunkard, kept asking the night, "What is life?" Then eventually he would answer himself, "So this is life!" and the cycle would begin over again. He must have been at the window below Henry's. To reply to him, Henry leaned against the bars of his own window and called down, "Well, what *is* life then?"

No reply. Finally there was blessed silence in the cell below. Henry lay back down.

They slept with the window shutters open. Henry could hear every detail of the activity in the bustling kitchen of the nearby hotel. He lay in the dark, in a reflective dreamy mood, and felt that he had never before fully heard the voice of the village at night. It seemed as if he might be traveling through time, hearing the nighttime scurry of a walled medieval town; the Concord became the Rhine, his neighbors burghers and knights. Finally he drifted off to sleep.

HENRY HAD REACHED his conclusions about the poll tax over time, weaving together a variety of inspirations. He had read Charles Lane's letter to *The Liberator*, explicating Alcott's motives: "This act of non-resistance, you will perceive, does not rest on the plea of poverty. . . . But it is founded on the moral instinct which forbids every moral being to be a party, either actively or permissively, to the destructive principles of power and might over peace and love." Henry had carefully considered how much he agreed and disagreed with William Paley, who documented God's shaping nudges all over creation in his vast 1803 tract *Natural Theology; or, Evidences of the Existence and Attributes of the Deity*. He also owned Paley's earlier book *The Principles of Moral and Political Philosophy*, which had been a Harvard textbook in his junior year. It included a long and windy chapter, "The Duty of Submission to Civil Government Explained," which surveyed everything from dueling to polygamy to scriptural arguments on behalf of the Sabbath. At college Henry had written essays on Paley's theology and natural history, and he considered his social ethics just as carefully. "It may be as much a duty, at one time, to resist government," wrote Paley, "as it is, at another, to obey it; to wit, whenever more advantage may accrue to the community from resistance than mischief."

More recently, Henry had read with great attention Emerson's 1844 essay "Politics," in which his mentor lobbied on behalf of the virtues of individualism and democratic government, defended individual rights over the intrusion of the state, examined the nature of property ownership, and expressed skepticism about the trustworthiness of the church and the popular press.

"The less government we have, the better," argued Emerson, continuing,

> We live in a very low state of the world, and pay unwilling tribute to governments founded on force. There is not, among the most religious and instructed men of the most religious and civil nations, a reliance on the moral sentiment, and a sufficient belief in the unity of things to persuade them that society can be maintained without artificial restraints, as well as the solar system; or that the private citizen might be reasonable, and a good neighbour, without the hint of a jail or a confiscation. What is strange too, there never was in any man with sufficient faith in the power of rectitude, to inspire him with the broad design of renovating the State on the principle of right and love.

Ever since watching Bronson Alcott perform the same tax protest three years earlier, and Charles Lane a year later, Henry had sought ways to demonstrate his lack of allegiance to the state, his right to refuse governmental demands that he found intrusive and inhumane. For the previous few years, neglecting to pay his poll tax—after paying it since reaching adulthood—had been a relatively low-risk way to perform this symbolic gesture. For various reasons, many other Concordians did not pay their tax during the same period. For the tax year of 1834–35, for example, seventy-three people failed to pay, forty-six of whom owed only poll tax. Yet apparently Henry was the first since Alcott and Lane to make a point of refusing out of moral objections to the state's use of funds.

THE NEXT MORNING, the rectangular hole in the cell door proved to accommodate a tin pan a jailer pushed through it. It was laden with brown bread, a pint of chocolate, and an iron spoon. Soon the jailer returned to pick up the dishes. Henry had drunk his chocolate but eaten only half his bread, so he placed the remainder on the tray. Instantly his cellmate grabbed the bread and advised Henry that any extra provender should be hoarded to supplement the meager lunch and dinner.

Then Sam Staples came to the cell and explained to Henry that he was free to go because his overdue poll tax had been paid the previous night by someone else.

Surprised and angry, Henry refused.

Staples was dumbfounded. In all his time as constable, he had never met a prisoner who was not eager to leave jail once his cause for arrest had been attended to. But Henry stubbornly refused to accept his unexpected freedom.

"Henry," Staples finally sighed, "if you will not go of your own accord I shall put you out, for you cannot stay here any longer."

Staples released Henry's cellmate to his assigned daytime task of haying in a nearby field. Each day some inmates were temporarily released to do jobs for the town or even for the jailer himself. Before he left, the man told Henry good-bye. He wouldn't be back until noon, he explained, and he doubted that Henry would still be around then.

Henry was furious at this turn of events, but he realized he could not win. Finally he bade farewell to his cell and started down the street. Formerly it had been the custom in Concord to greet debtors emerging from the jail by holding up both hands, crossing the fingers over each other until they resembled barred windows, peering through them, and mockingly asking the former prisoner, "How do ye do?" The villagers did not respond thus to Henry's reappearance on the street, but he imagined that they looked askance at him even more than usual. People had been raising their eyebrows at his antics for his whole life, however, and most of the time he took their surprise as a testament to his extraordinary virtues.

He walked to the cobbler's, retrieved his mended shoe, and fell back into his daily routine. His arrest and brief incarceration amounted to almost nothing, but he began turning over in his mind ways to magnify the experience and make it symbolic for literary purposes. Soon he had caught and saddled the family horse and was two miles away, on the high slopes of one of his favorite places, Fair Haven Hill, leading a huckleberry party high above the village and its jail.

AFTER A WEEK in which Henry thought long and hard about freedom and responsibility, he demonstrated his commitment to abolition by making his cabin available for an important rally. Inviting both members and guests, the Concord Female Anti-Slavery Society hosted the event on the first of August, their second commemoration of the tenth anniversary of the end of British slavery in the West Indies. Mrs. Thoreau, as well as Sophia and Helen, helped organize the event, as part of their long-standing involvement in the organization they had helped to found.

Like the first such event two years earlier, at which Emerson had officially joined the abolitionist ranks after Henry rang the bell to attract a crowd, this one drew heartening support. "All who love freedom and hate slavery" were invited, *The Liberator* had declared in its article about the upcoming event. The radical newspaper had lured readers to Walden Pond by promising speeches by several fiery speakers. They included the former slave Lewis Hayden, who had once been owned by the Kentucky legislator Henry Clay, who in 1840 had failed in his Whig candidacy for president against William Henry Harrison. The Transcendental Club member and Unitarian minister Caleb Stetson, who had been a brother in the Emerson circle, was there. Ellery Channing's uncle, the liberal theologian William Ellery Channing—whose views on abolition had grown ever stronger since emancipation in the British West Indies—was a big draw. In his 1835 book *Slavery*, Channing had argued passionately, "If human affairs are controlled, as we believe, by Almighty Rectitude and Impartial Goodness, then to hope for happiness from wrong-doing is as insane as to seek health and prosperity by rebelling against the laws of nature, by sowing our seed on the ocean, or making poison our common food."

From the door of Henry's cabin, the speeches rang out across the bean field. There followed a picnic lunch during which attendees could meet speakers and all could further unite their spirits against what they perceived as the most despicable enemy of civilization. Henry's desire for a more natural life was uniting with his resistance to what he and other Transcendentalists perceived as unnatural laws. A man of principle, Henry had come to believe, could not live his own life with pride and dignity if he turned his back on the suffering of others.

Chapter 27

CHAOS AND ANCIENT NIGHT

G EORGE THATCHER AND Henry landed their borrowed
canoe on the shore of Mattanawacook Island and climbed
out. They had been asking around for an Indian village and finally
spied one from across the Penobscot River, amid handsome elms
and quiet meadows. A dark Indian girl of ten or twelve lay in
sunlight on a boulder in the water, washing and softly singing an
aboriginal song that sounded almost like humming. On the shore
lay a salmon spear with a point of only sharpened wood. Like the
girl's song, the spear showed no sign of the Indians' many decades
of contact with Europeans. It might have come out of the lost
native past that captivated Henry.

He had been in Maine for only a few days, having left Concord
on the last day of August 1846, a month after the abolitionist rally at
his Walden cabin. George Thatcher, who was married to Rebecca
Jane Billings, one of Henry's cousins on his father's side, was a
Bangor lumberman. Knowing Henry's love of the woods and interest in Indians, he had invited Henry to accompany him to examine
property he was considering buying on the west branch of the
Penobscot River, about a hundred miles—by river—north of
Bangor. Thence Henry planned to forge into the wilderness to
climb Mount Ktaadn. It was in Piscataquis County in north central

Maine, although Henry thought it was Penobscot County because he was using John Hayward's outdated 1839 *New England Gazetteer.* Henry knew that it was easier to climb Ktaadn from the Wassataquoik River and the Aroostook road on the northeast side, but he wanted to experience more of the wilderness and sample the boatman's life.

The Penobscot word *ktaadn* meant greatest or highest mountain. A mere handful of white men had ascended the peak since the first, Charles Turner and his party in 1804, or at least few had bragged about it. They included Maine's state geologist, Charles T. Jackson, who was the brother of Lidian Emerson and Lucy Jackson Brown. Henry had met Jackson in 1843, when he lectured at the Concord Lyceum, and he owned some of Jackson's books. He was hoping to follow in his footsteps.

Jackson had measured the altitude of Ktaadn as 5,300 feet, a mile above sea level. Ktaadn was the tallest mountain in Maine, with the second highest, Sugarloaf, more than a hundred miles south and west toward the Vermont border. Henry was excited to venture so far from his home village. Here on the northern edge of the nation and the eastern rim of the continent, far from his path by the railroad cutaway behind Stow's Woods in Concord, he hoped to find the primeval world of his dreams.

Henry and George left their canoe on the shore and walked toward the closest hut. A dozen large, threatening dogs clamored at their approach. They seemed as feral as wolves and perhaps only recently derived from them. Always a walking compendium of travel literature, Henry thought of a line in Thomas Hariot's sixteenth-century *Brief and True Report of the New Found Land of Virginia,* a reference to European settlers devouring the wild lion of the New World and sometimes eating the natives' "Wolves or wolfish Dogs." Hariot's was the first book published by an English colonist in North America, the beginning of the long line of natural and social history that preoccupied Henry. Hariot had learned enough of the Algonquian language from natives brought to England to be able to serve as an interpreter in the New World and then as its first anthropologist, concentrating mostly on the ordinary lives of the natives.

A sturdy-looking Indian man came to the door with a long staff, with which he beat a number of the dogs, who then scattered and grew quieter. Like a Concord laborer, he was dressed only in pantaloons and shirt. Although Henry had daydreamed about the noble savages of the past ever since he and John gleaned arrowheads from Concord's fields, he still responded with distaste to many of the actual Indians he encountered. What he saw as their habitual woebegone expression and sullen response to questions reminded him of the proverbial girl who cried over spilt milk. Henry envisioned a circle of wigwams with dancing braves torturing a captive, thinking that even that dark scene would be more respectable than the cluster of squalid, tumbledown shacks that met his eye along the Penobscot. He had read that in 1837, only nine years earlier, there had been 362 members of the tribe on this island. Only a few remained.

This man didn't invite his visitors indoors. Henry thought he looked greasy and slow-witted as he responded sluggishly to their questions.

Did he know of any Indians heading upriver soon?

Yes, the Indian replied, he was going himself, with one other person, this very day and before noon.

Who is the other? they asked.

"Louis Neptune, who lives in the next house."

Henry recognized the name as that of the Indian who had replaced Charles Jackson's first guide during his ascent in 1837.

"Well, let us go over and see Louis together."

They followed the man next door, where they were greeted by more yelping dogs. Louis Neptune was short and wiry, dressed like his neighbor, with a face so wrinkled it seemed puckered like an old apple. The first man's behavior indicated that Neptune was his chief or at least a superior of some kind. Yes, Neptune said, they were departing as described, in two canoes, to hunt moose around Chesuncook for perhaps as long as a month.

One of the men said, "Well, Louis, suppose you get to the Point," meaning Mattawamkeag Point, "to camp. We walk on up the West Branch tomorrow—four of us—and wait for you at the dam or this side. You overtake us tomorrow or the next day and take us into your canoes."

Louis Neptune regarded them.

"We stop for you, you stop for us," Henry's companion said. "We pay you for your trouble."

Neptune added, "Maybe you carry some provision for all—some pork, some bread—and so pay. Me sure get some moose."

In the account of his own ascent, Charles Jackson had written of Neptune's response to a snowstorm, "Louis declared that Pomola was angry with us for presuming to measure the height of the mountain, and revenged himself upon us by this storm." Pomola was said to be a storm god dwelling atop Ktaadn, a bird spirit although at times described in Abenaki religion as a gryphon sort of hybrid—the feet and wings of an eagle but with the body of a man and the head of a moose. Earlier, Charles Turner recorded the local tradition that once upon a time seven Indians tried to ascend the mountain and were killed by Pomola. "The two Indians, whom we hired to pilot and assist us," wrote Turner, "refused to proceed ahead—however, when they found that we were determined to proceed, even without them, they again went forward courageously, and seemed ambitious to be first on the summit." As advised, Turner donated a corked bottle of rum to the deity, alongside the initials of each member of his party cut upon sheet lead and left as proof of their ascent.

Nine years later, Henry cheekily asked Neptune if he thought that Pomola would allow this new party to climb his mountain. The Indian replied with equal solemnity that the group must leave on the summit a bottle of rum for the god, that he had himself seen such a gift disappear overnight.

EARLY SEPTEMBER WAS just past the summer plague of mosquitoes and black flies. Lumbering season was also gone, but there was still a lot of activity. Spring had brought a drastic flood to the region, and parties of men were working to repair the damage—rude little houses wet halfway up or washed off their foundation and settled down elsewhere. Henry and George were able to stay briefly with a group of these men, at a camp farther into the woods than they would normally have found at this time of year. Then they encountered other travelers who joined them.

At first the Penobscot River seemed quiet, rocky and shallow, broken only by rapids flashing sparks of sunlight. Ospreys circled overhead and plummeted to a white splash in the river, sometimes catching a wriggling silver fish and sometimes missing their lunch and having to start over. Woodpeckers hammered the towering trunks. Loons laughed and eagles screamed. As the sun went down, the whistling of duck wings was replaced by owl hoot and wolf howl.

The tall dark evergreens were mixed with the striking black-mottled white trunks of silver birch. The forest was so damp—there were no dry boots in these woods—that Henry often felt as if he were slogging through a swamp. Loggers' winter camp huts, which were available to all travelers, seemed to have grown naturally from the forest. Fifteen feet wide and twenty long, constructed of stacked and interlocked tree trunks, they were festooned with lichen and moss, the uncured logs dripping resin that to Henry smelled as primordial as toadstools. Aromatic evergreen shingles, well made with cleaver and sledgehammer, sheathed the roof. The door latch resembled an iron one, but was actually carefully whittled wood, because iron would quickly rust in this damp environment. Inside, the center of the hut was a fireplace, at least three feet wide, surrounded by a fence of logs with benches beyond. Above gaped a square hole in the roof, open to snow and rain that were usually sizzled away by the roaring fire before they could reach it. Fragrant beds of flat arbor vitae branchlets lay under the eaves on each side. Most loggers left a dirty pack of damp playing cards for the entertainment of the next visitor. Henry noted the bare furnishings, not unlike his own at Walden—basin, pail, barrel—although his was a far more finished cabin.

Naturally the camps were short of reading material. In one, however, Henry was fluffing his bed of arbor vitae leaves when he found, half buried among the greenery, a copy of Emerson's address on West Indian emancipation, from two years earlier. Apparently it had been left by Charles Jackson, Emerson's brother-in-law, and someone in the party mentioned that Emerson's eloquence had converted two more people to the abolitionist stance.

Henry felt a wild excitement in trekking these sopping paths so far from domesticated Concord. This brutish and forbidding land was wild in a way that Walden could no longer be. Even some well-traveled areas had no path, because the loggers' saws and chains, provisions and livestock, were brought upstream on the ice at the beginning of winter and taken back downstream before the spring thaw. Hiking by a river, the group encountered the skeleton of a moose, its white bones scattered where Indians had felled it. At times every rod of ground seemed covered in moose tracks—like a cow's, but larger—mingled with the smaller half-moon tracks of their calves. Settlements along rivers in various directions had driven the moose to this region, and Henry guessed that probably their population in these woods was the highest it had ever been. There were also countless bear tracks. When the men wanted to leave provisions or equipment behind for a while, they had to perch them high atop saplings to protect them from bears.

As Nathaniel Hawthorne had observed when they met in the summer of 1842, Henry had a natural talent for boats, and here in Maine he had a chance to enjoy a new craft. The batteau—the usual American spelling of the French word *bateau*, "boat"—had long been the most popular watercraft for exploring America's northern rivers. Dating from the French and Indian Wars in the mid-eighteenth century, or even earlier, they may have been adapted from French fishing dories. More versatile than a canoe although not as fast, they had a shallow draft and flared sides for stability, a narrow long stern and bow for safely navigating rapids, and a flat bottom that could accommodate cargo, passengers, and livestock. In Oldtown, George and Henry had stopped to explore a batteau manufactory.

Henry admired the countryside and wildlife, but he loved the river. He reveled particularly in shooting the rapids. With the less experienced crew positioned like barrels to lend ballast and ordered not to move, the batteau raced along like a spawning salmon, with one man in the bow and another in the stern on the same side, working their twelve-foot iron-tipped spruce poles. Henry realized that no matter what one's boating experience elsewhere, reckless attempts to navigate these rapids without experience could prove fatal. With these stalwarts in charge, however, he not only took courage but finally decided he had never experienced such exhilaration on a boat. Sometimes rapids were as long as a mile. Spray kept the boaters drenched. During stops they scraped splinters off the bottom and sides of the batteau with their well-oiled knives. At one point Henry and another inexperienced man tried their hand at poling the rapids, but with the batteau soon spinning dizzily in a whirlpool they had to surrender their position to the laughing experts.

After an afternoon of spectacular fishing for speckled and rainbow trout, that night Henry dreamed that he was fishing for them again, and he woke to the blurry sense that the fish's proximity to his rough bed was some kind of fable. He got up in the predawn darkness under a lingering moon. As his companions slept huddled in their blankets around the dying fire, he baited a hook to test the reality of the fish and of this whole heady wilderness experience. He cast his line. Soon fish were arcing through the air toward shore, with Henry's line invisible but their silvery forms sparkling against the dark face of Ktaadn. For now the fable was his reality.

EVEN IN THE wilderness, however, Henry did not escape from the rest of the world. The boatmen argued about how the United States congressional campaigns would turn out. The country was afire over the conflict with Mexico, following President Polk's declaration of war in May in the wake of the previous year's annexation of Texas by the United States. Just after Christmas 1845, following a ten-year stint as a sovereign nation, the Republic of Texas had transformed into the twenty-eighth state. Whigs and Democrats, Northerners and Southerners, were fiercely divided on such issues as the growing notion of white domination and expansion to the western coast, the moral complexities of imperialism, and the role of slavery in Texas and any other territories that might be acquired, such as Alta California.

Politics wasn't the only aspect of civilization that Henry failed to leave behind. Even advertising penetrated far into the forest. Near the roaring falls of the shallow Katepskonegan, halfway across the portage—locally called a "carry"—stood a naked pine, its bark stripped off. The exposed pitch had served as glue for a two-foot-long handbill for Oak Hall, a renowned clothing store in Boston, hundreds of miles away. Henry thought wryly that now the local moose and otter could learn where to buy the latest fashion—or at least where they might regain their own stolen hides. The store's founder, George W. Simmons, who was only three years older than Henry, was a pioneer in outdoor advertising. He was said to have signs painted along every road within fifty miles of Boston and his pasteups and posters could be seen throughout New England. Instead of rolling clothes racks out onto the sidewalk before an unimpressive storefront, in the manner of his predecessors and rivals, Simmons had renovated his store in 1842 with grand oak paneling and huge display windows. Renamed Oak Hall, it lured customers in for a new kind of retail experience. To attract attention to a sale, he might stand on the store's roof and throw down to crowds free clothing, or release flocks of balloons into the sky. Henry and his companions dubbed this portage the Oak Hall Carry. He was preoccupied with modern commerce, from the advertisements he could not resist reading in newspapers to the evocative glimpse of baled linen and whiff of salt fish from the Grand Banks brought to him at Walden by the groaning train cars.

Their few encounters with other people met with hospitality. They stayed briefly at the wilderness home of a Kennebec River waterman named McCauslin, who had settled in the wilderness to raise and supply provisions for lumbermen. His clearing at the mouth of the Little Schoodic River on the north bank of the Penobscot was bounded on three sides by straight tall pines; the travelers had to fire a gun to announce their arrival and wait for McCauslin to ferry them across in his batteau. Inside his house, the huge fireplace, fueled by four-foot-long logs, could have roasted an entire ox. The best meal of the Maine trip was eaten there—salmon and shad, ham and eggs, potatoes and cheese, stewed cranberries, white sweet cakes and yellow hotcakes. McCauslin's cows produced so much milk that butter was not only a staple at every meal but also in endless supply for waterproofing boots, which the men did again and again the next day, while waiting out a rainstorm and wondering what had become of Louis Neptune and his companions.

Finally, at Millinocket, they saw two canoes approaching—Neptune and his companion in one and two strangers in the other. They had outfitted themselves in Bangor almost to the point of disguise. From a distance they looked like Quakers in their heavy caped overcoats and wide-brimmed hats. Up close Henry found that the bottom of each canoe held several young muskrats, the Indians' primary food source during these river outings. They had dug them out of their riverbank burrows. The Indians reminded him of the urchins and beggars he had watched scrounging for paper and string in urban streets—a shocking way in which what he thought of as degradation crossed barriers of class and race. Henry found himself general-izing that perhaps he was wrong before, when he naïvely imagined that Indians had honor.

Their delay in reaching the rendezvous had been caused by a bout of drinking at Five Islands. "Me been sick," moaned Neptune. "Oh, me unwell now. You make bargain, then me go."

Soon, leaving the white men on the bank of the Penobscot, the Indians paddled up the Millinocket. As the real Indians slowly faded into the distance, Henry's imagination transformed them into figures he considered more worthy of his daydreams. Their canoes became bark sewn with spruce root, their paddles whittled of hornbeam. They slept in skin wigwams, not log huts; ate bear fat and moose flesh, not sweet cakes. These imaginary Indians paddled up the river and into the mist.

The white men continued on without native guides. McCauslin accompanied them, and he turned out to be an invaluable guide in some regions. During one peaceful, windless sunset, to avoid the likelihood that the wind would be against them on North Twin Lake the next day, they decided to row five miles on the river toward the lake. Red clouds flamed above the tree line and were reflected in the water. The men had passed all lumber camps and other sign of human habitation. Ahead lay only wilderness, with the summit of Ktaadn barely visible against the moonlit sky. Only McCauslin knew this region, and he proved his worth by navigating across the still water of the vast lake, which had no current to guide them.

The men took turns rowing. An owl hooted ethereally as their oars plashed. Henry imagined moose standing invisible in the darkness beneath the trees on shore, silently watching this strange craft. Together the men sang the verses they could recall from various boating songs. Thus, four and a half years after the death of his brother, Henry found himself rowing a boat while singing the very words that he and John had sung in the *Musketaquid*:

Row, brothers, row, the stream runs fast,
The rapids are near, and the daylight's past—

Together the men repeated the last line, and their voices echoed across the still lake that, ahead, reflected the full moon and the dreaming summit of Ktaadn:

The rapids are near, and the daylight's past . . .

FINALLY HENRY AND his companions tied their batteau to a tree along a creek called the Aboljacknagesic ("open-land stream") and, with compass in hand, aimed northeast, toward the southern face of the tallest peak. They crossed the creek, at a span of more than fifty feet, by walking along a titanic jam of logs and boulders, and plunged into the forest. Steadily the trail grew more steep. Because he had more experience on mountain trails, Henry took the lead. Nibbling the cranberries that eked out a living in every crevice, he thought they might prove a profitable crop when the region was settled with reliable avenues of commerce.

They camped in a ravine where the air played, Henry thought, like a nest of young whirlwinds. The wind kept the men restless. They slept fitfully, with one member of the party ill and huddled in a blanket. Suddenly in the darkness a fir tree on the fire burst into flames along its length with such a roar that it startled one of the campers into jumping up with a scream, thinking for a moment that he was in a nightmare about the world on fire.

The next morning Henry climbed on alone. He carried his entire heavy pack up the mountain, in case he was unable to find his friends again and had to descend solo toward the river. From where he left the others, he could see an Olympian panorama without a clearing or man-made habitation in sight. Many lakes were visible in their entirety, like puddles glimpsed from a carriage—Millinocket to the south, flecked with its dozens of islands; eighteen-mile-long Chesuncook, and Moosehead more than twice that length in the southwest. The dark green woodland seemed endless and untouched, as if no man had even whittled a walking stick there. Yet Henry knew the forest was already shrinking. Frequently sailors in Maine ports told of their ships having been becalmed offshore, surrounded by a clotted mass of floating timber carried by the rivers down to the sea. The white pines could reach two hundred feet in height and, when cut, proved sometimes as much as four hundred years old. But offshore they were a slaughtered jumble, each trunk seared with the brand of the man who had felled it.

Henry left his companions far behind. Everywhere loose rocks and boulders lay as if dropped from a great height—only there was no greater height. He was on top of the world. An earlier glimpse of Ktaadn's cloud-veiled summit, from the peaceful water of Quakish Lake, made it seem the link between earth and heaven. The mountain itself looked like the rough building materials of Earth, scattered around a primordial quarry. This was how God made the world. Eventually, Henry imagined, these raw materials would be refined and sent downhill to the happy tamed valleys below.

He knew that earlier visitors who had the good fortune to find the summit unclouded reported that it was about five miles long, comprising a thousand acres of tableland. But he saw only mist, felt only wind. The mountaintop was a cloud factory. When Henry scooped a dipperful of water from a trickling brook, he thought of his cold, refreshing drink as condensed clouds. Above, ahead, the summit was obscured by a whirling cloud that seemed always on the verge of departure, yet was somehow constantly replenished. Like the mountain, the clouds seemed hostile to human visitors. To Henry—a bookish village dweller—the rare glimpse of a dark crag to one side or the other conjured horrific visions of Vulcan hammering fire at his forge, of Prometheus chained by Zeus where an eagle could feed daily on his liver, even of Atlas bearing this rocky world upon his shoulders as punishment for his revolt in heaven. Mountaintops did not welcome puny men from the valley.

Why came ye here before your time? vast Nature seemed to demand of Henry. Later he described how, on this mountaintop, he imagined the voice of the wilderness admonishing him: *This ground is not prepared for you. Is it not enough that I smile in the valleys? I have never made this soil for thy feet, this air for thy breathing, these rocks for thy neighbors. I cannot pity nor fondle thee here, but forever relentlessly drive thee hence to where I am kind.*

Gradually, as he climbed onward through this alien realm, Henry felt he was losing grip on some aspect of his own identity. Some vital part of himself seemed to escape between his ribs like breath knocked out of him. He had never felt more alone or less important. Like the cloud at the summit, his reason seemed to waver but not quite disperse. Even birds had surrendered their autonomy to the whims of the gods. Small gray-brown sparrows, or sparrowlike birds, blew athwart his path like chips off the granite precipice. This was not the friendly nature of the wood pigeons and chipping squirrels of Walden. On this mountain there was no path because men were not supposed to be there. It was easy to imagine the summit as the home of Pomola. This was a place for dark heathen rites. Henry found himself thinking that perhaps only more primitive people than the white race—perhaps only a race closer akin to animals and earth—ought to be here.

Why seek me where I have not called thee, Nature seemed to demand, *and then complain because you find me but a stepmother? Shouldst thou freeze or starve, or shudder thy life away, here is no shrine, nor altar, nor any access to my ear.*

He began to feel in awe of matter itself—the mountain of solid earth beneath his feet, the world supporting it, the ancient stones of which the earth was carved. Rocks and trees were themselves worthy of reverence. He felt the wind on his cheek and marveled even at the movement of air. To touch this world every day seemed miraculous. *Who are we?* he asked himself. *Where are we?* Finally Henry understood why savages thought it an affront to the gods to climb mountains. There was a force there that did not feel kindness toward men. Was awe, he wondered, always mixed with fear?

In a dizzying panic, feeling possessed by a Titan, Henry thought of Satan's declaration to the spirits of the abyss in *Paradise Lost*:

> *Chaos and ancient Night, I come no spy*
> *With purpose to explore or to disturb*
> *The secrets of your realm . . .*

Probably Henry had reached the saddle between Ktaadn's two peaks, South and Baxter, a few hundred feet below the actual cloud-covered summit. Exhilarated, chastened, he began to tell himself that his companions would be worried, that he must about-face and return to camp with the others. Besides, he rationalized, clouds might obscure the summit for days, preventing him from ever seeing the full view of the valley. He might as well quit now. He turned his back on the peak belonging to the dark gods and started downhill toward his companions. Behind him the wind roared like a voice.

THE JOURNEY TO Maine left Henry shocked by his vision of nature on the mountaintop. He had planned and launched the adventure with the goal of experiencing wilderness and reaching further into the primitive within himself. He found it exciting to do so, but he also realized that wilderness alone was not enough—in fact, that raw wilderness might be more than a civilized sensibility could face, much less live within on a daily basis. The reality of wilderness, the notion of wildness, would always be a tonic for the quietly desperate people of the nineteenth century, he was certain, but tonics had to be imbibed in small restorative doses.

The rally at the cabin following his night in jail had reminded him of how important it was to engage fully with the crucial issues of his time. He was feeling a need to do more than observe society from its margin as a gadfly critic. He was moving toward becoming more of a participant in the daily struggle on behalf of principles he believed. He returned from this journey reminded that however much he loved the natural world and felt himself an integral member of the natural community, he was just as much a product of and participant in the life of a social community—several, in fact, from Concord to the larger world of American literature.

He still dreamed of writing something meaningful. His work had been progressing quickly on his account of the river voyage with John, and after the Maine trip he returned to it with renewed vigor. Emerson's encouragement helped. Lately villagers were asking Henry why he moved to Walden and how he spent his time there, and he had begun writing up an account of his goals and experience for a Lyceum lecture and a possible essay.

In Maine, although he had been able to keep up with the lumbermen, he was the most tamed among the travelers. He was the young man who lived on the doorstep of a village that he visited almost daily. Night and day the mud turtles' doze was startled by the wail of the Fitchburg train. In Maine, Henry had sometimes been the man who helped spin the batteau in a whirlpool, but back home in Concord he was considered tough and wild—the village skeptic, the heretic, the nonconformist, positions he cherished as antidotes to being called "Woods-burner!" and considered the local ne'er-do-well.

One evening shortly after his return to Walden, with his compact and well-built little cabin on the shore behind him, Henry pushed his boat gently into the still water. He paddled out into the pond that had been a golden vision in his dreams for a quarter century, since he had first glimpsed it during his fifth summer. A symbol as much as a reality to him, Walden always drew him back to its peaceful shores. This time, however, after his glimpse of a terrifying wildness at the heart of nature, he was returning with relief to his own secure, domestic home. These were the safe, predictable pathways that he could walk each day for a new glimpse of the divinity that, a long way down from the mountaintop, smiled upon him rather than scowled. The Hawthornes had been evicted from their personal Garden because of financial woes, but Henry was returning to his, with no money in the bank but with days rich in time and joy—with no love waiting for him at home, but with freedom and autonomy greeting him every morning.

Floating under the stars and above their reflections, as if flying through the night sky, he began to play his flute, and the wooded far shore of the lake flung back gentle echoes. The reflected music seemed stolen—how he ought to sound to others, he thought, not to himself. It was like hearing one of his poems read by someone else. Like the reflection in the pond—the dark uneven line of trees on its shore and the starry sky overhead—the echo was not a mirror of reality but an artful revision of it. More than he noticed the music itself, Henry heard its echo from the shore, and before it his own breath like a grace note.

Coda

AFTER THE CABIN

IN SEPTEMBER 1847, Henry Thoreau walked away from his cabin at Walden Pond. Emerson was departing for another European lecture tour and he invited Thoreau to return to Bush and help Lidian and the children in his absence. Thoreau accepted the offer. When he closed the door on the second of September, he had lived in his long-dreamed-of retreat for only two years, two months, and two days. "I left the woods for as good a reason as I went there," he declared in *Walden*. "Perhaps it seemed to me that I had several more lives to live, and could not spare any more time for that one." He continued to visit the pond almost daily, but he lived in the village for the remaining fifteen years of his life, most of it in the Thoreaus' big house on Main Street that the family bought after their rising income permitted them to rent out the Texas House.

Five years after moving out of the cabin, Thoreau revealed more to his journal:

But why I changed? why I left the woods? I do not think that I can tell. I have often wished myself back.... There was a little stagnation, it may be. About 2 o'clock in the afternoon the world's axle creaked as if it needed greasing, as if the oxen labored with the wain and could hardly get their load over the ridge of the day. Perhaps if I lived there much longer, I might live there forever....To speak sincerely, I went there because I had got ready to go; I left it for the same reason.

Although Thoreau had built upon Emerson's land rent-free, after he moved out his generous mentor bought the cabin from him. He sold it to his gardener, a rough countryman and drunkard named Hugh Whelan, who moved it to a bean field near Walden Street. But soon Whelan fled his family and job and abandoned the cabin. In 1849 a man named James Clark bought it and moved it to his family farm, turning it into a storage shed for grain. In 1863, a year after Thoreau's death, Ellery Channing visited the site and found the declining hut windowless. Five years later the Clarks took off the roof and used it to shield a pig yard. In 1876 an observer noted that the dilapidated cabin, with a new roof, served as a stable. By the mid-1880s, however, the former cabin had been torn down, and some of its wood was said to have been employed in rebuilding a barn.

Less than two years after his single night of jail in 1846, Thoreau incorporated the experience into a lecture, "The Rights and Duties of the Individual in Relation to Government." In 1849 it appeared in essay form as "Resistance to Civil Government," in *Aesthetic Papers*, edited by Elizabeth Peabody, alongside Emerson's essay "War" and Hawthorne's story/essay "Main-Street." Four years after Thoreau's death in 1862, the essay was re-titled "Civil Disobedience" in the first collection of his shorter writings, *A Yankee in Canada, with Anti-Slavery and Reform Papers*. It has been known by this title ever since.

Mohandas Gandhi wrote of the essay's influence on him, "Thoreau was a great writer, philosopher, poet, and withal a most practical man, that is, he taught nothing he was not prepared to practice in himself. He was one of the greatest and most moral men America has produced." Dr. Martin Luther King Jr. insisted that "Civil Disobedience," which he first read as a student at Morehouse College, was his "first contact with the theory of nonviolent resistance. . . . Fascinated by the idea of refusing to cooperate with an evil system, I was so deeply moved that I re-read the work several times. . . . The teachings of Thoreau came alive in our civil rights movement; indeed, they are more alive than ever before." King described bus boycotts and sit-ins as "outgrowths of Thoreau's insistence that evil must be resisted and that no moral man can patiently adjust to injustice." The incendiary essay has often been banned. In the 1950s, the United States Information Service reprinted it in a textbook to be stocked in all their libraries, but Senator Joseph McCarthy succeeded in having the book removed from many library shelves, specifically because it contained "Civil Disobedience," which McCarthy reviled.

AFTER YEARS OF struggle, in 1849 Helen Thoreau succumbed to the family legacy of tuberculosis and died at the age of thirty-six. During her last months, Henry insisted upon hiring a daguerreotypist to come to the house and photograph his sisters, so at least the family had a keepsake after Helen's death. The funeral was held in the home. During the service Henry sat expressionless, staring into space, until the pallbearers prepared to carry Helen's coffin out the door. Then he wound his music box and everyone waited while a melancholy minor-key tune played until it wound down.

The same year, James Munroe & Company in Boston, who had published Emerson's *Nature* in 1836, published *A Week on the Concord and Merrimack Rivers*—a decade after the journey Thoreau employed as a cord on which to string philosophy, poetry, and vignette. Despite Emerson's diligent support, Thoreau had to agree to reimburse Murray for printing costs out of sales of the book. He was never able to do so. Later he bought back the unsold copies of the one-thousand-copy first edition, prompting his now famous remark that he possessed "a library of some nine hundred volumes, seven hundred of which I wrote myself." He also claimed to appreciate his lack of success as an author: "It affects my privacy less, and leaves me freer."

The family's pencil business prospered in the late 1840s. For a time Thoreau's former student, Horace Hosmer, worked as their agent in New York City. In the early 1850s, the Thoreaus began receiving large orders for their high-quality ground graphite, and soon they learned that it was because the invention of electrotyping was increasing demand for raw product. By 1853 the Thoreau family concentrated on supplying this new need and ceased manufacturing pencils entirely. At about the same time, a group of German pencil manufacturers launched in New York City and quickly dominated the U.S. market. The Thoreaus bought a big house on Main Street and rented out the Texas Street house; they were even able to afford a couple of servants.

Thoreau spent roughly four times as long thinking about and writing *Walden* as he spent living at the pond. The book evolved through at least seven drafts. In early 1848, in a Concord Lyceum lecture entitled "Economy—Illustrated by the Life of a Student," Thoreau first publicly discussed his building of the cabin and his observations and goals surrounding it. Response was mixed, but soon he delivered a second lecture about his experience, "White Beans & Walden Pond." Gradually more venues invited him to deliver such lectures, and over the years he steadily revised them and added to his growing manuscript. On the ninth of August 1854, Ticknor & Fields in Boston published *Walden; or, Life in the Woods*, with a lithograph of Thoreau's survey map of the pond as frontispiece in each of the two thousand copies. On publication day, Henry

gave the event less attention than he devoted to plants whose matu-
ration he was following with his own system of notation: "To Boston.
Walden published. Elder-berries XXX. Waxwork yellowing X."

The book received considerable attention in newspapers and
magazines. One of the earliest reviews, in the *Boston Daily Evening
Traveller*, concluded, "It is a curious and amusing book, written in the
Emersonian style, but containing many shrewd and sensible sugges-
tions, with a fair share of nonsense." Bronson Alcott's verdict on
Walden and *A Week* has proven apt: "books to find readers and fame
as years pass by, and publish the author's surpassing merits." Many
reviewers agreed. "*Walden* is a prose poem," proclaimed the Worcester
Palladium in words that have been echoed thousands of times since.
"It has classical elegance, and New England homeliness, with a sparkle of Oriental magnificence in it. It is a book to be read and re-read,
and read again, until another is written like it."

Publication of *Walden* established Henry's reputation in the
United States and, to a lesser extent, abroad. He was increasingly in
demand in American magazines such as the *Atlantic Monthly*. Horace
Greeley, publisher of the New York *Tribune*, had become Thoreau's
unofficial agent, beginning by placing his essay "Ktaadn and the
Maine Woods" in the *Union Magazine* in 1848, the year Thoreau
began a regular career as a lecturer. From Salem, Hawthorne invited
Henry to lecture; other invitations came from as far away as Bangor,
Maine. Most lectures grew into essays. Besides "Civil Disobedience,"
Thoreau wrote other political and philosophical essays that would
prove influential over the next century and more: "Slavery in
Massachusetts," "Life Without Principle," and two essays—both of
which began as lectures—about the radical abolitionist John Brown.
In October 1859, Brown's violent raid on the U.S. arsenal at Harpers
Ferry, Virginia, galvanized both sides of the slavery issue and is
considered to have helped ignite the Civil War. Less than two weeks

after Brown's defeat, Thoreau delivered his first lecture on Brown's opposition to slavery and his mode of resisting governmental control. When he spoke at the Concord Town Hall, the selectmen refused to ring the town bell to notify the public, so Thoreau rang it himself. Almost no newspapers were willing to voice support for Brown's actions, but Thoreau said of him, "The Republican party does not perceive how many his *failure* will make to vote more correctly than they would have them. . . . For once we are lifted out of the trivialness and dust of politics into the region of truth and manhood. No man in America has ever stood up so persistently and effectively for the dignity of human nature, knowing himself for a man, and the equal of any and all governments."

In the early 1850s Thoreau committed himself more fully than ever to his journal. At the time of his death, he had written two million words in this private storehouse, filling seven thousand pages in forty-seven volumes between October 1837 and November 1861. He came to realize that his most important task was attending to the natural phenomena of everyday life, and at one point he half-jokingly complained that his observations were becoming more scientific and less poetic. Slowly, as funds permitted, he acquired the large, inadequate handbooks and technical manuals of the era to help him identify everything from grasses to small mammals. He created a huge calendar of annual natural events, recording the first blossoming of wildflowers and the return of migrating birds, the emergence of woodchucks and the duration of snowstorms. Today scientists are using his detailed journal records to analyze climate change during the nineteenth century.

At the age of seventy-two, after two years of illness, John Thoreau Sr. died of tuberculosis in 1859, so quietly that his watching family barely noticed the moment of his departure. Two days later Thoreau wrote in his journal, "When we have experienced many disappointments, such as the loss of friends, the notes of birds cease to affect us as they did." Thoreau stepped into the role of man of the house, taking over management of the graphite business, attending to correspondence and billing. But he continued to spend as much time as possible outdoors. The next year, before the Middlesex Agricultural Society, Thoreau delivered a lecture that is now considered his most original contribution to science: "The Succession of Forest Trees." Thoreau was one of the first people to document the means by which woodland growth proceeds upon a predictable pattern of succession.

GRADUALLY TUBERCULOSIS WORE Henry Thoreau down, as it had taken his sister and father—and likely would have taken his brother had tetanus not intervened. By early 1862, after months of decline, Henry knew his days were numbered. In March he replied to a letter from an admirer of *A Week on the Concord and Merrimack Rivers*, "I have not been engaged in any particular work on Botany, or the like, though, if I were to live, I should have much to report on Natural History generally. . . . You ask particularly after my health. I suppose that I have not many months to live; but, of course, I know nothing about it. I may add that I am enjoying existence as much as ever, and regret nothing."

Friends visited Thoreau often. Bronson Alcott brought cider and apples. Elizabeth Hoar worked to help Thoreau arrange his manuscripts, journals, and letters. The Boston publisher William Ticknor of Ticknor & Fields came to visit, to acquire the rights to all of Thoreau's writings in order to produce a uniform edition. Sam Staples, who had been a friend since before he put Thoreau in jail for a night sixteen years earlier, visited and told Emerson that he found Henry happy and serene, that he had never seen a man dying "with so much peace."

As Thoreau faded into immobility and near silence, some friends and family worried about his soul, but he was still impatient with orthodox religion. When a family friend demanded to know the state of his relationship with Christ, Thoreau replied that a snowstorm meant more to him. Aunt Louisa asked if he had made his peace with God and he replied cheekily, "I did not know we had ever quarreled, Aunt." A friend, Parker Pillsbury, visited and found Thoreau barely able to gasp replies to questions, as his sister sat nearby sorting papers and his mother stood guard with medicine and fan. But Pillsbury could not resist raising a provocative topic: "You seem so near the brink of the dark river, that I almost wonder how the opposite shore may appear to you."

"One world at a time," sighed Thoreau.

He died quietly on the sixth of May 1862, at nine o'clock in the morning, with his sister and mother and aunt by his side. He was forty-four. Until the end, he had been revising his accounts of journeys to Maine, and his last discernible words were "moose" and "Indian."

ACKNOWLEDGMENTS

W HILE I WORKED on this book, my mother suffered a severe stroke, which resulted in my writing while sitting beside her as she slept in a hospital and nursing home. At times I held her good hand in my left and typed with only my right. I extend heartfelt thanks from my brother David and myself to the doctors, nurses, therapists, and others who helped my mother and tried to make her last days comfortable, and to the friends and family who rallied around us, especially Jo and Harry Brown, and my aunt Iva Yow. A few months later, my wife gave birth to our son, Vance—and I found myself thankful to midwives and other medical professionals and other friends and family. Sleepless and bleary-eyed, I was soon typing again with one hand, while holding a sleeping newborn. As they typed this book, my hands linked my mother and my son, the past and the future. For me, these memories will always weave through *The Adventures of Henry Thoreau*.

Thanks first and foremost to Laura Sloan Patterson, my wonderful first reader and reality check and wife. At Bloomsbury, thanks to George Gibson, friend and editor, who patiently and insightfully critiqued several drafts; to George's assistant, Rob Galloway, his former assistant Lea Beresford, publicist extraordinaire Carrie

Majer, tireless managing editor Nate Knaebel, eagle-eyed copy editor Emily DeHuff. I applaud my wonderful agent, Heide Lange, who has guarded and assisted my career through twelve books, and her excellent assistants Stephanie Delman and Rachel Mosner, and former assistants Rachael Dillon Fried. Special daily thanks to the wonderful staff at the Greensburg Hempfield Area Library— Cesar Muccari, Diane Ciabattoni, and the tireless interlibrary loan crew: Linda Matey, Allyson Helper, Christine Lee, Donna Davis, and Janie Mason.

Many thanks to the fine Thoreau scholar and cordial human being Sandra Harbert Petrulionis, professor of English and American Studies at Pennsylvania State University, who critiqued early and late drafts of chapters and finally read the entire manuscript—with intelligence and generosity and humor. Jeffrey Cramer encouraged and his books were most helpful. Rebecca Solnit prompted me to think more about Thoreau's context. Several friends and scholars critiqued portions of the manuscript or encouraged the project in other ways: Ross King, John Spurlock, Christine Cusick, Josephine Humphreys, Maria Browning, Margaret Renkl, Serenity Gerbman, Jennifer Ouellette, Stephanie Wilson, Jerry Felton, Robert Majcher, and Ned Stuckey-French. Jon Erickson was essential, as usual, and invariably smart and entertaining, and the same description applies to Karissa Kilgore. Thanks to my brother David Sims, to Sarah Patterson and Jodi Sims (I have great luck in sisters-in-law), to my intrepid cousin J. R. Yow, and to Bill and Rhonda Patterson.

NOTES

B ECAUSE THOREAU'S WORKS are available in countless
editions, I cite them as follows: his journal entries by date, unless
the date is unknown; his letters by date, referring to the *Correspondence*
(q.v.), unless the date is unknown; his published writings by an essay's
or book's title and the relevant chapter; annotated editions of *Walden* or
collections of Thoreau's essays by the name of the editor; and biographies of Thoreau and other figures by the author's name. Occasionally
I tweak the punctuation in quoted conversation to suit contemporary
dialogue style. For queries regarding minor sources not clear in these
notes, email me via my website, www.michaelsimsbooks.com.

Abbreviations for Frequently Cited Sources

ESQ = *Emerson Society Quarterly*
Hawthorne = *American Notebooks*, edited by Simpson (q.v.)
JMN = *Journals and Miscellaneous Notebooks* of Ralph Waldo Emerson
Journal = Journal of Henry David Thoreau, edited by Bradford Torrey and F. H.
   Allen. I used Dover's 1962 edition, two giant volumes that reproduce four
   original 1902 pages per page, then checked against Princeton University
   Press's many volumes of *The Writings of Henry David Thoreau*.
RWE = Ralph Waldo Emerson
TSB = *Thoreau Society Bulletin*
Week = *A Week on the Concord and Merrimack Rivers*

Overture: DANCING ON THE ICE

3 **"Today, Thoreau's words are quoted"**: Ken Kifer, "Analysis and Notes on Walden: Henry Thoreau's Text with Adjacent Thoreauvian Commentary." At http://www.phred.org/~alex/kenkifer/www.kenkifer.com/thoreau/index.htm.

3 **"Thoreau was a superior genius"**: RWE, letter to George Stewart Jr., January 22, 1877.

Chapter 1: BEHIND THE STARS

9 **"I did not take it"**: Sanborn 1917, p. 41.

9 **Mrs. Wheeler was teaching a private class**: Sanborn 1917, p. 39.

9 **he failed to look at the face**: *Journal,* November 14, 1851. Numerous sources mention this trait, including Thoreau himself.

10 **At the age of three**: Channing, p. 19.

10 **Henry once carried a basket of young chickens**: Salt, p. 7.

10 **to nickname Henry "the Judge"**: Channing, p. 5.

10 **suffered baptism . . . without tears**: *Journal,* December 27, 1855; Hoeltje 1939, p. 350.

10 **"I don't feel well"**: Channing, p. 18.

11 **"Why, Henry dear"**: E. Emerson, pp. 14–15.

11 **his sisters' wavy brown hair**: See Sophia Thoreau's painting of her brother, Meltzer and Harding, p. 49, and portraits of the Thoreau family in Concord Free Public Library.

11 **Each Christmas Eve**: John Thoreau Jr., letter to George Sewall, December 31, 1839, in Harding 1982, pp. 22–23; Le Brun, p. 11; Hoar, p. 53.

13 **enunciated r's with a Gallic burr**: Channing, pp. 2–3.

13 **evolving into *thorough***: Edward Emerson, son of RWE, in letter dated October 11, 1918, wrote, "We always called my friend Thó-row, the *h* sounded, and accent on the first syllable." See *The Goddard Biblio Log,* Spring 1973, p. 7. Nathaniel Hawthorne, in a journal entry on September 1, 1842 after meeting Thoreau, spelled his name *Thorow*. His friend Daniel Ricketson addressed letters to "Mr. Thorough" and "Mr. Thoroughly Good."

13 **French one, from snuff box to shrug**: Hosmer, p. 79. I couldn't resist Hosmer's examples.

13 **An old building of unpainted gray boards**: E. Emerson 1917, p. 12; Meltzer, p. 14; *Journal,* May 26, 1857.

14 **Chelmsford**: *Journal,* January 7, 1856; Channing, chapter 1; Sanborn 1917, pp. 33–34; Marble, pp. 36–37.

14 **He also worked . . . with an inventor and chemist named Joseph Dixon**
Petroski 1989, especially chapter 9. See also Conrad 2005.

14 **vision of a beautiful lake**: In *Journal*, August 1845 (Thoreau 1906, vol. I, p.
380ff.), Thoreau says, "Twenty-three years since, when I was five years old";
in *Walden*, "Bean Field," he says, "When I was four years old, as I well
remember." His birthday was July 12. Whether one counts his age as four
or five during this first Walden visit depends upon the date of this first
glimpse of the pond, which was not recorded anywhere. But in 1845 it had
been twenty-three years since his fifth summer.

15 **briars of sweet blackberries**: Thoreau, throughout *Journal*; Hoar, p. 56.

15 **settlers who organized wolf hunt**: Shattuck, chapter 12.

15 **close to being born on Nawshawtuct Hill**: Horace Hosmer, quoted in E.
Emerson, n. 3.

15 **handsome brick house**: *Journal*, January 7, 1856.

15 **next door to Samuel Hoar**: Sanborn 1917, p. 36.

15–16 **Henry's father enjoyed village life**: *Journal*, October 21, 1856; February 3,
1859 (the day of his father's death); and Hosmer, in E. Emerson.

16 **He loved the first ball games of early spring**: *Journal*, April 10, 1856. For
games, see Hale, pp. 199–200, and Hoar, p. 52.

16 **Hosmer brothers**: Description of Hosmer brothers derives from various
places throughout Horace Hosmer.

18 **"It was the wild midnight"**: Sargent, p. 132ff. We do not know which lines
Thoreau recited. These are the opening lines and also in a passage reprinted in
Sargent's standard nineteenth-century anthology of excerpts for declamation.

18 **"the fine scholar with a big nose"**: Alfred Munroe, quoted in Harding 1989, p. 49.

18 **textbooks concerned natural philosophy**: Hoeltje 1948, p. 104.

19 **"The earth, and all bodies"**: Enfield, p. 141.

20 **"There are four Seasons in a year"**: Sanborn 1917, pp. 51–52.

Chapter 2: SEEK YOUR FORTUNE

22 **Harvard & Groton Accommodation Coach**: See company waybill, Concord
Free Library, http://www.concordlibrary.org/scollect/buildinghistories/
MiddlesexHotel/storyPages/stagecoachWaybill.html

22 **rowdy taverns and hostelries**: Paige, pp. 226–27.

22 **Cicero's orations . . . probation**: Sattelmeyer, p. 3.

23 **"You have barely got in"**: Josiah Quincy to Thoreau, quoted in Borst, p. 10.

23 **4,038 points . . . deducted for tardiness**: Cameron 1959, especially p. 14ff.

23 **Since the progressive Unitarians had become dominant**: Neil Brody
Miller, pp. 101–3, 244–45.

23 **addressed each other entirely in Latin**: Morison, p. 246.

23 **Quincy was tall and martial**: Morison, especially pp. 246–253; Metzger, p. 32.

24 **destroyed furniture . . . reined in the rowdy student body**: Pier, p. 128ff.

24 **he did collaborate in the occasional prank**: In a letter to Henry Vose, October 13, 1837, Thoreau said: "Can you realize that we too can moralize about college pranks, and reflect upon the pleasures of a college life, as among the things that are past? Mayst thou ever remember me as a fellow soldier in the campaign of 1837."

24 **He had a distinctive shape**: For description see Sanborn 1882, p. 263; Sanborn 1901, pp. 5–6; journals of Hawthorne, RWE, Alcott; Mrs. Edwin Bigelow and Elizabeth J. Weir, in E. Emerson, "A Different Drummer"; John Weiss, p. 9; Isaac Newton Goodhue, in Cummins, p. 2; Channing, pp. 2, 25; Ricketson, pp 14–15; Daniel Ricketson again, quoted in Sanborn 1882, pp. 261–66; John Shepard Keyes, letter to Francis H. Underwood, 15 November 1886, in *TSB*, CII, (Spring 1968), pp. 2–3; Hoar, pp. 70–72; Rose Hawthorne, in George Parsons Lathrop; E. Emerson 1917, p. 2.

24 **He tended to dominate a conversation**: Sophia Thoreau's former student Elizabeth J. Weir, in E. Emerson 1971; Robinson, pp. 12–13.

24 **his earnest excitement transcended**: Thoreau's neighbor Amanda P. Mather, letter to Daniel Mason, September 13, 1897; in Petrulionis 2012, p. 160ff.

25 **On many winter days at school**: Thoreau, letter to Horatio R. Storer, February 15, 1847.

26 **Each day at Harvard**: Hale, chapter 9, esp. pp. 136–37, 196–199; Pier, pp. 137–39; Thoreau, quoted by Salt, p. 16; Hoar, vol. 1, p. 125ff.

26 **each monthly installment of Charles Dickens's novel**: Hale was an almost exact contemporary of Thoreau's at Harvard, and on p. 199 he mentions the table buying a Dickens novel as it was published; the only one to be published during this time was *Pickwick*.

28 **a student would take out his small metal tinderbox**: Pier, p. 137.

28 **trying to puff dried lily stems**: Channing, p. 242.

28 **a black jacket was required**: Fellow student Marston Watson, quoted in Sanborn 1917, p. 154.

28 **seldom bothered to black his boots**: John Shepard Keyes, letter to Francis H. Underwood, November 15, 1886, in *TSB*, CII (Spring 1968), pp. 2–3.

28 **a kind of mystical arrogance**: Weiss.

29 **As a freshman at Harvard**: For Harvard's influence, see Sattelmeyer throughout, especially pp. 6–16; Cameron 1953 and 1959; Kwiat; Adams 1940; and overviews in Harding 1982 and Richardson 1986.

30 **wrote an essay on part of *Natural Theology***: Sanborn, p. 67.

31 **"It can surely not be right"**: Cicero, p. 78.

32 **"At the age of sixteen"**: *ESQ*, no. 2 (second quarter, 1957), p. 2.

32 **"You can buckle on your knapsack"**: Channing, pp. 11, 18.

33 **Concord boasted a lead pipe factory**: Richardson, p. 210.

33 **One-horse shays**: Sanborn, *Life*, p. 38. *Shay* was a corruption of the French word *chaise*.

33 **tall and handsome and plucky**: Hosmer, p. 92; Salt, p. 13.

33 **"enough to drive a man to Nova Zembla"**: Hendrick, 1.

33 **Mrs. Thoreau stated her opinion bluntly**: Every commentator makes this point, both friends such as Le Brun and critics such as Sanborn.

33 **eager to help a struggling servant**: Le Brun, pp. 11–12.

34 **"my David Henry"**: Concord neighbor Priscilla Rice Edes, quoted in Adams 1953, p. 2.

34 **His own beak jutted**: Various commentators mentioned above refer to his nose; his friend Hoar, p. 70, says, "He had a curved nose which reminded one a little of the beak of a parrot."

34 **He sat stiffly**: Curtis, p. 63; Channing, p. 25; Hawthorne called Thoreau "a cast-iron man"; Petrulionis 2012, p. 79, pp. 81–82.

35 **"I told my David Henry"**: Concord neighbor Priscilla Rice Edes, quoted in Adams 1953, p. 2.

35 **"You shall stay at home"**: Channing, p. 18.

Chapter 3: MORE BEAUTIFUL THAN USEFUL

36 **"Jones—a disquisition"**: Hale, p. 204ff.

36 **"The characteristic of our epoch"**: Sanborn 1894, pp. 6–10.

37 **center and side aisles**: http://www.harvardsquarelibrary.org/harvard-church/13.htm.

37 **covered hand carts and other vehicles**: Hale, p. 205.

38 **Quincy had already forbidden such carousal**: Harding 1982, p. 48–49.

38 **"The Commercial Spirit of Modern Times"**: See illustration, Meltzer p. 34.

38 **Rice, the son of a blacksmith**: Henry Williams, p. 25.

38 **Henry Vose**: See letters to and from Vose and Rice in Sanborn 1917, p. 54ff; Harding 1982, various comments; Lebeaux 1977.

38 **After every few speakers**: Hale, pp. 206–7.

39 **One, James Richardson**: James Richardson, letter to Thoreau, September 7, 1837, reprinted in Sanborn, *Familiar Letters*, p. 10.

39 **John Shepard Keyes**: For details about Keyes and his visit to Harvard, see John Shepard Keyes, in Amelia F. Emerson, pp. 73, 80; Harding 1989 p. 174; Keyes, *Autobiography*, pp. 49, 57; for background information, see Adams, p. 32; Keyes, letter to Francis H. Underwood, November 15, 1886, in *TSB* CII (Spring 1968), p. 1. See also Adams, p. 31ff.

41 **Boyish and round-faced**: Sattelmeyer, p. 4; Metzger, p. 29; Cameron 1959, p. 13; John Thoreau Jr., letter to George Stearns, October 18, 1833, in Sanborn 1917, pp. 215ff.; Eidson, pp. 472–73; Henry Williams, p. 24.

42 **a few weeks living with Wheeler**: Sanborn 1894, p. 68, n. 1, citing Channing; Cramer 2004, p. 188, n. 77; Eidson, pp. 479, 480.

43 **the image of a lakeside cabin**: How much time Thoreau spent at Wheeler's cabin is not known, but scholars conclude that he was there in summer 1837; he referred to these experiences later, and there is no record of his having spent time at anyone else's lakeside cabin.

Chapter 4: MEADOW RIVER

44 **after the death of their mother in 1830**: Harding 1982, p. 21.

44 **rushing from one meeting to another**: Thoreau, *Correspondence*, p. 131.

44 **known as "comeouters"**: Adams 1953, p. 2; Sanborn 1917, p. 45.

44 **abolitionists had boarded with the Thoreaus**: Petrulionis 2001, p. 387. Details about abolition in this scene derive from Petrulionis unless otherwise cited.

45 **Reverend Ezra Ripley**: For physical description of Ripley, see Jarvis, p. 79, 81; see portraits on p. 39 of Meltzer and on the online Unitarian historical site http://www25.uua.org/uuhs/duub/articles/ezraripley.html. Unless otherwise cited, details about Ripley's behavior derive from RWE, "Ezra Ripley, D. D."

45 **Washington commandeered Harvard's dormitories**: See First Parish history at http://www.firstparish.org/cms/about-first-parish/history-of-fp/ministers.

45 **performed the marriage service for John Thoreau**: Meltzer, p. 39.

46 **Ripley climbed up a long flight of stairs**: Description of the church from Hoar, pp. 47–49, and RWE.

46 **bayonets "bagnets" . . . "Let every critter jine"**: Hoar, p. 49

46 **The now wrinkled and bent Amos Barrett**: Barrett's recollection is recorded in Swayne, pp. 49–51.

47 **Musketaquid**: Thoreau, *Week*, chapter 1; see also Mattesen, p. 86.

47 **Its current was so slow . . . water lilies**: Hawthorne, August 6, 1842.

47 **mail arrived and departed sixteen times a week**: Shattuck, chapter 13.

48 **Concord Bank and Middlesex Mutual Fire Insurance Company**: Concord Mill Dam Company Records, Concord Free Public Library.

48 **town pump . . . swimming hole**: *Journal,* February 9, 1851; Hoar, p. 51.

48 **required to muster for militia inspection**: Hoar, pp. 55–56; Jarvis, p. 21.

48 **fife and drum, their volume rising and falling**: *Journal,* May 27, 1857.

48 **boys played soldier**: Hoar, pp. 54–56.

49 **planted on the nineteenth of April**: Keyes, *History*, chapter 45; Swayne, p. 281, n. 2.

49 **Loring had manufactured first lead pipes and then wooden pails**: See the Loring-Barrett-Sherman-Smith Family Papers, Concord Free Library, Vault A45, Loring, Unit 1.

49 **barns soon filled with horses**: Hoar, p. 56.

50 **Temperance leaders made no more headway**: Jarvis, p. 167ff.

50 **prominent Concordian Nathan Brooks**: Meltzer, pp. 39, 42, and Hoar, p. 56.

50 **catered to locals and stage travelers**: Jarvis, p. 32.

50 **flip**: Keyes, Middlesex Hotel talk; Jarvis, p. 162.

Chapter 5: THE NEW SCHOOLMASTER

51 **Centre Grammar School**: Details on the school derive mostly from Jarvis, p. 125ff.

51 **$2,132.55 during the upcoming academic year**: Richardson 1986, p. 35.

51 **Most Concord teachers were recent graduates**: Jarvis, p. 110.

52 **Nehemiah Ball**: Details about Ball's appearance and quirks derive from Keyes 1888 p. 236ff. and Wheeler, p. 29ff.; see also Jarvis, p. 137 n., and E. Emerson 1971, especially the Daniel Potter interview.

52 **replaced the village's Debating Club**: Jarvis, pp. 26–27, 135ff.

52 **holidays**: Jarvis, pp. 145–146; Hoar, pp. 53–55.

53 **The school committee found the stench**: Jarvis, pp. 126–27.

54 **elicited a violent response**: Hoar, p. 52ff.

55 **"I will not sit down"**: Jarvis, pp. 110–15.

55 **regulations advised teachers**: Marble, pp. 78–79.

56 **"When I'm grown up, I'll whip you for this"**: E. Emerson 1971, pp. 80–90; see also Harding 1982, p. 53, and n. 6, citing an interview with Daniel F. Potter by Allen French, in manuscript in Harding's own files. In old age, Daniel Potter spoke with Edward Emerson on November 17, 1904, recounting this story and adding, "I never saw the day I wanted to do it. Why, Henry Thoreau was the kindest-hearted of men."

57 **a necessary return to the pencil business**: Details not otherwise cited derive from Petroski 1989, especially chapter 9, pp. 104–25. See also Conrad 2005. Harding 1982 devotes attention to the business throughout his biography.

57 **Dixon mixed plumbago from Ceylon**: See Petroski, but also the Jersey City historical page on the Dixon Crucible Company at http://www.njcu.edu /programs/jchistory/pages/d_pages/dixon_crucible_company.htm.

58 **"The Lead Pencils exhibited"**: See photograph of magazine notice, Meltzer, p. 138.

59 **the Thoreaus extended the chamber**: Details of the grinding process derive from E. Emerson.

Chapter 6: SAVAGE BROTHERS

60 **His quick sympathy**: Description of John's personality derives from E. Emerson 1917, p. 21; Myerson 1994, pp. 371–72; Priscilla Rice Edes, reprinted in Adams 1953, p. 2.

60 **"flat and insipid"**: John Thoreau Jr., letter to George Stearns, October 18, 1833; in Sanborn 1917, pp. 215–18.

60 **enjoyed playing the flute**: Myerson 1994, pp. 370–71. For its appearance, see flute in Concord Museum.

61 **John frequently suffered**: John Thoreau, letter to George Stearns, October 18, 1833; in Sanborn 1917, p. 215ff.

61 **Consumption, or tuberculosis**: The disease was named tuberculosis in 1839. For background in this era, see Bowditch and Cardwell; for overall history see Dormandy.

61 **Henry and John's grandfather had died of consumption**: Sanborn 1917, p. 109.

61 **Henry bragged that he could carry a rifle**: E. Emerson 1917.

61 **He had developed a strong, muscular body**: Sanborn 1882, p. 253ff.

61 **childhood introduction to hunting and fishing**: Thoreau, *Walden*, "Higher Laws."

62 **yielded mainly firewood**: Maynard, p. 17.

63 **Ahead, beyond the village**: Thoreau describes the vew in *Journal,* August 29, 1838, and elsewhere; see also Joseph Hosmer; and Roman 2007, quoting David R. Foster, and Foster himself, pp. 10–14.

64 **"the state of rude uncivilized men"**: See Sayre, p. 3, for Webster's definition and example, and for Rousseau's criticism of Europe behind the fanciful descriptions of savages.

65 **"This great mortality"**: Shattuck, chapter 1. Sanborn, in *Life*, p. 507, reproduces Thoreau's 1840 list of books in his personal library, which include Shattuck's history.

68 **"If men have dared"**: Thoreau, letter to Charles Wyatt Rice, August 5, 1836.

68 **"There on Nawshawtuct"**: Thoreau's reconstruction of his words, written in journal October 29, 1837, concerning an event "some four or six weeks ago." He spells Nawshawtuct variously; usually nowadays it is spelled Nashawtuc.

69 **"I do not see where you find your Indian arrowheads"**: Channing, p. 271.

69 **In mid-November**: Thoreau, letter to John Thoreau, November 11–14, 1837. See also Myerson 1995 for background on Thoreau's information about Tahatawan.

Chapter 7: GOD AND NATURE FACE TO FACE

71 **"I hear . . . that you are comfortably located"**: James Richardson Jr., letter to Thoreau, September 7, 1837.

71 **Emerson was among those examining Henry**: Cameron 1959, p. 15.

72 **"I have sometimes thought"**: RWE, *JMN*, June 2, 1832.

73 **"Adam called his house, heaven and earth"**: Emerson 1836, p. 92.

74 **Lucy Jackson Brown, from Plymouth**: Sanborn 1917, pp. 128ff.

74 **After her husband spent their money**: Harmon Smith, p. 5.

75 **a plain, white two-story house**: Swayne, pp. 70ff.

78 **Samuel Hoar gave a speech**: Ruth Haskins Emerson (RWE's mother), letter to her son William, June 27, 1837; Concord Library.

78 **"Do you keep a journal?"**: *Journal*, October 22, 1837. I follow scholarly consensus that the speaker was RWE.

79 **"friendship is good which begins on sentiment"**: RWE, *JMN*, October 21, 1837.

79 **"Shall We Keep Journals?"**: Sanborn 1917, p. 735ff., reprints the essay; he discusses its context in Sanborn 1882, p. 150ff.

80 **"To be alone"**: *Journal*, October 22, 1837; **"We have always a resource"**: November 17; **"Crossed the river today"**: December 23; **"a new note in nature"**: December (otherwise undated); **"jugular vein of Musketaquid"**: November 16; **"gray twilight of the poets"**: October 30; **"Just before immersion"**: October 29; **"So when thick vapors"**: October 27; **"How cheering it is"**: December 31; **Goethe's 1790 play**: October 25; **"I am at home"**: November 17; **ancient Latin and Greek**: e.g., *Journal*, October 25 and December 18, 1837. **"This shall be the test"** . . . **"I yet lack discernment"**: November 12–13.

82 **"Poverty was her lot"**: See reproduction of newspaper page in Meltzer and Harding, p. 69.

83 ***"Jam laeto turgent"***: *Journal*, November 20, 1837. He translated Virgil's lines later for *Week*.

84 *Henry could see the same rituals enacted: Journal*, September 2, 1851.

84 **music** (details in this note from Perry Miller's volume of 1840 journal): **hymnlike opening march**: description of music mine, not Thoreau's; **remind him of the Hindu Vedas**: August 16, p. 155; **crickets . . . frogs . . . "A flitting maiden"**: August 8, p. 148, and August 13, p. 153; **music in the clang of tools**: December 31, p. 201; **Working by the pond**: December 15, p. 193.

Chapter 8: HOW COMIC IS SIMPLICITY

89 **"I delight much in my young friend"**: RWE, *JMN*, October 27, 1837. RWE's quotation, in the style of the time, was "Henry Thoreau merely remarked that 'Mr Hosmer had kicked the pail over.'" I changed "had" to "has."

89 **In December, Emerson informed Henry**: Smith 1999, p. 13. These two paragraphs closely follow points made by Smith.

90 **the hall that divided the house down the center**: Bartlett 1885, p. 50.

90 **one side of the room**: See Bartlett 1885, p. 49ff and RWE photographs and the Concord Museum reconstruction of the study with original furnishings.

90 **criticism for, and misrepresentation of, his recent essays . . . his favorite exclamation: "Baaaaaa. . . ."**: Lidian Jackson Emerson, letter to Lucy Jackson Brown, [February 13, 1838]; in *Selected Letters*, p. 70ff.

90 **"My good Henry Thoreau"**: RWE, *JMN*, February 11, 1838.

91 **Seventy percent of the signatures on a petition**: Petrulionis 2001, p. 391.

91 **Massachusetts had banned slavery in 1783**: Petrulionis 2006, p. 10.

91 **1814 and the founding of the Concord Female Charitable Society**: ibid, p. 389.

91 **Wilder's Trinitarian church had hosted**: ibid, p. 388.

91 **Sarah and Angelina Grimké**: Petrulionis 2006, p. 17ff.

92 **"I think I shall not turn away my attention"**: Lidian Emerson, in Beck, p. 32.

92 **"bigoted, rash, and morose"**: Sermon by Albert Folsom, in *Annual Report of the Boston Female Anti-Slavery Society* (Boston: Isaac Knapp, 1837), pp. 55–56.

92 **a mob stormed Lovejoy's office**: See newspaper story from November 1837, online at http://www.altonweb.com/history/lovejoy/a01.html. For murder of Lovejoy, see Simon, pp. 128–33.

93 **"In nature all the growth"**: RWE, *JMN*, June 6, 1838; vol. 7, p. 9.

94 **"We must use the language of facts"**: RWE, *JMN*, immediately before October 27, 1838; in vol. 7, p. 121.

94 **"Is not the Vast"**: RWE, *JMN*, after September 16, 1838; in vol. 7, p. 75.

94 **Yet his eureka revelation**: Richardson, p. 143.

94 **"Then retire & hide"**: RWE, *JMN*, June 12, 1838; in vol. 7, p. 14.

94 **"Men are constantly dinging"**: *Journal*, August 13, 1838.

94 **"Nature is the beautiful asylum"**: RWE, Journal D, September 24, 1838; in vol. 7, p. 83.

95 **forced Helen to abandon her own teaching**: Cameron 1957, p. 48.

95 **Haskins had had no expectations of Henry**: Haskins 1887, p. 109ff.

97 **Many other people noticed Henry's imitation of Emerson**: Curtis, in Petrulionis 2012, p. 78ff.

97 **his handwriting even came to resemble his mentor's**: Sanborn 1901, p. 4.

97 **"I saw Thoreau last night"**: James Russell Lowell, letter dated July 12, 1838, in Howard, pp. 18–19.

Chapter 9: WE CAN TEACH YOU

98 **In June 1838, having failed to find a job teaching**: Sanborn 1917, p. 201.

98 **"I have four scholars"**: Thoreau, letter to John Thoreau, July 8, 1838; reprinted in Sanborn 1906, p. 23.

98 **"for the reception of a limited number of pupils"**: Advertisement repro-
      duced in Borst, p. 39.

98 **first interviewed by John**: Interview dialogue from Sanborn 1917, pp. 203–4.

99 **Some students reported home**: School details and quotations not otherwise
      cited derive from student reminiscences preserved by E. Emerson and Horace
      Hosmer.

99 **School was in session from half past eight**: Edmund Hosmer, letter to his
      family, in Hoagland, p. 482.

100 **"trainer" had become a synonym for "militiaman"**: Hoar, p. 70; De Vere, p. 24.

101 **Henry read aloud**: Edmund Hosmer, letter to his family, quoted in Hoagland,
      p. 482.

101 **He spoke of his own belief**: Former student Thomas Hosmer, in E. Emerson,
      "A Different Drummer."

103 **"Not having been privy"**: RWE, *JMN*, undated, November 1838.

103 **held it up to the nearest student, Henry Warren**: Warren's account appears
      in Sanborn 1917, pp. 206–7.

105 **Young Thomas Hosmer**: In E. Emerson, "A Different Drummer."

106 **a likely spot to have once held an Indian fishing village**: Sanborn 1917, pp.
      205–7.

107 **For Caroline, it was a homecoming**: Koopman, p. 61.

107 **Edmund was writing in one often**: Details about Edmund's education not
      otherwise cited derive from Hoagland, pp. 474ff.

109 **"I have within the last few days"**: *Journal,* June 22, 1839.

110 **imitation of the classical elegiac mode**: Hodder, pp. 36–39; Lebeaux 1977.

110 **"Lately alas I knew a gentle boy"**: *Journal,* June 24, 1839; printed in *The Dial*
      in 1840.

110 **"Last night . . . came to me"**: RWE, *JMN,* August 1, 1839.

Chapter 10: NO REMEDY FOR LOVE

111 **Ellen Sewall**: Sewall, diary entry for July 5, 1832, in Stewart, p. 6; letter from
      Samuel Sewall to Edmund Quincy Sewall, August 23, 1839, in Stewart;
      Raysor, p. 458; Koopman, p. 62.

113 **He took Ellen and Aunt Prudence on the river**: Harding 1965, p. 101.

113 **"All outdoors is a church"**: Koopman, p. 67. Koopman could not recall
      whether her mother said that Henry said "All outdoors is a church" or "All
      outdoors should be a church." I picked one.

113 **"this famous animal"**: Ellen Sewall, letter to her father, in Raysor, p. 458.

114 **"Oh, I can not tell you half"**: Letter from Ellen Sewall to her father, July 31,
      1839; in Stewart.

114 **classmate Robert Barnwell**: RWE, *JMN*, in an undated entry between February 22 and 25, 1839.

115 **Ellen must be either an absolute genius or some kind of idiot**: Koopman, p. 67.

115 **"Our rays united" . . . "There is no remedy"**: *Journal,* July 24 and 25, 1839.

115 **John Keyes**: Most of the information on Keyes's response to Ellen Sewall comes from complete letters in Harding 1965.

116 **Josiah Bartlett asked Henry**: RWE, *JMN*, September 14, 1839; see Plumstead and Hayford, vol. 7, p. 238.

117 **On Thursday the twenty-ninth of August**: Details of melon party from Keyes, *Diary*; and Elizabeth Hoar, undated letter to Bowles family in *TSB*, Winter 1977, p. 5.

117 **departed on the last day of August 1839**: Description of voyage not otherwise cited derives from *Journal*, beginning August 31, 1839, and *Week*.

122 **"We are shut up in schools"**: RWE, *JMN*, September 14, 1839.

Chapter 11: GIVE HER A KISS FOR ME

124 **"The house seems deserted"**: Ellen Sewall, letter to Prudence Ward, December 26, 1839.

124 **"Flee to the mountains"**: Richardson, p. 303.

124 **"If sister has read it through"**: Harding 1965, p. 104.

125 **"By another spring I may be a mail-carrier in Peru"**: *Journal,* March 21, 1840.

126 **"The other day," Henry wrote**: *Journal,* June 19, 1840.

127 **John and Ellen strolled on the beach**: Koopman, p. 63.

127 **"These two days that I have not written"**: *Journal,* July 19, 1840.

128 **"Tonight I feel doleful"**: John Thoreau journal, July 22, 1840; reprinted in Blanding, p. 5. I have inserted a couple of periods to make the entry more intelligible.

129 **she received a romantic letter from Henry**: Koopman, p. 64.

129 **Ellen consulted her father**: Letter from Ellen Sewall to Prudence Ward, November 18, 1840, in Stewart, p. 9.

130 **"When we are amiable"**: *Journal*, January 19, 1841.

130 **"That is the first piece Henry gave me"**: Ellen Sewall, journal entry for July 25, 1841; reprinted in Harding 1982, p. 103. Quotation marks appear in Sewall's original.

Chapter 12: MY FRIEND'S LITTLE BROTHER

131 **"A very pleasant schoolmaster"**: Edmund Sewall, letter to his aunt, April 5, 1839; in Sanborn, *Life*, p. 202.

132 **writing book his aunt gave him**: Edmund Sewall, letter to his parents, March 28, 1840; in Hoagland, p. 478ff.

132 **Henry saw a slate-colored sparrow**: Edmund Sewall, letter to his parents, March 28, 1840; reprinted in Hoagland, p. 478ff. Thoreau described its song in journal entries such as March 23, 1852.

133 **descendant of Concord's first regular paper**: See Concord Free Library page http://www.concordlibrary.org/scollect/concord-pre-civil-war-newspapers/index.html.

133 **"How shall I help myself?"**: *Journal,* April 8, 1840.

134 **"I was not at all interested"**: Edmund Sewall, journal, April 8, 1840; in Hoagland, p. 477.

134 **Henry and John's childhood friends**: Unless otherwise cited, details about Horace Hosmer's early life and involvement with the Thoreau school, as well as dialogue involving him, derive from Hosmer, pp. 10–12, 72–74, 85–94, 115, and from various places throughout his interviews quoted in E. Emerson.

Chapter 13: LOG CABINS AND CIDER

137 **youngest and smallest pupil**: For national issues in 1840 campaign, see Formisano, especially p. 680ff., and Gunderson throughout. For neologisms, many of which became standard in U.S. political discourse, see Dillard, especially p. 176ff.

139 **a silk lapel ribbon . . . Newspaper cartoons**: Gunderson, illustrations opposite p. 116.

140 **On the fourth of July**: *Journal,* July 4, 1840. For details on Concord events, see Hosmer, p. 19 n. 8, and p. 31 n. 3, and pp. 26, 72; Jarvis, p. 166ff; *Yeoman's Gazette,* Saturday July 11, 1840, quoted in RWE, *JMN,* vol. 7, p. 379 n (n.d., between entries dated June 29 and July 10); RWE, *JMN,* vol. 7, p. 379, n. 302; Keyes, unpaginated diary, Concord Public Library, and Keyes, *Autobiography,* pp. 81–83, pp. 69–70.

141 **"You're not the man"**: Hosmer, p. 72.

141 **"The simplest things are always better than curiosities"**: RWE, *JMN,* vol. 7, p. 378 (n.d., between entries dated June 29 and July 10).

141 **"A man's life should be a stately march"**: *Journal,* June 30, 1840.

142 **"The line of beauty is a curve"**: *Journal,* July 4, 1840.

142 **"When this old hat was new"**: Silber, p. 44. I have slightly changed the punctuation.

143 **"Oh, no, he never lost a fight"**: http://www.mudcat.org/thread.cfm?threadid=83400.

143 **court dress of white satin waistcoat**: Fuess, vol. 2, p. 75; Gunderson, p. 173, contrasts Webster's clothing in these settings to great effect, and I couldn't

resist consulting his sources for my own examples. Also see Gunderson, pp. 174ff., for evolution of oratorical styles, especially Webster's.

143 **Webster was still best known in the Thoreau family**: Louisa Dunbar, quoted in Sanborn, *Life*, p. 46.

145 **more pro-Whig than its former incarnations**: Concord Free Library, "Concord, Massachusetts Newspapers up to the Civil War," at http://www. concordlibrary.org/scollect/concord-pre-civil-war-newspapers/index.html.

145 **"The Great Harrison Barbecue"**: *Yeoman's Gazette*, Saturday July 11, 1840, quoted in RWE, *JMN*, vol. 7, p. 379 n. (n.d., between entries dated June 29 and July 10).

145 **Alcott . . . moved to Concord in early April**: Details about Bronson Alcott's Temple School and the Alcotts' arrival in Concord not otherwise cited derive from Matteson, primarily pp. 55–85.

145 **modest annual rent of fifty-two dollars . . . Smug in a near-messianic sense**: Sanborn 1908, p. 9, 14.

148 **"our bold bible for The Young America"**: RWE, letter to Margaret Fuller, [editors uncertain] April 21? and 23?, 1840.

149 **"I believe we all feel much alike"**: RWE, letter to Margaret Fuller, December 12, 1839.

149 **"a very accomplished and very intelligent person"**: RWE, *JMN*, August 12, 1836.

149 **"One grave thing I have to say"**: RWE, letter to Margaret Fuller, May 8, 1840.

150 **"When he talks he is great"**: Reisen, p. 61.

Chapter 14: MELODIES AND INVENTIONS

151 **"The present seems never to get its due,"** February 3, 1841; **bronchitis**, February 14; **"as any out doors,"** February 10.

152 **"If wisely executed"**: George Ripley, letter to RWE, November 9, 1840. Frothingham reprints Ripley's proposal on pp. 307ff. For Brook Farm background, see Myerson 1987 and Delano.

153 **"What a brave thing Mr. Ripley has done!"**: RWE, letter to Margaret Fuller, May 27 and 29, 1840; in RWE, *Complete Works*, vol. 10, p. 581.

153 **"As for these communities . . . To be associated with others,"** *Journal*, March 21, 1841.

154 **"Dec. 8, 1840—Owe Father"**: Sanborn 1901, p. 28.

155 **tap the tea kettle**: *Journal*, April 4, 1841.

155 **shoveling manure**, *Journal*, April 20, 1841.

155 **"He is to have his board"**: RWE, letter to William Emerson, June 1, 1841.

155 **"a noble manly youth"**: RWE, letter to William Emerson, May 30, 1841.

156 **"I am living with Mr. Emerson"**: Thoreau, letter to Isaiah T. Williams, September 8, 1841.

156 **no pressure in his family to marry**: Harding 1982 makes this point, p. 112; see also discussion in Lebeaux 1977.

156 **"I do not want to feel"**: *Journal,* December 25, 1941; **"sturdy English wit,"** December 30.

157 **"I am about five feet"**: Borst, p. 74.

Chapter 15: NEAR TO THE WORLD OF SPIRITS

159 **he read Walter Raleigh**: *Journal,* January 5, 1842.

159 **"a more rapid blossoming"**: *Journal,* January 3, 1842, notes that he popped corn for the Emerson children at this time, but some details derive from RWE's daughter Edith Emerson Forbes's later accounts; and from E. Emerson and RWE, *JMN,* January 30, 1842.

159 **to name her Lucy Cotton**: Lidian Jackson Emerson, letter to Lucy Jackson Brown, December 3, 1841; in *Selected Letters,* pp. 96–97.

160 **"My music makes the thunder dance!"**: RWE, *JMN,* January 30, 1842

160 **"The practical faith of men . . . no infidelity so great"**: *Journal,* January 1, 1842.

161 **On Saturday, the eighth of January, Henry was at home**: Lidian Emerson, letter to Lucy Brown, in Petrulionis 2012, p. 2. She said he reported some details to her, others to RWE.

162 **devastating effects of drink**: Jarvis, pp. 167–75; Sanborn 1882, pp. 42–43.

162 **John . . . temperance pledge**: Myerson 1994, p. 372–73.

162 **reported John's horrifying new symptoms . . . "Now sit down and talk to me"**; Lidian Emerson, letter to Lucy Brown, in Myerson, p. 6, 106

164 **glimmers of John's calm former self**: Thoreau, letter to Isaiah T. Williams, March 14, 1842.

164 **"None at all" . . . "composed by the deceased"**: Lidian Emerson, letter to Lucy Jackson Brown, January 16, 1842; in *Selected Letters,* p. 100.

165 **Frost was ordained as a colleague of Dr. Ripley**: Most details about Frost derive from Myerson's 1994 article, including the only lines extant from John's poem.

166 **"Did John love her too?"**: Koopman, p. 66.

166 **a lock of his brother's hair**: Borst, p. 605.

167 **"You may judge we were all alarmed"**: RWE, letter to William Emerson, January 24, 1842.

167 **"I wish you would tell Cousin Willie" . . . sighed his last small breath**: RWE, *JMN,* January 30, 1842.

168 **"Shall I ever dare to love"**: RWE, letter to Margaret Fuller, January 28, 1842.

169 **"I do not wish"**: Thoreau, letter to Mrs. Lucy Brown, March 2, 1842.

170 **"Where is my heart gone"**: *Journal,* March 26.

Chapter 16: Hawthorne's New Boat

175 **"Great, grim, earnest men"**: RWE, *JMN,* September 21, 1841; vol. 6, pp. 52–53.

176 **parsonage's high paneling and heavy beams**: Hawthorne, August 8, 1842, and "The Old Manse," preface to *Mosses*; McFarland, p. 10; Bartlett 1885, pp. 53–54.

177 **Emerson rented it to them** : Megan Marshall, p. 428.

177 **"He seems pleased with the colony"**: Quoted in Wineapple, p. 160.

177 **"Upon the whole we look upon him"**: Poe, vol. 10, p. 104. Originally published in *Graham's Magazine,* April 1842.

177 **Panic of 1837 . . . Hawthorne also swore to himself**: Wineapple, pp. 93–97.

178 **Emerson had hired John Garrison**: Petrulionis 2006.

178 **"Henry Thorow"**: Tharp, p. 151.

178 **"You never saw anything so splendid"**: Julian Hawthorne, vol. 1, p. 178.

179 **"There is something that kindles the imagination"**: Hawthorne, June 1, 1842.

180 **"We are as happy as people can be"**: Hawthorne, letter to Louisa Hawthorne, July 10, 1842.

181 **"Would that my wife would permit"**: Hawthorne, August 5, 1842.

181 **Sophia was a talented artist**: Tharp, p. 54; Julian Hawthorne, p. 279; Hoar, p. 69.

182 **sounds they heard around the house . . . his fictions seemed light**: Hawthorne, August 8, 1842.

183 **"Mr. Thorow dined with us yesterday"**: Hawthorne, September 1, 1842; **"A perfect pond-lily"**: August 13.

185 **"the Indian name of which I have forgotten"**: Hawthorne, September 18, 1842.

185 **"reflection is indeed the reality"**: Hawthorne, undated entry in 1841–52 notebooks; in Simpson, p. 251.

Chapter 17: A Skating Party

186 **The homely local boy taught the handsome author**: Hawthorne, "The Old Manse," introduction to *Mosses.*

186 **"There is a gentleman in this town"**: Hawthorne, letter to Epes Sargent, October 21, 1842; in *Selected Letters,* pp. 106–7.

187 **wrote to a friend about John's death**: Thoreau, letter to Isaiah Williams, October 10, 1842.

187 **"Last night," Emerson wrote**: RWE, *JMN*, undated entry, vol. 6, p. 304.

188 **"A letter, written a century or more ago"**: Hawthorne, December 6, 1837; **stray leaf from the book of Fate**: June 1, 1842; **"What moral could be drawn"**: December 6, 1837; **"It might be made emblematical"**: October 16, 1837.

189 **"dithyrambic dances" . . . "Mr. Hawthorne is such an Ajax"**: Sophia Hawthorne, letter to Mary Foote, December 18, 1842; in Rose Hawthorne Lathrop, p. 50ff.

190 **Every year Henry was thrilled anew**: A few details in this section derive from later journal entries—e.g., December 19, 1854; January 14 and February 1, 1855—but Thoreau spoke years earlier about his love of skating.

191 **"Plainly the fox belongs"**: *Journal*, vol. 1, p. 470.

192 **to understand the snow itself**: Channing, p. 264.

192 **Swedenborg . . . had studied crystallization**: Eric G. Wilson, p. 100ff.

193 **"For it consists, as it were"**: Swedenborg, vol. 2, p. 542.

193 **"In one place you might see"**: also mist etc., *Journal*, December 16, 19, 23.

193 **Separate volumes by various authors**: Rusk, *Letters of RWE*, vol. 3, p. 47, n. 175; Hyde's notes, pp. 315–19, as well as his book's introduction.

194 **"By what chance or lucid interval"**: RWE, letter to Margaret Fuller, April 10, 1842.

Chapter 18: STATEN ISLAND

197 **"No incidents worthy of note"**: Richard Fuller 1972, pp. 1–4.

198 **"He is a good writer"**: Hawthorne, September 1, 1842.

198 **Richard Fuller had sent him a music box**: Thoreau, letter to Richard Fuller, January 16, 1843, and Harding and Bode's note following.

199 **shortly after he met the Hawthornes**: Thoreau, letter to Lucy Brown, January 24, 1843.

199 **"My heart really warmed with sympathy"**: Lidian Emerson, letter to RWE, January 15, 1843.

199 **family pressure for gainful employment**: E.g., Lebeaux 1977, p. 209.

199 **"I have to say that Henry listens"**: RWE, letter to William Emerson, March 13, 1843; in *Letters*, vol. 3, p. 157ff.

200 **"a diseased bundle of nerves"**: Thoreau, January 1, 1843; in Bridgman, p. 284.

200 **Later he gave Henry seven dollars**: RWE, letter to William Emerson, May 6, 1843; in *Letters*, vol. 3, p. 172; **"procure for himself literary labor"**: p. 157ff.

201 **"We have become better acquainted"**: Letter from Elizabeth Hoar to Thoreau, May 2, 1843.

201 **"I love Henry, but I do not like him"**: RWE, *JMN*, March 1843.

201 **"I am sure no truer & no purer person"**: RWE, letter to William Emerson, May 6, 1843.

201 **"Mr. Thoreau was discussed"**: Hawthorne, April 8, 1842.

202 **"the first time that I ever came home"**: Hawthorne, October 10, 1842.

203 **"Man's accidents are God's purposes"**: The scratched inscriptions on the window, dated April 3, 1843, can still be seen at the Old Manse in Concord.

203 **Hawthorne . . . was receiving no payment**: McFarland, p. 88ff.

205 **"Want a cab, sir?"**: Thoreau, letter to Cynthia Thoreau, May 11, 1843. Details about arrival and William Emerson's house not otherwise cited derive from this letter.

206 **the house was halfway up a hill . . . "From 9 to 2 or thereabouts" . . . "I do not feel myself especially serviceable"**: : Thoreau, letter to his parents, June 8, 1843.

206 **"There are two things I hear" . . . He claimed to be unimpressed by New York**: Thoreau, letter to RWE, May 23, 1843. Details in beach description derive from this letter and from next source below.

207 **"The crowd is something new"**: Thoreau, letter to RWE, June 8, 1843.

207 **wide and sunlit Broadway**: Dickens, chapter 6.

207 **on the wooden blocks**: Thoreau, letter to Cynthia Thoreau, May 11, 1843; see also "Manhattan's First Experiments with Wooden Streets," at http://www.manhattanpast.com/2012/manhattans-first-experiments-with-wooden-streets/.

208 **flocks of fashionable women**: Description of women's clothes here comes from Dickens, chapter 6, as do details about vehicles below and description of pigs beyond Thoreau's.

208 **could not walk past them in the kitchen**: RWE, 1843 (otherwise undated); in *JMN*, vol. 6, p. 371.

208 **"It must have a very bad influence"**: Thoreau, letter to Cynthia Thoreau, October 1, 1843.

210 **hundreds of new immigrants**: Thoreau, letter to Helen Thoreau, July 21, 1843.

210 **"In place of something fresher"**: Thoreau, letter to Helen Thoreau, May 23, 1843. See also Thomas, pp. 101–3.

211 **"You seem to speak"**: Thoreau, letter to Lidian Emerson, June 20, 1843.

211 **locusts crawled out of the earth**: Thoreau, letter to his mother, July 7, 1843. He was actually observing seventeen-year periodical cicadas, *Magicicada* genus.

212 ***Phar-r-r-a oh—Pha-r-r-aoh***: Thoreau's phonetic representation.

213 **Emerson complained about the profanation of his Eden**: RWE, letter to Thoreau, September, 8, 1843.

213 **"But no matter let them hack away"**: Thoreau, letter to RWE, October 17, 1843.

214 Hawthorne . . . came upon a makeshift village: Hawthorne, October 6, 1843.

215 "I think of you all very often": Thoreau, letter to Cynthia Thoreau, August 6, 1843.

215 Thanksgiving . . . in Concord: Hoar, pp. 57–58.

216 "Henry T. thanks you for the purse": RWE, December 17, 1843.

216 his father's pencil factory occupied: Sanborn 1917, p. 327.

Chapter 19: FIRE

217 They forgot to take matches: Details of fire not otherwise cited derive from *Journal,* undated June 1850 entry, vol. II, p. 21ff.

217 Edward Hoar: Sanborn 1917, p. 371, 416ff.

218 "Where will this end?": *Journal,* undated entry, 1850 (vol. II, p. 21ff., MSL I, 149); stacked cords of firewood: Sanborn 1917, p. 419.

219 "Who are these men": Thoreau says that these were his thoughts at the time.

220 frustration with property owners' restrictions: RWE, *JMN,* undated, November 1838.

221 "The fire, we understand": *Concord Freeman,* May 3, 1844; for extent of damage, Sanborn 1917, p. 419.

221 the only reason that Edward and Henry evaded prosecution: Sanborn 1917, p. 422.

222 "Cyrus Hubbard and others": Harding 1982, p. 161.

222 "Don't talk to me of Henry Thoreau!": Mary Hosmer Brown, p. 109.

222 he felt an inconsolable grief: Thoreau, "House-Warming," in *Walden.*

222 "damned rascal": Thoreau's quotation; see also Cramer 2007, p. 55, n. 38.

Chapter 20: A POOR MAN'S HOUSE

223 "Some were marked S for Soft": Petroski 1989, pp. 118–19.

223 An advertisement in 1844 declared: Petroski, p. 120.

224 refuge in part to escape censure or even reprisal: A speculation raised by various commentators, especially Lebeaux 1984, p. 118ff.

224 "I only ask a clean seat": *Journal,* April 5, 1841.

224 "The rich man's house": *Journal,* August (no date), 1840.

225 "I have thought," he sighed to his journal: *Journal,* January 19, 1842.

225 broken-down old Hollowell farm: *Walden,* "Where I Lived, and What I Lived For"; Van Doren Stern, p. 214, n. 5, 7.

227 "Come, now, can't you lend me": Sanborn 1873, p. 26.

228 **The empire's trade in slaves**: See Petrulionis 2006 for background on abolition of slavery in the British Empire. Text of Slavery Abolition Act available at http://www.pdavis.nl/Legis_07.htm.

228 **William Lloyd Garrison, the founder of both**: Petrulionis 2006, p. 9.

229 **"the editor or publisher of a certain paper"**.. . . Arthur Tappan . . . nine-foot-high double gallows . . . burned in effigy: Garrison, vol. 1, pp. 247, 485, 492, 519.

229 **"a collation in the woods"**: *Concord Freeman*, July 12 and 26, 1844..

229 **paid a quarter apiece to attend**: *Herald of Freedom*, August 16, 1844, p. 86.

230 **his mother and both sisters had journeyed to Boston**: Petrulionis 2001, pp. 397–98.

230 **Henry himself ran to the steeple**: Sanborn 1903, p. 88; Cabot, vol. 2, p. 430, n. 1.

231 **One observer, twenty-year-old George William Curtis**: Curtis, p. 193.

231 **despite Transcendentalism's insistence upon an individual's ability**: Beck, pp. 32–33, makes this point about RWE's philosophical inconsistency.

231 **"I think it cannot be maintained"**: RWE, December 2, 1836, in *JMN*, vol. 12, p. 152.

232 **"Madmen, madwomen, men with beards"**: RWE, "Chardon Street and Bible Conventions," in *Miscellaneous Pieces* (vol. 4 of *Works*), p. 155.

232 **a number of those took refuge near Walden Pond**: Unless otherwise cited, details of inhabitants near Walden derive from *Walden*, "Former Inhabitants; & Winter Visitors."

234 **Cynthia selected an otherwise appealing spot**: Sanborn 1909, vol. 2, pp. 400–401.

234 **signed a mortgage on the property**: *TSB*, No. 19 (Spring 1990), pp. 5–6;.

236 **"landlord & waterlord of 14 acres"**: RWE, letter to William Emerson, October 4, 1845.

236 **"I see nothing for you in this earth"**: Letter to Thoreau from Channing, March 5, 1845; in *Correspondence*, p. 161.

237 **began construction by borrowing an ax**: Thoreau, *Walden*, "Economy." Thoreau never specified who lent the ax. Alcott claimed that he did, Channing that he did, and both Townsend Scudder and George Willis Cooke credited Emerson. But Alcott had referred to it earlier and indeed quotes Thoreau's precise words when he came to him. Cramer 2004, p. 39, n. 213; Harding, *Annotated Walden*, p. 38, n. 1, for precise citations. Thoreau mentions a larger ax and then later his smaller felling ax. Cramer points out virtues of a broad ax over a felling ax. Logging and woodworking sites online provided information on the ax's use and the rationale of its design. An example: http://www.orionn49.com/choosing_an_axe.html.

238 **Henry's father had bought a couple**: Cramer 2004, p. 42, n. 224.

239 **"Good boards overhead"**: Thoreau, *Walden*, "Economy." Details not otherwise cited derive from Thoreau's account.

239 **machined at this time instead of handmade**: Cramer 2004, p. 43, n. 228.

249 **At dawn one morning in early May**: Mary Hosmer Brown.

240 **Hosmer was one of Henry's closest friends**: Sanborn 1882, p. 117.

240 **George William Curtis**: Petrulionis 2012, p. 78.

241 **"The best part of an animal"**: Mary Hosmer Brown, p. 205.

241 **Bronson Alcott, brothers George and Burrill Curtis**: Sanborn 1882, pp.
116–17.

Chapter 21: FAVORED BY THE GODS

242 **a man of the largest rents**: Julian Hawthorne, p. 280; from letter by Sophia
Peabody to her mother, April 4, 1844.

242 **"It is as simple as a name can be"** . . . **"As for myself, who have been a
trifler"**: Hawthorne, letter to George Stillman Hillard, March 24, 1844; in
Complete Writings, vol. 17, p. 423.

243 **"What would you say to go out as a consul to China?"**: Letter from John
L. O'Sullivan to Hawthorne, March 21, 1845; in Julian Hawthorne, p. 284.

243 **"for the avowed object of thwarting"**: O'Sullivan.

245 **Henry optimistically planted crops**: Thoreau, *Walden*, "Bean Field"; *Journal,*
spring and summer 1845.

245 **The field had been sown with rye**: Joseph Hosmer, p. 1.

246 **"If those beans were mine"**: *Journal*, vol. 1, p. 367.

246 **metaphor of self-cultivation**: Richardson explores this point, p. 57ff.

247 **"There is one chance in a thousand"**: Hawthorne, letter to Evert Duyckinck,
July 1, 1845.

247 **Henry hid some of the crevices**: Joseph Hosmer.

248 **There were no curtains**: Channing 1902, p. 7.

249 **"fit to entertain a traveling god"**: *Journal*, July 5, 1845.

Chapter 22: DEATH ON THE RIVER

252 **"A gump"**: Hawthorne, letter to Sophia Hawthorne, June 2, 1844, in *Letters,*

252 **Martha Emmeline Hunt**: Quotations from Hunt's diary, and many details of her
last days, derive from August 1, 1845, obituary in *Concord Freeman*. Hawthorne's
observations derive from his journal entry on July 9, 1845. He fictionalized
this incident in his 1852 novel *The Blithedale Romance* (the novel based in part

upon his experience at Brook Farm). Details not otherwise cited derive from Curtis 1853, p. 308ff.

252 **Her parents, Daniel and Clarissa Hunt . . . ten brothers and sisters . . . descended from early settlers**: Leslie Perrin Wilson, unpaginated.

253 **Buttrick, who had inherited the family farm**: Simpson, p. 621, n. 262.13.

253 **found the smell of burning gunpowder exciting**: *Journal*, July 22, 1851.

Chapter 23: LIVING FIREWORKS

257 **its big black eyes wary**: Behavior described derives from *Walden* except for mouse responding to music, from Joseph Hosmer.

258 *putchee nashoba . . . wuskówhàn*, **"wanderers"**: Roger Williams, p. 91; Schorger 1938, p. 471ff.

258 **"How thick the pigeons are!"**: *Journal*, vol. 1, p. 367. Thoreau's description of the pigeons' appearance and behavior derive from numerous journal entries, including August 6, 1845, the source of most of his pigeon comments in *Walden*, in which see also "Spring," "Sounds," and "Brute Neighbors." See Graig, Schorger 1955, and Wilson.

259 **"I have seene them fly"**: Wood, pp. 31–32.

260 **like a farmer winnowing**: Thoreau, *Week*, "Tuesday." Contrast Audubon's description, p. 324, of a giant flock at a distance sounding like "a hard gale at sea, passing through the rigging of a close-reefed vessel."

261 **He loved insects**: Channing, p. 265; also for lichen and Thoreau kicking through leaves.

262 **Emerson thought that Henry had mastered the art**: RWE, *JMN* 1853; Petrulionis 2012, p. 19.

263 **"An abode without birds"**: Quoted in Thoreau, *Walden*, "Where I Lived and What I Lived For." This is Thoreau's own translation from Simon Alexandre Langlois' French translation, *Harivansa, ou Histoire de la Famille de Hari*. See Cramer 2004, p. 83, n. 30.

263 **the magic of fireflies**: Thoreau writes fondly of fireflies throughout his journal.

263 **akin to reading Virgil and Homer**: Thoreau, *Week*, "Tuesday."

Chapter 24: LUNCHEON AT THE CABIN

265 **"Henry T. has built him a house"**: Prudence Ward, letter to Ellen Sewall, January 1846.

265 **baked goods and other treats**: Marble, p. 129.

265 **dined frequently at the Emerson's house**: Curtis, chapter 5.

265 George Keyes . . . came to visit him at Walden: E. Emerson 1917, p. 24.

266 During winter holidays he trekked: Hoar, p. 72.

266 "Why, sixty old women like Nabby Kettle": Quoted in Hoar, p. 72.

266 Hosmer . . . to the pond to visit Henry: Most details from Mary Hosmer
       Brown, p. 94ff.

267 expeditions to find the most delicious chestnuts: Hoar, pp. 70–72.

267 Bill Wheeler hobbling into town: *Journal*, January 16, 1852.

267 he bathed every day until cool weather set in: *Journal*, September 26, 1854.

268 Henry started cleaning early in the morning: Thoreau, *Walden*.

268 his childhood friend Joseph Hosmer Jr.: Thoreau, *Walden*, "Economy" and
       "Housewarming"; Channing, p. 7; *Journal*, July 10, 1852; *Week*, "Saturday."

271 Indians . . . carried nocake: Wood, p. 76.

271 he came upon a worrisome scene: Ricketson, pp. 252–53.

272 "They were a disgrace to their sex": *Journal*, January 17, 1852.

272 "Sir . . . I like your notions": *Journal*, July 14, 1845.

272 Alek Therien: *Walden*, "Reading" and "Visitors"; Harding 1995, p. 141, n. 1;
       Journal, July 14, 1845; Cramer, p. 143 n. 27.

273 heading, Henry figured, for the slaughterhouses in Brighton: *Walden*,
       "Solitude"; Harding 1995, p. 130, n. 2.

274 Hawthorne did not share Emerson's high opinion: Hawthorne, letter to
       Sophia Hawthorne, June 2, 1844, in *Letters*.

274 George Curtis, amused by the gathering of oracles: Curtis 1898, p. 95ff.

Chapter 25: My Muse, My Brother

275 "I wish to meet the facts of life": *Journal*, July 6, 1845.

275 Early in 1846: Wineapple, p. 193.

276 To reach Walden's depths: Most details derive from *Walden*, "The Pond in
       Winter."

278 Usually they didn't analyze an adventure: See Hovde for analysis of how
       Thoreau transmuted journal entries into material for *Week*.

279 "We have authentic intelligence": Sophia Peabody Hawthorne to her
       mother, March 23, 1846, in *Letters*.

279 "baptized in the deep waters of *Tragedy*": Delano, p. 85.

280 "no more brains than a cabbage": Mellow, pp. 233–34; "original at *all*
       points": p. 193.

280 "I admire you rather as a writer of Tales": Hawthorne, letter to Edgar Allan
       Poe, June 17, 1846. in Quinn, p. 511.

280 "Here, in some unknown age": Hawthorne, "The Old Manse," preface to
       Mosses from an Old Manse.

281 **he and Emerson sat down together . . . s**: RWE, letter to Charles King
      Newcomb, July 16, 1846; in *Letters of RWE*, vol. 3, pp. 337–38.

283 **Benjamin Hosmer . . . walked the seven miles from Bedford**: Horace
      Hosmer, p. 14.

Chapter 26: A Night in Jail

284 **One warm evening late in July 1846**: S. A. Jones, in Petrulionis 2012, p.
      157ff.; Sanborn 1882, p. 207; *Journal*, June 12, 1846.

284 **Staples, the constable**: Broderick, p. 621–626; *Journal*, December 31, 1857; E.
      Emerson, p. 65ff., and p. 136, n. 1; S. A. Jones, from 1890 interview with
      Staples, in Petrulionis 2012, p. 157ff; Sanborn 1917, p. 328; Harding 1975;
      "Middlesex Hotel Story" among the Building Histories on the website of
      the Concord Free Public Library, http://www.concordlibrary.org/
      scollect/buildinghistories/MiddlesexHotel/index.html.

285 **"I'll pay your tax, Henry"**: E. Emerson, p. 65.

285 **Hoar . . . paid Alcott's tax**: Harding 1975.

285 **Alcott had been deliberately rejecting the government's right**: Matteson,
      p. 189.

285 **he had threatened Alcott**: Broderick, p. 621, n. 35.

286 **Staples had a higher, more affectionate opinion of Henry**: Cooke, p.
      1672.

286 **Henry if you don't pay**: Anonymous, "An Evening with Thoreau," in the
      Concord *High School Voice* of November 15, 1895; in Harding 1989, p. 78.

286 **past the local poor farm and poor house**: Sanborn 1882, p. 207; Roman,
      map.

286 **the jail tavern . . . Supreme Court in March**: Jarvis, p. 159, p. 6.

286 **"The Comparative Moral Policy"**: Sanborn 1917, pp. 78–82.

286 **jail**: For jail description, see Sanborn 1917, p. 167; Van Doren Stern, p. 468, n.
      37; Keyes, *Brief History*, chapter 45; Thoreau, "Civil Disobedience"; E.
      Emerson, p. 65.

288 **"Sir, I do not wish to be considered"**: In "Civil Disobedience," Thoreau
      exaggerates the text of this note to the clerk: "Know all men by these
      presents, that I, Henry Thoreau, do not wish to be regarded as a member of
      any incorporated society which I have not joined." But the Concord
      library has the original note in Thoreau's handwriting.

288 **During the same six years, Henry had also refrained**: Details not otherwise
      cited derive from "Civil Disobedience."

288 **In 1780, immediately after the war . . . "Ministers of the Gospel" . . . Fiscal
      policy**: Broderick, p. 613ff.

290 **When Mrs. Thoreau learned of Henry's arrest**: Letter by Jane Hosmer in Harding 1989, p. 167.

290 **probably Maria**: Oehlschlaeger, pp. 197–202; Todd, p. 11.

290 **running an errand in the village**: Petrulionis 2012, p. 158; E. Emerson, p. 65.

291 **"find sufficient goods"**: quoted in Broderick, p. 615.

291 **"What is life?"**: Dialogue from this interaction, E. Emerson, p. 65.

292 **"This act of non-resistance"**: Cain, p. 155.

293 **after paying it since reaching adulthood**: Broderick, p. 625.

294 **The next morning, Samuel Staples explained**: Anonymous, "An Evening with Thoreau," in Concord *High School Voice*, November 15, 1895.

294 **Staples was dumbfounded . . . Henry was furious**: Staples, p. 23; "mad as the devil" was his phrase.

295–296 **Lewis Hayden . . . .Caleb Stetson**: *Concord Freeman*, August 7, 1846.

297 **A man of principle, Henry had come to believe**: Thoreau, "Life without Principle" and *Journal*, summer 1846.

Chapter 27: CHAOS AND ANCIENT NIGHT

297 **Mattanawacook Island**: Cramer 2009, p. 6, n. 43.

297 **on the last day of August**: Thoreau's thoughts and observations in Maine not otherwise cited derive from "Ktaadn," published in *Sartain's Union Magazine of Literature and Art,* July–November 1848.

297 **George Thatcher**: Cramer 2009, p. 1, n. 2.

298 **Charles Turner and his party in 1804**: Cramer 2009, p. 2, n. 7.

298 **Henry had met Jackson in 1843**: Hyde, p. 325, n. 64.

298 **hoped to find the primeval world of his dreams**: This is the critical consensus regarding Thoreau's ideas about Maine and wilderness prior to this journey. See Nash, especially pp. 90ff.; Lebeaux 1984, p. 137ff; Harding 1965.

300 **"Louis declared that Pomola"**: Hyde, p. 325, n. 69. I use Thoreau's spelling, "Pomola," although sources list many others. Mount Katahdin now has a Pamola Peak.

300 **"The two Indians, whom we hired" . . . a corked bottle of rum**: Cramer 2009, p. 8.

303 **batteau**: Thoreau; and see also history on the New York State Museum site, http://www.nysm.nysed.gov/research_collections/research/history/three/bat3.html, and http://www.bairnet.org/organizations/leonardsmills/bateau.htm.

305 **The store's founder, George W. Simmons**: Allaback, pp. 546–47.

308 **Henry climbed on alone**: For more on Thoreau's response to the wilderness, see Nash, especially pp. 90–95.

310 **"Why came ye here before your time?"**: Thoreau wrote these words (italicized within my text) later, in "Ktaadn," but he presents them as his thoughts at the time.

311 **Probably Henry had reached the saddle**: Hyde, p. 329, n. 107; see also discussion in Cramer 2009.

312 **One evening shortly after his return to Walden**: *Journal*, 1845; no date given, but immediately precedes August 6; see Thoreau 1906, vol. I, p. 375.

Coda: AFTER THE CABIN

314 **"But why I changed?"**: *Journal*, January 22, 1852.

315 **Emerson . . . bought the cabin**: Sanborn 1917, quoting Channing, pp. 329–30. Most details of cabin's fate derive from Channing, but see also Harding 1982.

315 **"Thoreau was a great writer"**: Mohandas Gandhi, p. 279; see also Rajmohan Gandhi, pp. 113–14, 142.

316 **"first contact with the theory of nonviolent resistance"**: King, p. 13.

316 **McCarthy succeeded in having the book removed**: Harding 1967, p. 24.

316 **Then he wound his music box**: Harding 1982, p. 258.

317 **"a library of some nine hundred volumes"**: *Journal*, October 28, 1853.

317 **Horace Hosmer, worked as their agent**: Raymond Adams, *Thoreau Newsletter*, April 1937.

317 **"Economy—Illustrated by the Life of a Student" . . . "White Beans and Walden Pond"**: Concord Lyceum records, Borst, p. 140ff.

317 **ninth of August 1854 . . . 2319 copies**: Tryon, p. 289.

318 **"To Boston. Walden published"**: *Journal*, August 9, 1854.

318 **"It is a curious and amusing book"**: Borst, p. 303.

318 **"It has classical elegance"**: *TSB*, Fall 1971 (No. 117).

319 **"The Republican party does not perceive"**: Thoreau, "A Plea for Captain John Brown," in Hyde, p. 259ff.

319 **scientists are using his detailed journal records**: Miller-Rushing and Primack.

319 **"When we have experienced many disappointments"**: *Journal*, February 5, 1859.

320 **"I have not been engaged in any particular work"**: Thoreau, letter to Myron Benton (dictated to Sophia Thoreau), March 21, 1862.

320 **Elizabeth Hoar worked to help; Ticknor . . . came to visit Henry**: *Concord Saunterer*, vol. 14, no. 3 (Fall 1979), p. 1.

320 **Staples . . . found Henry happy and serene**: RWE, *JMN*, March 24, 1862.

BIBLIOGRAPHY

Adams, Raymond. "Thoreau and His Neighbors," *Thoreau Society Bulletin* XLIV (Summer 1953).

———. "Thoreau at Harvard: Some Unpublished Records." *New England Quarterly,* vol. 13, no. 1 (March 1940).

———. "Thoreau's Sources for 'Resistance to Civil Government.'" *Studies in Philology,* vol. 42, no. 3 (July 1945).

Allaback, Steven. "Oak Hall in American Literature." *American Literature,* vol. 46, no. 4 (January 1975).

Audubon, John James. *Ornithological Biography, or An Account of the Habits of the Birds of the United States of America.* Philadelphia: E. L. Carey and A. Hart, in multiple volumes beginning in 1832.

Bartlett, George B. *The Concord Guide Book.* D. Lothrop, 1890.

———. *Concord: Historic, Literary, and Picturesque.* Boston: D. Lothrop, 1885.

Blanding, Thomas. "Passages from John Thoreau, Jr.'s Journal." *Thoreau Society Bulletin* 136 (Summer 1976).

Borst, Raymond R. *The Thoreau Log: A Documentary Life of Henry David Thoreau 1817–1862.* New York: G. K. Hall, 1992.

Bowditch, Henry I. "Consumption in America," *Atlantic Monthly* 23 (1869): 51 (pt. 1), 177 (pt. 2), 315 (pt. 3).

Broderick, John C. "Thoreau, Alcott, and the Poll Tax." *Studies in Philology* 53 (1956).

Brown, Mary Hosmer. *Memories of Concord.* Boston: Four Seas, 1926.

Cabot, James Elliot. *A Memoir of Ralph Waldo Emerson.* Two volumes. Boston: Houghton Mifflin, 1887.

Cain, William E., ed. *A Historical Guide to Henry David Thoreau.* Oxford: Oxford University Press, 2000.

Cameron, Kenneth Walter. "Chronology of Thoreau's Harvard Years." *Emerson Society Quarterly* 18 (Summer 1959).

———. "Helen Thoreau Writes to Dr. Shattuck in 1838." *Emerson Society Quarterly* VI (1957).

———. "Thoreau Discovers Emerson." *Bulletin of the New York Public Library*, vol. 57, no. 7 (June 1953).

———. *Thoreau's Harvard Years* (two parts). Hartford: Transcendental Books, 1966.

Channing, Ellery. *Thoreau: The Poet Naturalist*. Revised edition, Boston: Charles E. Goodspeed, 1902; originally published, Boston: Roberts Brothers, 1873.

Cicero. *The Nature of the Gods*. Translated by P. G. Walsh. Oxford: Oxford University Press, 1997.

Conrad, Randall. "Machine in the Wetland: Re-Imagining Thoreau's Plumbago-Grinder." *Thoreau Society Bulletin* (Fall 2005)

———. "Realizing Resistance: Thoreau and the First of August, 1846, at Walden." *The Concord Saunterer: A Journal of Thoreau Studies*, Thoreau Society, new series vol. 12–13 (2004–2005).

Conway, Moncure Daniel. *Autobiography*. Boston: Houghton Mifflin, 1904.

Cooke, George Willis. "The Two Thoreaus." *Independent*, December 10, 1896.

Cosman, Max. "Apropos of John Thoreau." *American Literature* 12 (1940).

———. "Thoreau and Staten Island." *Staten Island Historian*, vol. 6, no. 1, serial no. 21 (January–March 1943).

Cramer, Jeffrey S., ed. *I to Myself: An Annotated Selection from the Journal of Henry D. Thoreau*. New Haven: Yale University Press, 2007.

———, ed. *The Maine Woods: A Fully Annotated Edition*. New Haven: Yale University Press, 2009.

———, ed. *Walden: A Fully Annotated Edition*. New Haven: Yale University Press, 2004.

Cummins, Roger W. "Thoreau and Isaac Newton Goodhue," *Thoreau Society Bulletin* CXXIII (Spring 1973).

Curtis, George William. *Early Letters of George William Curtis to John Sullivan Dwight: Brook Farm and Concord*. Edited by George Willis Cooke. New York: Harper & Brothers, 1898.

———. *Literary and Social Essays*. New York: Harper & Brothers, 1895.

———. "Nathaniel Hawthorne." In *Homes of American Authors; Comprising Anecdotal, Personal, and Descriptive Sketches*, by Various Writers. New York: Putnam, 1853.

———. "Thoreau and My Lady Cavaliere." In *From the Easy Chair*. New York: Harper, 1892.

Dean, Bradley P. "Rediscovery at Walden: The History of Thoreau's Bean Field." *Concord Saunterer: A Journal of Thoreau Studies*, Thoreau Society, new series vol. 12–13 (2004–2005).

Delano, Sterling F. *Brook Farm: The Dark Side of Utopia*. Cambridge, MA: Harvard University Press, 2004.

De Vere, Maximilian Schele. *Americanisms: The English of the New World*. New York: Scribner's, 1872.

The Dial. The University of Pennsylvania hosts an online archive of *The Dial* at http://onlinebooks.library.upenn.edu/webbin/serial?id=thedial.

Dillard, Joey Lee. *Toward a Social History of American English.* Berlin: Walter de Gruyter, 1985.

Dormandy, Thomas. *The White Death: A History of Tuberculosis.* New York: New York University Press, 2000.

Eidson, John Olin. "Emerson's 'Good Grecian.'" *New England Quarterly,* vol. 27, no. 4 (December 1954).

Emerson, Amelia F. "John Shepard Keyes," in *Memoirs of Members of the Social Circle in Concord.* Fifth series. Cambridge: Riverside, 1940.

Emerson, Edward Waldo. "A Different Drummer." In Harding 1971.

———. *Henry Thoreau as Remembered by a Young Friend.* Boston: Houghton Mifflin, 1917.

Emerson, Lidian Jackson. *The Selected Letters of Lidian Jackson Emerson.* Edited by Delores Bird Carpenter. Columbia: University of Missouri Press, 1987.

Emerson, Ralph Waldo. *Nature.* Boston: James Munroe & Co., 1836.

———. *Ralph Waldo Emerson: Essays and Journals.* Edited by Lewis Mumford. Garden City, NY: Doubleday, 1968.

———. *Journals and Miscellaneous Notebooks.* Cambridge: Harvard University Press, 1960–1982. Sixteen volumes.

———. *Nature.* Boston: James Munroe, 1836.

Formisano, Ronald P. "The New Political History and the Election of 1840." *Journal of Interdisciplinary History,* vol. 23, no. 4 (Spring 1993).

Foster, David R. *Thoreau's Country: Journey through a Transformed Landscape.* Cambridge: Harvard University Press, 1999.

Frothingham, O. B. *George Ripley.* Boston: Houghton Mifflin, 1882.

Fuess, Claude Moore. *Daniel Webster.* Boston: Little, Brown, 1930.

Fuller, Richard. "The Younger Generation in 1840: From the Diary of a New England Boy." *Atlantic Monthly,* August 1925.

———. "Visit to the Wachusett, July 1842." *Thoreau Society Bulletin* 121, Autumn 1972.

Gandhi, Mohandas. "For Passive Resisters." *Indian Opinion* 7, October 26, 1907.

Gandhi, Rajmohan. *Gandhi: The Man, His People, and the Empire.* Berkeley: University of California Press, 2007.

Garrison. *William Lloyd Garrison, 1805–1879: The Story of His Life, Told by His Children.* New York: Century Company, 1885.

Gunderson, Robert Gray. *The Log-Cabin Campaign.* Lexington: University of Kentucky Press, 1957.

Hale, Edward Everett. *A New England Boyhood.* New York: Cassell, 1893.

Harding, Walter. *The Days of Henry Thoreau: A Biography.* Princeton: Princeton

University Press, 1992. A reprinting of the 1982 revision with a new afterword; original edition published New York: Alfred A. Knopf, 1962.

———, ed. *Henry David Thoreau: A Profile*. New York: Hill & Wang, 1971.

———. "Henry Thoreau and Ellen Sewall." *South Atlantic Quarterly* LXIV (Winter 1965).

———, ed. *Thoreau as Seen by His Contemporaries*. New York: Dover, 1989. Revised and enlarged edition, originally published by Holt, Rinehart and Winston in 1960 as *Thoreau: Man of Concord*.

———. "Thoreau's Sexuality." *Journal of Homosexuality* 21 (3) 1991.

———, ed. *Walden: An Annotated Edition*. Boston: Houghton Mifflin, 1995.

———. "Was It Legal? Thoreau in Jail." *American Heritage*, vol. 26, no. 5 (August 1975).

———, and Carl Bode, eds. *The Correspondence of Henry David Thoreau*. New York: New York University Press, 1958.

Haskins, David Greene. *Memoir of Ralph Haskins*. Cambridge: John Wilson and Son, 1881.

———. *Ralph Waldo Emerson: His Maternal Ancestors, with Some Reminiscences of Him*. Boston: Cupples, Upham and Company, 1887.

Hawthorne, Julian. *Nathaniel Hawthorne and His Wife: A Biography*. Boston: James R. Osgood and Company, 1885.

———. *Passages from the American Notebooks*. Edited by Sophia Hawthorne. Boston: Houghton Mifflin, 1883. See Randall Stewart's edition (Cambridge: Harvard University Press, 1932, 1960).

Hendrick, George. "Pages from Sophia Thoreau's Journal," *Thoreau Society Bulletin* LXI (1957).

Hoagland, Clayton. "The Diary of Thoreau's 'Gentle Boy.'" *New England Quarterly*, vol. 28, no. 4 (December 1955).

Hoar, George F. *Autobiography of Seventy Years*. New York: Scribner's, 1903.

Hodder, Alan D. *Thoreau's Ecstatic Witness*. New Haven: Yale University Press, 2001.

Hoeltje, Herbert H. "Thoreau and the Concord Academy." *New England Quarterly*, vol. 21, no. 1 (March 1948).

———. "Thoreau in Concord Church and Town Records." *New England Quarterly*, vol. 12, no. 2 (June 1939).

Hosmer, Horace. *Remembrances of Concord and the Thoreaus: Letters of Horace Hosmer to Dr. S. A. Jones*. Edited by George Hendrick. Urbana: University of Illinois Press, 1977.

Hosmer, Joseph. "Henry D. Thoreau." In Harding 1989.

Hovde, Carl F. "Nature into Art: Thoreau's Use of His Journals in 'A Week.'" *American Literature*, vol. 30, no. 2 (May 1958).

Hyde, Lewis, ed. *The Essays of Henry D. Thoreau*. New York: Farrar, Straus and Giroux / North Point Press, 2002.

Jarvis, Edward. *Traditions and Reminiscences of Concord, Massachusetts 1779–1878*. Amherst: University of Massachusetts Press, 1993.

Jones, Samuel Arthur (as S. A. J.). "A Belated Knight-Errant." *The Inlander* (a Michigan University student publication), vol. 5, no. 5 (February 1895).

———. *Pertaining to Thoreau*. Detroit: Edwin B. Hill, 1901.

———. *Thoreau: A Glimpse*. Concord, MA: Albert Lane / Erudite Press, 1903.

——— (as S. A. J.). "Thoreau's Incarceration." *Inlander* 9 (December 1898): 97–100, in Petrulionis 2012.

Keyes, John Shepard. *Autobiography*. Transcription of holograph manuscript, John Shepard Keyes Papers, William Munroe Special Collections, Concord Free Public Library.

———. *A Brief History of Concord*. Originally included in *History of Middlesex County, Massachusetts, with Biographical Sketches of Many of Its Pioneers and Prominent Men*. Philadelphia: J. W. Lewis & Co., 1890. Concord Free Public Library.

———. "Memoir of Nehemiah Ball." In *Memoirs of Members of the Social Circle in Concord: Second Series, from 1795 to 1840*. Cambridge, MA: Riverside Press, 1888.

———. A talk about the Middlesex Hotel (untitled). Delivered before the Concord Antiquarian Society on April 2, 1900. Concord Free Public Library.

King, Martin Luther, Jr. *The Autobiography of Martin Luther King, Jr.* Edited by Clayborne Carson. New York: Warner Books, 1998.

Koopman, Louise Osgood. "The Thoreau Romance." *Massachusetts Review*, vol. 4, no. 1 (Autumn 1962).

Kwiat, Joseph J. "Thoreau's Philosophical Apprenticeship." *New England Quarterly*, vol. 18, no. 1 (March 1945).

Lathrop, George Parsons. "Lecture." *Brooklyn Citizen*, December 12, 1894.

Lathrop, Rose Hawthorne. *Memories of Hawthorne*. Boston: Houghton Mifflin, 1897.

Lebeaux, Richard. *Thoreau's Seasons:* Boston: University of Massachusetts Press, 1984.

———. *Young Man Thoreau*. Boston: University of Massachusetts Press, 1977.

Le Brun, Jean Munroe. "Henry Thoreau's Mother." *Collectanea*, no. 2. Lakeland, MI: Edwin B. Hill, 1908. Reprint of article that appeared in *Boston Advertiser*, February 14, 1883. Apparently original appeared anonymously, but this source and others cite Le Brun as author.

Marble, Annie Russell. *Thoreau: His Home, Friends, and Books*. New York: Thomas Y. Crowell, 1902.

Marshall, Ian. "Winter Tracings and Transcendental Leaps: Henry Thoreau's Skating." *Papers on Language and Literature*, vol. 29, no. 4 (Autumn 1993).

Marshall, Megan. *Margaret Fuller: A New American Life.* Boston: Houghton Mifflin, 2013.

——. *The Peabody Sisters: Three Women Who Ignited American Romanticism.* Boston: Houghton Mifflin, 2005.

Matteson, John. *Eden's Outcasts: The Story of Louisa May Alcott and Her Father.* New York: W. W. Norton, 2007.

——. *The Lives of Margaret Fuller: A Biography.* New York: W. W. Norton, 2012.

Maynard, W. Barksdale. *Walden Pond: A History.* New York: Oxford University Press, 2004.

McFarland, Philip. *Hawthorne in Concord.* New York: Grove, 2004.

Mellow, James R. *Nathaniel Hawthorne in His Times.* Boston: Houghton Mifflin, 1980.

Meltzer, Milton. *Nathaniel Hawthorne: A Biography.* Minneapolis: Lerner Publishing / Twenty-First Century Books, 2007.

——, and Walter Harding. *A Thoreau Profile.* New York: Thomas Y. Crowell, 1962.

Miller, Edwin Haviland. *Salem Is My Dwelling Place: A Life of Nathaniel Hawthorne.* Iowa City: University of Iowa Press, 1991.

Miller, Neil Brody. "'Proper Subjects for Proper Inquiry': The First Unitarian Controversy and the Transformation of Federalist Print Culture." *Early American Literature*, vol. 43, no. 1 (2008).

Miller, Perry, ed. *Consciousness in Concord: The Text of Thoreau's Hitherto "Lost Journal" (1840–1841).* Boston: Houghton Mifflin, 1958.

Miller-Rushing, Abraham J., and Richard B. Primack. "Global Warming and Flowering Times in Thoreau's Concord: A Community Perspective." *Ecology*, vol. 89, no. 2 (February 2008).

Morison, Samuel Eliot. *Three Centuries of Harvard, 1636–1936.* Cambridge: Belknap Press of Harvard University Press, 1936.

Myerson, Joel. "Barzillai Frost's Funeral Sermon on the Death of John Thoreau Jr." *Huntington Library Quarterly*, vol. 57, no. 4 (Autumn 1994).

——, ed. *The Brook Farm Book: A Collection of First-Hand Accounts of the Community.* New York: Garland, 1987.

——, ed. *The Cambridge Companion to Henry David Thoreau.* Cambridge: Cambridge University Press, 1995.

——. "More Apropos of John Thoreau." *American Literature*, vol. 45, no. 1 (March 1973).

Nash, Roderick. *Wilderness and the American Mind.* Third edition. New Haven: Yale University Press, 1982.

Oehlschlaeger, Fritz, and George Hendrick, eds. *Toward the Making of Thoreau's Reputation: Selected Correspondence of S. A. Jones, A. W. Hosmer, H. S. Salt, H. G. O. Blake, and D. Ricketson.* Urbana: University of Illinois Press, 1979.

O'Sullivan, John L. "Annexation." *United States Magazine and Democratic Review*, vol. 17, no. 1 (July–August 1845).

Paige, Lucius R. *History of Cambridge, Massachusetts, 1630–1877, with a Genealogical Register*. Boston: Houghton and Company, 1877.

Petroski, Henry. "H. D. Thoreau, Engineer." *American Heritage of Invention and Technology*, Fall 1989.

———. *The Pencil*. New York: Knopf, 1990.

Petrulionis, Sandra Harbert. "'Swelling That Great Tide of Humanity': The Concord, Massachusetts, Female Anti-Slavery Society." *New England Quarterly* 74 (September 2001).

———, ed. *Thoreau in His Own Time: A Biographical Chronicle of His Life, Drawn from Recollections, Interviews, and Memoirs by Family, Friends, and Associates*. Iowa City: University of Iowa Press, 2012.

———. *To Set This World Right: The Antislavery Movement in Thoreau's Concord*. Ithaca: Cornell University Press, 2006.

Pier, Arthur Stanwood. *The Story of Harvard*. Boston: Little, Brown, 1913.

Poe, Edgar Allan. *The Complete Works of Edgar Allan Poe*. Edited by James A. Harrison. New York: Thomas Y. Crowell & Company, 1902.

Quinn, Arthur Hobson. *Edgar Allan Poe: A Critical Biography*. Baltimore: Johns Hopkins University Press, 1998. Reprint of the original 1941 edition.

Raysor, T. M. "The Love Story of Thoreau." *Studies in Philology*, vol. 23, no. 4 (October 1926).

Reisen, Harriet, and Nancy Porter. *Louisa May Alcott: The Woman Behind "Little Women."* New York: Henry Holt, 2009.

Richardson, Robert D. *Emerson: The Mind on Fire*. Berkeley: University of California Press, 1995.

———. *Henry Thoreau: A Life of the Mind*. Berkeley: University of California Press, 1986.

Ricketson, Anna and Walton, eds. *Daniel Ricketson and His Friends: Letters, Poems, Sketches Etc*. Boston: Houghton Mifflin, 1902.

Robinson, Mrs. W. S. *"Warrington" Pen-Portraits: A Collection of Personal and Political Reminiscences from 1848 to 1876, from the Writings of William S. Robinson*. Boston: Robinson, 1877.

Roman, John. *Map of Concord and Environs*. Concord, Massachusetts: Thoreau Society, 2006.

———. "Mapping Thoreau's World: An Artist's Journal on Making an Illustrated Map of Historic Concord." *The Concord Saunterer: A Journal of Thoreau Studies*, Thoreau Society, new series, vol. 15 (2007).

Rusk, Ralph L. *The Life of Ralph Waldo Emerson*. New York: Charles Scribner's Sons, 1949.

Salt, Henry Stephens. *The Life of Henry David Thoreau*. London: Walter Scott, 1896. Revised and enlarged edition of the 1890 biography.

Sanborn, Franklin B. *Bronson Alcott at Alcott House, England, and Fruitlands, New England (1842–1844)*. Cedar Rapids, IA: Torch Press, 1908.

———, ed. *Familiar Letters of Henry David Thoreau*. Boston: Houghton Mifflin, 1894.

———. *Henry David Thoreau*. Boston: Houghton Mifflin, 1882.

———. *The Life of Henry David Thoreau, Including Many Essays Hitherto Unpublished and Some Account of His Family and Friends*. Boston: Houghton Mifflin, 1917.

———. *The Personality of Thoreau*. Boston: Goodspeed, 1901.

———. *Recollections of Seventy Years*. Boston: R. G. Badger, 1909.

Sargent, Epes. *The Standard Speaker; Containing Exercises in Prose and Poetry for Declamation*. Philadelphia: Thomas, Cowperthwait & Co., 1852.

Sattelmeyer, Robert. *Thoreau's Reading: A Study in Intellectual History*. Princeton: Princeton University Press, 1988.

Sayre, Robert F. *Thoreau and the American Indians*. Princeton: Princeton University Press, 1977.

Schorger, Arlie W. *The Passenger Pigeon: Its Natural History and Extinction*. Madison: University of Wisconsin Press, 1955.

———. "Unpublished Manuscripts by Cotton Mather on the Passenger Pigeon," *The Auk* 55 (July 1938).

Scudder, Townsend. *Concord: American Town*. Boston: Little, Brown, 1947.

Sewall, Edmund Quincy. Diary, 1840. A single folder, covering March 28 to May 16, 1840, in the American Antiquarian Society in Worcester, Massachusetts.

Shattuck, Lemuel. *A History of the Town of Concord. . . .* Boston: Russell, Odiorne & Co., 1835.

Silber, Irwin. *Songs America Voted By*. Harrisburg PA: Stackpole Books, 1971.

Sidney, Margaret. *Old Concord: Her Highways and Byways*. Boston: D. Lothrop, 1888.

Simon, Paul. *Freedom's Champion*. Revised edition. Carbondale: Southern Illinois University Press, 1994.

Smith, Harmon. *My Friend, My Friend: The Story of Thoreau's Relationship with Emerson*. Boston: University of Massachusetts Press, 1999.

Staples, Samuel. Quoted in "An Evening with Thoreau." *High School Voice* (Concord, MA), November 15, 1895.

Stewart, Shawn. "Transcendental Romance Meets the Ministry of Pain: The Thoreau Brothers, Ellen Sewall, and Her Father." *Concord Saunterer: A Journal of Thoreau Studies*, Thoreau Society, new series vol. 14 (2006).

Swayne, Josephine Latham, editor. *The Story of Concord Told by Concord Writers*. Boston: E. F. Worster, 1903.

Swedenborg, Emmanuel. *The Principia*. Translated by James R. Rendell and Isaiah Tansley. London: Swedenborg Society, 1912.

Tharp, Louise Hall. *The Peabody Sisters of Salem*. Boston: Little, Brown, 1950.

Thatcher, B. B. *Indian Traits: Being Sketches of the Manners, Customs, and Character of the North American Natives*. London: O. Rich, 1834.

Thomas, William S. "Thoreau as His Own Editor." *New England Quarterly*, vol. 15, no. 1 (March 1942).

Todd, Mabel Loomis. *The Thoreau Family Two Generations Ago*. Berkeley Heights, NJ: Oriole Press for the Thoreau Society, 1958.

Torrey, Bradford. "Thoreau as a Diarist." *Atlantic Monthly* XCV (January 1905).

————, and F. H. Allen, eds. *The Journal of Henry David Thoreau*. New York: Dover, 1962. Reprint in two oversize volumes of 1902 complete edition.

Tryon, Warren S., and William Charvat. *The Cost Books of Ticknor and Fields*. New York: Bibliographical Society of America, 1949.

Underwood, John. "The Subversive Encyclopedia." *Science Museum Library & Archives Newsletter* (Spring/Summer 2010).

Uva, Richard H., Joseph C. Neal, and Joseph M. DiTomaso. *Weeds of the Northeast*. Ithaca: Cornell University Press, 1997.

Valenti, Patricia Dunlavey. "Sophia Peabody Hawthorne: A Study of Artistic Influence." *Studies in the American Renaissance* 1990.

Van Doren Stern, Philip, ed. *The Annotated "Walden."* New York: Random House, 1970.

Weiss, John. "Thoreau." *Christian Examiner* LXXIX, July 1865.

Wheeler, Marion. "Old Burying Grounds of Concord." Concord: Concord Historical Commission, 1999.

Wheeler, Ruth. "Thoreau's Concord," in *Henry David Thoreau: Studies and Commentaries*. Edited by Walter Harding et al. Associated University Press, 1972.

Whelpley, Samuel. *A compend of history, from the earliest times; comprehending a general view of the present state of the world, with respect to civilization, religion, and government: and a brief dissertation on the importance of historical knowledge*. Boston: Richardson & Lord, 1822.

Williams, Henry. *Memorials of the Class of 1837 of Harvard University*. Prepared for the Fiftieth Anniversary of Their Graduation, by the Class Secretary. Boston: George H. Ellis, 1887.

Williams, Roger. *A Key into the Language of America: or, An Help to the Language of the Natives in That Part of America, Called New-England*. London: Gregory Dexter, 1643.

Wilmes, D. R. "F.B. Sanborn and the Lost New England World of Transcendentalism." *Colby Quarterly*, vol. 16, no. 4 (December 1980).

Wilson, Alexander. *Wilson's American Ornithology, with Notes by Jardine* . . . Boston: Otis, Broaders & Co., 1840.

Wilson, Eric G. "Thoreau, Crystallography, and the Science of the Transparent." *Studies in Romanticism* 43 (Spring 2004).

Wilson, Leslie Perrin. "Concord Cameos: Martha Hunt." *Concord Magazine,* March–April 2001.

Wineapple, Brenda. *Hawthorne: A Life.* New York: Alfred A. Knopf, 2003.

Zboray, Ronald J., and Mary Saracino Zboray. "Whig Women, Politics, and Culture in the Campaign of 1840: Three Perspectives from Massachusetts." *Journal of the Early Republic,* vol. 17, no. 2 (Summer 1997).

INDEX

Note: The initials HDT in subheadings refer to Henry David Thoreau.

ABOUT THE AUTHOR

Michael Sims's several nonfiction books include *The Story of Charlotte's Web*, which the *Washington Post*, *Boston Globe*, and other venues chose as one of the best books of 2011; *Adam's Navel*, which was a *New York Times* Notable Book, a *Library Journal* Best Science Book, and was translated into several languages; and *In the Womb: Animals*, a companion to the National Geographic Channel TV series. He created and edits the Connoisseur's Collection Victorian anthology series for Bloomsbury, which includes *Dracula's Guest*, *The Dead Witness*, and the forthcoming *The Phantom Coach*; and has also edited *The Annotated Archy and Mehitabel*, *The Penguin Book of Gaslight Crime*, and other volumes. His writing has appeared in many periodicals, including the *New York Times*, the *Times* (London), the *Chronicle of Higher Education*, the *New Statesman*, *Orion*, *American Archaeology*, *Health*, and the *Washington Post*. Please visit his website at www.michaelsimsbooks.com or follow him on Twitter at @michalesimsbook.